Reading on the Farm

ROSE AND EVELINE ON THE RAMPARTS.

"Let me be sentinel for a while," she said, "my sweet lady—I will at least scream louder than you if any danger should approach."

Reading on the Farm

Victorian Fiction and the Colonial World

Lydia Wevers

Victoria University Press

TE WHARE WĀNANGA O TE ŪPOKO O TE IKA A MĀUI
VICTORIA
UNIVERSITY OF WELLINGTON

VICTORIA UNIVERSITY PRESS
Victoria University of Wellington
PO Box 600 Wellington
http://www.victoria.ac.nz/vup

First published 2010
Reprinted 2010, 2012

National Library of New Zealand Cataloguing-in-Publication Data

Wevers, Lydia
Reading on the farm : Victorian fiction and the colonial world / Lydia Wevers.
Includes bibliographical references and index.
ISBN 978-0-86473-6352
1. Brancepeth family—Library. 2. Reading interests—New Zealand—History—19th century. I. Title.
028.90993—dc 22

Edited by Jolisa Gracewood
Index compiled by Tordis Flath

Printed by PrintStop, Wellington

This book is for Seb, Lizzie and Tom

It is also for Ed

And in memoriam John Vaughan Miller 1839–1923

Contents

Illustrations

Acknowledgements

My first and deepest thanks go to Ed Beetham. Ed has given me extraordinary help at every stage of writing this book. I have had open access to Brancepeth and everything that remains there, including family papers, without which this book could not have been written. Ed has been my first audience for many discoveries and an indefatigable research assistant in innumerable ways. His generosity and enthusiasm have been exceptional.

Without Ed I would not have known about John Vaughan Miller, on whom this book rests. I owe more than I can say to Miller, who became a part of my life. I would like to acknowledge him here.

I have had enormous help from Louise Grenside, the Stout Research Centre administrator, whose research knowledge, superb editing skills and unending good humour have been a constant part of the writing process.

I owe a huge debt of thanks to Nicola Frean, the Special Materials Librarian in charge of the J.C. Beaglehole room, where the Brancepeth Library is held, and to her assistants, especially Nick Wotton and Rachael Fabish. They have dealt with my thousands of requests with speed, expertise and good temper. I also owe a debt of thanks to Nicola's predecessor, Kathleen Coleridge, who first suggested I take a look at the Brancepeth Library.

My other great professional debt is to Gareth Winter, the Wairarapa Archivist. Gareth's knowledge of Wairarapa history and materials is unrivalled, matched only by the speed and accuracy with which he delivers information. Much of this book is reliant on the resources he supplied.

I would also like to thank other friends and colleagues

who have been generous with their time, expertise and enthusiasm, particularly those from the Stout Research Centre, Richard Hill, Jamie Belich, Brad Patterson, Lana Le Quesne, Brian Easton, John Newton and Maureen West; and also Brigitte Bonisch-Brednich, Roger Blackley, Kate Hunter, Penny Boumelha, Pamela Wood, Sydney Shep, Rebecca Rice, Jane Stafford, Matthew Trundle, Deborah Willis, Mark Williams, and my dear friend Margot Thompson. Russell Marshall was a very kind unpaid research assistant in London and in the Turnbull Library in the early stages of finding out about John Vaughan Miller, and Jan Miller has been very helpful with family details. Carrie Wainwright helped me with the Castlepoint Purchase and some early Wairarapa land history, and Liz Mellish, Wellington Tenths Trust, gave generous feedback on William Beetham's portrait of her tūpuna, the Te Ātiawa chiefs Wi Tako Ngatata and Honiana Te Puni.

Staff from Image Services have helped with a galaxy of scans and enhanced digital reproductions, part of the copious resource material I have needed; I am very grateful to Les Maiden, Kerie McCombe and Robert Cross. I would also like to thank Chris Szekely and the staff of the Alexander Turnbull Library who have, as always, provided expert help when needed.

Tony Ballantyne read the manuscript, and I am greatly indebted to him for his encouraging, acute and generous report. Jolisa Gracewood is an ace editor. I would like to thank her for her meticulous and extremely helpful work, and of course it is always a pleasure to work with Fergus Barrowman, superb reader, excellent editor and generous friend.

I have presented conference papers and public talks on the subject of this book at Sydney, Melbourne, Tasmania, Claremont California, Auckland, Otago and Masterton, and in my inaugural professorial lecture at Victoria University, Wellington, in May 2008.

Early versions of the research were published as 'Beetham of Brancepeth'. *Turnbull Library Record* 38 (2005) 57–63; and 'Reading on the Farm: A Study of the Brancepeth Farm Library'. *Bulletin of the Bibliographical Society of Australia and New Zealand*, Special Issue 28: 1,2 (2004) 184–194.

Finally, I am always lucky to have Alastair, Seb, Bry, Max, Lizzie, Tom, Jeremy, Francis, Maarten & Nick on my side.

CHAPTER ONE

The Romance of the Archive

On a summer morning in the twenty-first century, Brancepeth is not far away, only nineteen kilometres from Masterton, yet still remote, reached by quiet roads that wind through cuttings and over the limestone hill country of the east Wairarapa. This is sheep and beef land, scattered with English trees and the occasional farmhouse. At the intersection known in the 1890s as 'the Cross' there are stockyards, a hall, a small country school; this is Wainuioru. The bridge over the river is flanked by poplars that flame gold in the autumn. Soon after, the road comes to a T-junction; straight ahead is a cattle-stop and an unprepossessing wooden fence bearing the sign 'Brancepeth'. A steep and narrow dirt road to the top of the ridge and there it is: tall white gates and behind them the house, manorial, imposing, with three red gables and a crenellated turret.

This is not the original homestead: the first low double-gabled house was built from green sapwood in the 1860s. In 1905, parts of it were pulled down because the sapwood had rotted, and it was replaced by the red-roofed, two-storeyed house you see today. A carriageway sweeps past vast trees planted in the middle of the nineteenth century, the rose garden and the tennis court. I drive around to the right, through a cluster of farm buildings—the old barn and cookhouse, the schoolhouse, the men's whare—and into the yard behind the house, where I pull up beside the farm office. It is quiet, apart from the occasional shout, bark or cry of a peacock. From time to time, a quad bike or a ute clatters noisily down the road. In the porch of the office I find the rusty key and unlock the door.

The office at Brancepeth occupies half of a long, low, weatherboard shed, built of heart totara logged on the farm. The building fulfils two functions—on the far side of the office wall is the old library, entered from another porch that opens onto the road at the back, so readers could kick their muddy boots off. The library is now empty of books and filled with obsolete farm tools, but the office still contains the remnants of what was once a very important job. Pigeonholes line the wall above the desk, stuffed with ancient invoices, receipts and letter books, containing flimsy carbon copies of letters posted a hundred years ago. The shelves beside the fireplace hold row upon row of ledgers and station diaries, labelled by year; I reach for one, and it brings with it a shower of silverfish and dust. The room is full: memoranda and old bills hang on hooks, clipped together in bundles; there are cardboard labels, metal cash boxes, an antiquated safe, two ancient kneehole desks and a bentwood chair, a binding press, mailbags, and, on the dusty desktop, untidy piles of books. On the walls hang framed photographs of prize stock, an undated black and white photograph of the gate of the farm piled high with snow, and two torn posters from the *Illustrated London News*: one is Lord Tennyson, and the other might be Gladstone—perhaps the last survivors of a gift of four 'pictures of literary men' mentioned by the clerk in the station diary of 1901.

The Australian historian Greg Dening writes of the romance of the archive and what you find there—'lives, caught like dried flowers between the pages of a book'[1]. Dening's image applies quite literally to the Brancepeth library, where I did find flowers between the pages of books, but the romance of the archive at Brancepeth includes the contents of the office, the outbuildings, gardens and the homestead itself, where almost nothing has changed or been thrown away, and the artefacts and daily objects of a long-gone era are everywhere. Ralph Beetham's pipe-rack, with his initials carved on it, was given to him in 1901 when he was twenty-one, and hangs by the back door, still full of his pipes. The back stairs of the house are covered with nineteenth-century wallpaper, the cellar holds racks of hock and claret made more than a hundred years ago, and the station store's shelves are stacked with tins of long-vanished commercial brands of flour and treacle and ant poison. There is a buggy in the stables, and rows of bridles and saddles hang on pegs, the property of long-dead riders, whose names are engraved on their tackle. A crosscut saw, brought by the Beetham brothers on foot over the Rimutakas in the 1850s, is nailed to the wall. Though it is still a working farm, the station has something of the air of a museum—it is listed in the Historic Places Trust register as a Category I site[2]—and on every hand there is evidence of the lives that have been lived there since it was founded.

Walking into the office at Brancepeth, it is as if the clerk has only just closed the door and gone for lunch, except that a layer of dirt covers everything, insects scramble for the corners at my approach, and tatters of scrim hang off the walls. But John Vaughan Miller, who worked in the Brancepeth office for thirteen years from the first of January 1894, and Frank Garnett, who succeeded him in 1908, would still recognise the room they worked in and the files they created. Open any one of the ledgers or diaries at random, and the handwriting, in black ink with emphatic points made in red, is distinctively the hand of a clerk, with beautifully spaced names, ornate capitals, and lavish use of clerical abbreviations, including, in

Miller's hand, the long double s (ʃ) of the eighteenth century. The columns are neatly filled with long tables of accounts, and page after folio page records the small transactions of the many people who worked on the farm when it was at its largest: from the mid 1880s to 1905, before the Lands for Settlements Acts forced the break-up of the big estates.[3]

Up to 1905, when the Williams–Beetham partnership that owned the station had been dissolved and it was partitioned into separate farms, Brancepeth was one of numerous large settler estates that attempted to recreate an English rural gentry in New Zealand. Traditionally, the larger country estates were sheep stations. Sheep farming had the largest cost of private entry—James Belich notes that £2000–5000 was the minimum required to set up a run[4]—so the industry attracted a class of settler with either personal wealth or the necessary connections for raising capital. The Beetham family had emigrated from Surrey in 1856, driven by the universal motive of improving themselves, but also equipped with gentlemanly ambitions and influential networks. Their first piece of land, the 10,000 acres on which the homestead was built, was a leasehold block deriving from the Castlepoint purchase[5] that had not been taken up by its original holder, Matthew Hill. The station was run as a partnership between two families: the Williams–Beetham partnership, referred to by the family and their employees as The Firm. It supported two major homesteads: Brancepeth, where the family of Hugh Horsley Beetham and Ruth Bidwill Beetham lived; and Te Parae, the home of Annie Palmer Beetham (Hugh's oldest sister) and her husband T.C. (Thomas Coldham) Williams, son of the missionary Henry Williams. Over the initial thirty-odd years of the Williams–Beetham partnership, as the estate began to make money, they bought up surrounding land as it became available, until at its largest, Brancepeth covered about 76,000 acres and employed two to three hundred people.

Brancepeth, or 'Brawn's Path', is said to have been named for an early incident when a wild boar charged through a clearing where the Beethams were bushfelling.[6] By the 1890s, it was not only the organisational centre for the whole estate, but a social hub for the wider district. On any one day, at least twenty or thirty people came and went from Brancepeth, going about their business—bringing stores and mail, looking for work, organising chores on the farm, touting their wares, swagging, visiting the Beetham family, inspecting the sheep, surveying the property, passing the time. The clerk, John Vaughan Miller, who worked very long hours seven days a week (though he took things a little easier on Sundays), bitterly resented anyone who spent too much time in his office 'jawing', as he put it in the diary. Because Brancepeth was home to a whole community of people—the family, their house servants, the shepherds, bushfelling or rabbit-poisoning gangs, shearers, clerk, garden staff, grooms, cowmen, bullock drivers, roadmen—it provided a whole range of facilities for the people who belonged to it. There were cottages on the out-stations for the farm workers, and a schoolhouse with a schoolmaster for their children; a store at which you could buy clothing, food, tobacco, stationery and other small wants and necessities; the usual cookhouse and sleeping whares; and a substantial station library.

Station libraries were not a singular phenomenon in nineteenth-century New Zealand. In her 1971 thesis, 'The Colonial and his Books', Dulcie Gillespie-Needham identifies and discusses several station libraries including Brancepeth.[7] However, Brancepeth was exceptional in that it was never dispersed. Also, unlike some of the other station libraries studied by Gillespie-Needham, the Brancepeth library was not predominantly a self-improvement library. It carried a large number of books (just over 2000), most of which were contemporary Victorian fiction. The editor of the *Wairarapa*

Daily Times asserted in 1895 that the Brancepeth library was superior to the publicly funded library in Masterton, containing no 'rubbish', and run by 'managers with literary ability and business aptitude'.[8] It was believed by the people who used it to be the 'best of any station in New Zealand'.[9]

For these and many other reasons, the Brancepeth Station Library offers an extraordinary opportunity to reconstruct the lives of readers in a particular community at a specific historical moment. As Jonathan Rose has pointed out, it is 'relatively easy to recover the reading experiences of professional intellectuals', but the recovery of 'ordinary readers in history'—what they read and how they read it—has been a largely unanswerable question.[10] The remarkable thing about the Brancepeth library is not so much that it existed, but that it still exists as an intact collection, complete with tears and stains and reader debris. As such, it provides a material portrait of reader use and offers a wealth of information about who individual readers were, and what they liked, and didn't like, to read. Because the dirty books were not discarded by fastidious librarians, as was the case with damaged copies in many other private and municipal libraries, they bear evocative witness to the life of the station. Scribbled on, torn, falling apart, they embody their vanished readers, moments in whose lives are sometimes literally caught (or placed) between the pages, in the form of a dried flower, an insect or a blade of grass.

Even more exceptionally, the library is just one of the many interconnected archives of the station. These combined records—the multiple volumes of the station diary, ledgers, letters, invoices and family books—make for enticing glimpses of everyday life a hundred years ago. If the library opens windows on individual readers, the station records flesh out their social world. Reading was only one of the many occupations and activities taking place in a community that had a number of layers and was also physically bounded. The intensive record-keeping at Brancepeth opens out a localised micro-history of colonial relationships, which can add fresh nuances to the more generalised narratives of a national history. More particularly, the Brancepeth records offer some detail of the intellectual and emotional lives of these readers.

In another sense too, the history of the Brancepeth books, their readers, and their reading habits, provides an opportunity to address the obvious gap in the broader history of reading, which has primarily relied on borrowing patterns and reader autobiographies to chase down the elusive historical reader, but has paid almost no attention to content.[11] Any investigation of what Brancepeth readers preferred inevitably raises the question of reading taste: why did these people living and working on a New Zealand sheep station like what they liked (or not)? The comment and opinion provided in various forms by the station clerk, John Vaughan Miller, sheds an unusually sharp light on this question. More broadly, the narrative preoccupations of Victorian fiction, in what was the golden age of the novel, are suggestive about how fiction might naturalise imperial interests and ambitions in the minds of readers. Books, newspapers and their seductive companions, the illustrated magazines, ensured that readers everywhere stayed connected to Britain, and particularly to London's intellectual culture—and, thanks to the ubiquity of lending libraries, the circulation of ideas and narratives about Britishness and the empire was a normal part of daily life wherever you lived. This truism is demonstrated as vividly and powerfully by the life of a sheep station as it is by Sir George Grey's private library, or by the public libraries and mutual improvement societies that mushroomed throughout New Zealand and the British Empire in the latter half of the nineteenth century.

The growth of public libraries in New Zealand in

the nineteenth century, as J.E. Traue has shown, was exceptionally fast—an 'explosion', he dubbed it—with the highest density of libraries relative to total population 'ever reached in any country or state in the world'.[12] These libraries were subscription libraries, controlled by incorporated or unincorporated societies of subscribers, and later subsidised by municipal authorities. Traue notes that census figures indicate that, between 1873 and 1896, the number of volumes per head of population in New Zealand varied between one book to 1.72 and one to 3.05 people, which was more than for the colony of Victoria, making New Zealand a 'veritable paradise' for readers (152). In answer to the obvious question—why was this the case?—Traue begins with New Zealand Company propaganda from 1844:

> A well-conducted colonist is of necessity a reading man . . . None but they who have resided in a new colony can appreciate the value of a new book; and we are happy to bear testimony, that in no colony is literature more appreciated than in New Zealand . . .[13]

The Beethams were a literary family; their history is filled with minor literary and artistic figures, and literary culture, perhaps at its height in Victorian England, was something they participated in as a matter of course. Like many settlers, they brought their own books with them to New Zealand, which included books borrowed from (and never returned to) lending libraries in Britain. But the establishment of the subscription station library at Brancepeth along with many other libraries like it in New Zealand is not fully explained by the New Zealand Company's blandishments to prospective settlers. Traue persuasively draws a parallel with California, which also sprouted libraries and, like New Zealand, had an abnormally low percentage of women in its population, leaving a large number of men with little recreational diversity. At Brancepeth, likewise a disproportionately masculine community, a library was a socially approved diversion from the daily round of hard physical work. But as Traue also points out, by the second half of the nineteenth century, reading for pleasure, as opposed to reading for self-improvement, had established itself as the predominant reading culture and thus a primary market for book publishers. Advances in print technology and transport meant that large supplies of cheap novels could be quickly available in New Zealand by means of the low-cost 'Colonial Edition' reprints of popular novels. Once the hard physical labour of 'breaking in' the land had been achieved, what James Belich has referred to as the 'leisure ethic' of the colonial gentry[14]—an elegant marriage of work, respectability, public service and what Lady Barker called 'station amusements'[15]—took a more dominant place. At Brancepeth, the increasing leisure of the runholders is suggested by an expansion of household and administrative staff from the end of the 1880s, which is documented both in the station records and in the increase of files, diaries, ledgers and written records. There was also an exponential growth in book orders and library space about this time; by 1890, the library required a separate building. The collection consisted mainly of fiction (about 88%[16]), more evidence of the 'leisure ethic' as well as an eloquent witness to the steady popularisation of reading that took place in the latter half of the nineteenth century.

The Brancepeth library was moved off the station as an intact collection in 1966, partly for preservation reasons and perhaps because there were no more readers for its time-worn Victorian novels. Hugh Beetham, grandson of Hugh Horsley Beetham, gifted the library, along with its original wood and glass bookcases made by joiners working on the farm, to Victoria University of Wellington. The books now inhabit the ground floor of the University Library, a multi-storey concrete block designed in the 1960s and a world away from the cosy wooden farm library room, with its armchairs round the fireplace and central newspaper table spread with a patterned cloth. A stipulation of the gift was that the library be kept in its tall glass cases. The books, covered in red 'linenette' now faded to a dirty yellow-brown, neatly numbered and with the title and author handwritten across the top of the spine, are the object of idle curiosity from staff and students who stray from the history stacks. They are seldom read and not often handled, but their presence quietly evokes the difference between reading for pleasure and reading in an academic institution. The books are clearly part of a private (although not personal) library, and collectively speak their particular history—published in the last two decades of the nineteenth century, read on site by long-dead readers, and kept together, complete with damaged copies and a catalogue, in matching faded jackets in their antique hand-made cases. When the cases are opened, the look, feel, and smell of the books is redolent of the nineteenth century. Alongside the cases, photographs of the station library *in situ* on the farm, taken shortly before it was transported to Wellington, give the passing student a glimpse of the collection's former life.

Some elements of the library archive and the book collection are now missing. The lending book, which the station clerk described as sitting on the central table together with the catalogue, has disappeared. Some of the books, too, are missing, and many are damaged. Other than a few nineteenth-century repairs, there are only light signs of a librarian's hand in the physical management of the collection. The books are numbered according to an alphabetical list of authors, so for example Mrs Henry Wood's phenomenally popular *East Lynne* (1861) would be marked 449/19: she is the 449th author on the list, and this was the last of her nineteen books to be purchased and added to the collection when the catalogue was published in 1895. It is, however, also one of the books that no longer exist, probably because it was either read to death or filched by an ardent reader. The missing volumes are almost more evocative in their absence than their presence.

Because reading is often a solitary occupation, the trajectory a reader takes through books on the shelf mostly vanishes from view, as do their reactions to what they read. But the life of a book can also be written on its pages and covers. Most of the remaining books have had rough lives, shown by their wrinkled, stained and sometimes torn covers, ash-grey edges and numerous greasy fingerprints. Together with the ghosts of their missing fellows, they are tangible proof that these books had eager readers. The varying wear and tear offers many clues as to reading taste, individual reader reactions, and the use the community made of its resource, and though the Brancepeth library no longer inhabits the narrow purpose-built totara reading room with its central table and armchairs by the fireplace, the station archives are full of its presence and the books are, often literally, full of the farm.

Reading is a situated activity: it happens *somewhere*. By a fire, in the grass, over dinner, in the smoking room, in the country, the city or on the train. Other things happen around it. People talk, argue, work, get drunk and eat; they quarrel with each other, worry about their pay and their health, get distracted, work too hard. And the place in which they do all these things is, in this case, also a colony, part of a worldwide network—an 'imperial web' as Tony Ballantyne has called it[17]—comprising different and distinct peoples and cultures, and a power dynamic that writes itself into all aspects of life, including not only the choice of books for a library but what was printed on their pages.

Greg Dening has observed, 'there is in history no resurrection. There is only cultivated meaning . . . History . . . is independent of our knowing, as wild as reality, controlled and ordered like life, but not by us.'[18] At every point, the Brancepeth library archive demonstrates this truth: it is tantalisingly detailed but frustratingly incomplete, with its missing books and records. Both what remains in the record and what is absent from it suggest a number of questions that this book pursues, but cannot always answer. What was the shape and nature of the library, and what can we know about how it was used? Who were the readers? What was the social world of the reader and what kind of place and society did the library service? What sort of interactions occurred in this diverse community? What connections were there between the novels these readers enjoyed and the place in which they read them? What was *in* the books they read and how it did those stories connect to the larger world of Victorians and their books? And what, ultimately, is it possible to know about everyday life in the late nineteenth century in rural New Zealand?

Brancepeth station a hundred years ago can neither be revisited nor fully understood from the twenty-first century. Even the noises of the station have changed, both in volume and urgency, the thunder and grunt of a bullock-team giving way to the roar of quad bikes and utes. There are no more horses, no laundry maids, no grooms in pale blue suede coats, nor whares full of swaggers. The library building is empty of books and readers, filled instead with rusty bits of equipment among which float a few stray issues of the *Illustrated Sporting and Dramatic News*. But it is possible to read the intersecting social and literary histories of Brancepeth in the 1890s—incomplete as histories always are, and restricted to certain particular points of view—from the many different textual archives created on the station. Via the details and omissions, and in the anonymous fingerprints and marginalia covering the books, the station readers and their fellow workers, in their many guises, occupations and diversions, come into view.

Archivally, the richest period at Brancepeth is the years from 1893 to 1908, when the job of farm clerk and record-keeper was held by John Vaughan Miller. Miller liked to write. He had been a clerk in the Admiralty before emigrating to New Zealand in the 1880s, and his ledgers and diary volumes bear the marks of professionalism. After Miller's first year, he upgraded the record books to a folio format, probably because the A4-sized Rough Diary from Whitcombe and Tombs he used in his first year didn't give him enough space. The newer folios are Commercial Diaries in hard cover, with the year printed in gold on the spine. Written mostly in black ink and interleaved with blotting paper that retains tantalising glimpses of crossed out phrases, the folios record the weather, daily events, visitors, financial transactions, chores (a regular entry concerns the winding of the clock), mail deliveries, people and stock movements, tasks, gossip, and some details of Miller's own life—letters received and written to his family, articles written and dates of publication, and small or large irritations of the day. Miller cross-references diary entries with the ledgers, which contain the personnel records; these tell what each employee spent in the store, for example, or the various costs that were deducted from their pay, one of which was the library subscription. Details about how men lost their jobs, or where they moved to, are sometimes recorded in the ledgers, although the events leading up to being 'paid off' or 'po'd', which is how Miller always referred to it, are generally recorded in the diary. The library collection itself is full of marginalia, much of it written by Miller, who also spent his spare time writing opinion pieces, articles and letters for the local paper. Most of the men on the farm did not produce written records themselves (though a few letters survive), but they all had dealings with Miller, which are faithfully recorded in the diaries. Lost are the great library lending book and the notices and lists of subscribers Miller posted in the library, but an astonishing number of documents remain, even the small pocket diaries Miller ordered for the shepherds to keep their tallies and notes in.

The station library was not the only collection of books on the farm. The Beethams had a sizeable family library in the smoking room that was used as a study and office. Some family members also kept intermittent diaries, and the family vault holds an extensive collection of wills, survey plans, passports, photographs, postcards, letters, scrapbooks, poems and small objects, the accumulated memorabilia of an affluent nineteenth-century family, members of the class Belich has dubbed 'sheeplords'.[19] The Beethams, part of the closely-networked colonial and Anglo elite, were literary and artistic, and enthusiastically well-connected both at home in New Zealand and at 'Home' in England. Their sense of landedness, position and heredity made them good archivists —nothing was thrown away, and they zealously collected records of their own origins, documentary history and textual artefacts. Hugh Horsley Beetham's son Ralph became a book and curio collector in later life, and the smoking room contains many early New Zealand books as well as books the family brought with them on the journey to New Zealand. Books and paper artefacts are of course not the only objects that were preserved, but the sheer quantity of textual objects and the care taken of them speaks eloquently of the esteem in which literacy and literariness were held on the farm.

The way the homestead and its surrounding buildings are laid out also says much about the importance of reading on the farm. The house faces west across the Wainuioru River to the hills and the Tararua mountain range beyond. The building that contains the office and the library sits behind the house, at right angles to the back door and separated from it by the drying lawn, which lies between the house and the laundry. A little gate divides the office from the store, but, like the laundry, the office is inside the gate, and thus part of the larger space occupied by the house. John Vaughan Miller could look out his window and see what was happening in the kitchen, the laundry and the back garden, as well as who might be coming across from the house. Anyone approaching the house from the rear—which was most of the working population of the farm—also had to pass his office; in the yard behind him, the daily traffic poured in and out from the lane which ran down the back of the farm buildings. Brancepeth's huge kitchen gardens spread out across the paddock northeast of the house, while out the front of the homestead was a more formal, decorative garden with extensive shrubberies and rose beds, and a paddock, known as 'Tempest paddock', where horses were grazed. The formal part of the grounds also featured a tennis court to the left of the main drive, and there was a fernery in the garden at the back of the kitchen and a vineyard on the hill behind the house. The stables, the cookhouse, the schoolhouse, the original whare built by the Beetham brothers on the site, and the large whare where the men and the swaggers slept (the latter one of the few buildings no longer standing), are grouped round the drive at the back.

The homestead is the first thing a visitor sees. Large, imposing, with a square tower above the front porch (it is said to have been modelled on a Scottish hunting lodge), it is the picture of colonial success. Cresting a gentle rise, it overlooks a landscaped garden of enormous exotic and native trees planted in the nineteenth century, with sweeping lawns and a lovely rural outlook beyond. Tucked behind the homestead are the working parts of the farm, neatly arranged in a loose semi-circle, connected but not crammed together, with the library and the schoolhouse down the lane. The station office is located at the point of intersection between the shared working buildings and the grand house. Everything related to the business of the farm spreads out from that little gate that opens on to the office porch. At the other end, the library faces outward towards the working area of the farm, with its own porch opening on to the road. Anyone wishing to visit the library would have had no difficulty in finding it, but it was a little secluded from the continual business of the office. The library acted as a social space for men working on the farm, who could sit by the fire in the evening or on Sundays reading the papers; it is likely, too, that women from the homestead, family members and the governesses, browsed the shelves peacefully during the day. The library building also hosted meetings of the Library Committee and other gatherings, some of which are mentioned by Miller in the station diary, and seems to have been used as a reading room by visitors to the station, such as the vicar. The library rule specifying that no one is to have a newspaper for more than fifteen minutes suggests there was considerable demand for the papers and consequent traffic in and out of the library. The local paper arrived every day and the British and Scottish papers came in each month, as well as a range of illustrated papers such as *The Graphic*. Despite the sense of busyness around the library, where readers competed for the newspaper while the station clerk catalogued, labelled or packed up orders of books for sending out to men working in remote areas, it was well situated for moments of privacy, solitude and concentration, offering a separateness appropriate to the life of the reader, while remaining at the heart of station life.

Not all reading activities were private and personal. The collection contains a marked-up copy of Dickens's *A Christmas Carol*, suggesting at least one seasonal performance, and Miller noted in his diary entry for Saturday, 6 January 1900, that there was great excitement in the house about a 'book title' dinner that evening, which he attended. What exactly a 'book title' dinner was Miller failed to explain, but perhaps they dressed up or performed charades. Miller also wrote articles for the *Wairarapa Daily Times* and a few other papers based on books he had read or articles from the British papers. And the library was admired and used by visitors to the station. Ellis Rowan, the Australian flower painter (1848–1922), visited Brancepeth in the mid 1890s; she produced two watercolours of the homestead that still hang on the walls of the morning room, and recorded in the book she wrote about her travels that she was taken to see the 'well-stocked station library, where all the new books and papers were to be seen.'[20] Many visitors contributed to the library's holdings, inscribing their gifts with names and dates. Books also accrued by accident, exchange, or were left behind by the shifting population of the station, sometimes on purpose. In the office, for example, a large family Bible has been left by the cowman, George Mallory, who presented it to the Brancepeth library on his departure for England.

Oral tradition on the station claims that the library was established in part out of a wish to improve literacy among the workers, and that the schoolmaster gave classes in adult literacy (although there is no firm evidence of the latter). Literacy rates in New Zealand were probably similar to those in Britain (census responses in New Zealand estimated the overall rate of illiteracy in 1858 was 25%),[21] but improved across the century. For comparison, Martyn Lyons has claimed that by the end of the nineteenth century, 95% of adult Australians could read and write, although the measure of literacy was simply being able to write your own name.[22] Certainly John Vaughan Miller, who wrote some articles about education, did not believe that the standard of literacy in New Zealand was high. Literacy varied by gender as well as class: over 80% of single-women migrants to Canterbury between 1857 and 1871, for example, were unskilled and probably had little chance of subsequent education.[23] The female household servants at Brancepeth may well have been illiterate; according to Miller, many of them had minimal social or professional skills. It is worth noting here that no female subscribers to the station library are recorded in the ledgers—which does not, of course, mean that no women borrowed books. Of those who might have subscribed, the governess probably had free access courtesy of her job, and the wives of men on the station perhaps regarded a single membership as a family subscription.

Even if the existence of a subscription library on a sheep station suggests an intention to facilitate literacy and self-improvement among the workforce, the collection actually contains very little in the way of self-improving texts. There are a few books which might have been connected to the schoolroom and used for learning to read (adventure stories by Captain Mayne Reid, and improving tales like Frederic Gammon's very popular *The Canal Boy Who Became President*), but given the subscription rate of £1 per annum, and explicit rules barring non-members, it is unlikely that any children were borrowers. The collection has a 'backbone' of the English canon (poetry, history, biography, general reference), but as a whole the Brancepeth library conforms to the tastes of Daphne Lawford, heroine of M.E. Braddon's 1881 novel *Asphodel*, who remarked crossly on receiving a box of new books from Mudie's circulating library:

> 'More "Voyages to the North Pole"; more "Three Weeks at the Top of the Biggest Pyramid"; more "Memoirs of Philip of Macedon's Private Secretary"', cried Daphne, sitting on the ground beside the newly-arrived box, and tossing all the instructive books on the carpet, after a contemptuous glance at their titles. 'Here is Browning's new poem, thank goodness! And a novel, "My Only Jo". Told in the first person and the present tense, no doubt; nice and light and lively. I think I shall take that and Browning, if you don't mind, Lina; and you shall have all the Travels and Memoirs.' (179–80)

No doubt the primary reason for the predominance of fiction at Brancepeth is simply that these were the books people wanted to read, the popularity of bestsellers as potent on a sheep station in New Zealand as in the big circulating libraries and family collections in Britain. As Amy Cruse perspicaciously observed in her 1935 study of the reading habits of Victorians:

> The Victorian reader . . . did not confine himself to 'great' books. It is the great books we know, that make up the literature of a country, but there is a sense in which the lesser books are equally important. For a book does not become effective, does not really come to life, except in its contacts with the reader . . . the books that figure largely in the histories of literature are, in many households, those which are placed respectfully behind the glass doors of the best bookcase . . . . . . while the family reads and rereads old favourites in tattered covers, and devours by dozens new volumes from the circulating library.[24]

What people *actually* read is a subject of great interest to scholars of book history.[25] But reading is not easy to study—unless the reader has what Dening called 'performance consciousness', that is, unless they kept a reading diary or otherwise made their reading public, as John Vaughan Miller did by writing occasional articles about it for the paper, reading tends to lie invisibly in someone's life. Like Cruse's Victorian family with their 'best bookcase' and their tattered favourites, the books at Brancepeth illuminate a layered history of reading, and reveal a layered world. To understand something about what Brancepeth embodied and how it worked, we must begin with the people who created it.

CHAPTER TWO

Willie's Diary

> I have made several unsuccessful attempts to keep a diary, but after having made a very spicy commencement I have got worse and worse and when very far behind have given it up. How I wish I had from the time of first commencing October 8th, 1851, kept a regular diary, dotting down my different thoughts and doings. Every day I see fresh advantages that would arise from such a course, I might have improved in writing, spelling and composition and have had the pleasure of being able to refer to the different periods in my eventful life.[1]

William Beetham, often known as Willie, second son of William and Mary Horsley Beetham, wrote this entry when he began his new diary in 1852. Attaching what he thought were the most interesting entries from his previous attempt, Willie began the story of his life again on 15 April, but broke off at 3 May. He began a fresh effort on his birthday in August, which he kept up for another eleven days. In July the following year, he started another diary and kept it going until the end of April 1854; at the time, the family was living on a farm at Frimley Hill, which Willie calls Finnley Hill, in Surrey. As he notes ruefully, 'it was a kind of farm diary and giving up the farm I of course gave it up also'. He was 17.

Willie's diary is full of laments about his lack of application—to his diary, to reading and writing, to the progress of his life. He berates himself for carelessness, idleness, despondency and being a 'poor hand at learning languages':

> Sept 17th, 1854. . . . I feel wretchedly out of love with myself; what time I have wasted and how deficient I am, oh! That I could improve the passing moment and banish these despondent thoughts—fool that I have been to neglect so long my own improvement . . .

During the years that he spent worrying about his personal failings and recording them in his diary, Willie's family was likewise in a state of indecision. Richmond, the eldest son, who was trained as an engineer, left for Australia in May 1852 in the hope of work on the goldfields. Two years later, there was talk of Willie following him overseas—'I hope New Zealand', wrote Willie—but despite reading a pamphlet on sheep farming in New Zealand that he liked 'much', little headway was made on a decision about his future. In the meantime he was sent to stay with relatives in Doncaster, went to church, helped househunt, mucked about with his brothers and felt idle and useless.

Willie's father, William Beetham, was a professional portrait painter who had achieved some success, working for a time at the Court of the Tsar in St Petersburg and exhibiting at the Royal Academy. Even so, in the manner of many fathers in Victorian novels, he was always anxious about money and constantly looking for ways to support his large family of seven sons and three daughters. On his 60th birthday in 1869, William would note that it was the 'first moment of my life which occurred as being free from grinding anxieties . . . '[2] It would be a long journey, both temporally and geographically, to that sense of ease. In a letter to Willie (17 November 1854) he declared that making a home for the family was his passion and yet 'there is little likelihood of my doing it here in this country'—so, like many of his class and generation, he turned his gaze to the British colonies. Stories of sons doing well elsewhere circulated amongst people they knew—for a time there was talk of Willie going with another boy to join Richmond in Australia, or trying the American West—and while William senior worried and deliberated, young Willie wrote intermittently in his diary and tried to prepare for life on the frontier, by attempting to learn algebra, 'drilling' in sums, reading books about the goldfields and building a model of a wooden frame house.

Willie's anxieties about being a burden to his parents and applying himself insufficiently to writing, languages, algebra—spring not only from boredom and inactivity, but also the general emphasis placed by Victorians on self-improvement and duty, reinforced by the specific expectations of his family. He frequently noted injunctions from his father to, for example, 'spend your present moments in improving your mind and helping your brothers and sisters with their studies' (17 November 1854). While William senior was away from home looking for work and advice (he considered Australia, Nova Scotia, and America, as well as buying a farm in England), Willie tried to improve himself through reading and writing. He read useful books like *The Gold Colonies of Australia*, as well as Byron's poems, Scott's *Waverley*, a novel called 'Margaret Waldegrave'[3] of which he said 'was much interested—think some of the characters rather sage for their years', and a book he names as 'Earncotness',[4] while lamenting, on 29 August 1854:

> I am very much afraid I am getting careless with my diary the fit is going off . . . I again resume my pen. I put off again and again and the more I am behindhand the more disinclined I feel to set to it. I don't suppose there is much worth writing about but I must try what I can remember.

Willie's sense of intellectual duty partly reflects his family environment, in which reading for instruction was common (though they also read for pleasure: in 1851, Willie described a peaceful domestic scene—'in the evening rubbed my chillblains while Annie read sense and sensibility'[5]). It was also no doubt exacerbated by the particular circumstances in which he found himself: conscious of the family's unfavourable financial situation; envious of his older brother's freedom and purpose in Australia; and itching for his father to make a decision that would settle his future. Willie's earnestness was also, of course, a product of the cultural and social norms of his class and society. As Beatrice Webb wrote, referring to the mid-Victorian middle class,

> It was the bounden duty of every citizen to better his social status . . . Only by this persistent pursuit by each individual of his own and his family's interest would the highest general level of civilization be attained.[6]

When Willie visited his uncle's printing works at Lincoln in September 1854, he declared he would write letters from New Zealand which would be published in the newspaper. The expansion of his own life into print and the print culture in which he lived was a source of both anxiety and pleasure, but was also taken for granted as a necessary ambition and expression of experience and success.

In the winter of 1854, recovering from a serious bout of smallpox which made his head feel like a 'vast soft ball', Willie lay in bed in reading the *Edinburgh Journal* and the *Illustrated London News* (both of which would be continued as long-term subscription journals at Brancepeth).[7] His mother also read to him from the church service and from 'Dick's diffusion of knowledge',[8] but Willie's thoughts constantly turned to New Zealand, mostly on practical matters. On 19 December he records reading 'London's Enciclopaedia' [sic].[9]

> Spent the day in reading 'london's' looking into the formation of orchards, draining etc. Draining will probably be useful in New Zealand. I am afraid I scarcely comprehend it, read a small portion of 'Ultima Thule'. I will continue to peruse it.

> Dec 20th. . . . Spent a greater part of the day in reading 'Ultima Thule'. I should very much like to go to New Zealand.
>
> . . . If Georgic and I go, it will be very nice to work hard and get a portion of land and build a house to receive them, I should be proud to do it. Land is very dear . . . I wonder how in small portions we could procure land.
>
> Dec 21st. Reading 'Ultima Thule' a great part of the day, he says in one part that land is from 5/- to 10/- per acre and in another part of his book he states Pounds without saying what kind of land it is . . . Papa says we shall never be able to accomplish New Zealand and must be content with the Far West of America.

When he was better, Willie was sent off by his father for lessons from the blacksmith and it was also suggested he take instruction from a carpenter, but the carpenter 'sent a very polite message that he would not have anything to do with me'. William senior's attention was clearly focusing on the kinds of skills that would be needed by emigrants, and if they could not be gained by experience, they could at least be learned from books. Among the reading matter that the family would eventually bring to New Zealand were useful practical texts: *The Complete Measurer* by Thomas Keith (London: 1824); *Cottage Building* (London: 1849–50), which has both W. Beetham and R. Beetham (probably Willie and his brother Richmond) written on the inside front cover, with a handwritten list of what might be estimates for 'Weather Bds, Partition, Roofing and Flooring'; and *The Useful Arts and Manufactures of Great Britain* (London: 1851), published by the Society for Promoting Christian Knowledge. Such texts would be put to good use when Brancepeth was established. The Beethams manufactured gas for lighting the house and established a water supply from a hilltop bore which still provides the main water source for the homestead. But their lack of practical experience was also illustrated by the fact that they built their first homestead from sapwood, not realising it would rot; this was perhaps a result of Willie's failure to ingratiate himself with the carpenter.

Reading aloud was a family activity recorded by Willie, and as the winter proceeded with a decision about where to go seeming no closer, he notes 'Papa read in Marjorie Stickland's life in America[10] and discussed the capabilities of Nova Scotia' (11 January 1855). After 'Papa' returned to London, 'we read aloud French Hay[11] as we have continued to do every evening during the week' (12 January), moving on to Sir Walter Scott's *Guy Mannering* when it was finished. William also read 'Tenison's Poems' (an 1842 copy of Tennyson with 'W. Beetham' written in it still exists in the Beetham family library), but found the quotidian progress of his diary tedious: 'I really see no use in recording each day separately[;] one will suffice for all' (12 January 1855). After a false start in April 1855 when 'Papa' proposed going to America by himself, there to 'pursue untrammeled his professional career [although] this plan does not exactly meet with Mama's approbation', Mary Beetham came home from London in May with the news that 'we were all to start for NZ on the 16th July in the WILLIAM AND JANE.'

Unsurprisingly, the diary goes into a hiatus until the family were underway, when Willie began again. Travel narratives were all the rage in the nineteenth century,[12] and as the experience of travel became less unusual, accounts of seasickness and other privations of travelling were made tedious by repetition. By 1886, for example, Edward Wakefield, the nephew of Edward Gibbon Wakefield, objected to the historian James Froude's book about New Zealand, *Oceana*, on the grounds that Froude's preoccupation with the dirty and uncomfortable conditions he traveled under was a 'most trivial narrative of everyday occurrences on steamers, the sort of stuff a hobbledehoy who has never been abroad before would write home to his little sisters'.[13] Wakefield's point about the tiresomeness of travel clichés is germane, but Willie's description of the trials of life on board a sailing ship—a rougher and more arduous proposition than a steamer—is refreshingly candid:

> I must say the wretchedness and misery far surpassed anything I imagined it was certainly terrific; everyone as ill as could be; the table covered with dirty pots, the pos full, the slop pail do [ditto]; everyone calling for the spueing utensil at the same [time] and none well enough to pass it; the ship pitching and rolling terrificly; everything tumbling about in the greatest confusion—there was several scenes in our cabin that would defy the pen of the ablest writer to describe much more than me . . .
>
> I have rendered myself wretched by neither keeping a log or writing letters with little difficulty I might have made a most interesting record. I cannot excuse myself I have put off from day to day as if frightened of it—as it is little good lamenting I will give it up and try what energy and perseverance will do for the future—turning over a new leaf as I enter the Southern Hemisphere.
>
> The chief thing we have to complain of has been caused by the wet coming through the roof of our cabin causing us an immense amount of trouble and stink; all our stores got wet, the bedding likewise in fact there was scarcely a rag in the cabin that was not sodden and before we could get them dry they were anything but sweet . . . (29 July 1855)

Willie's intentions of learning 'Latin, Greek, French, German, algebra and I don't know what all' on the voyage fell by the wayside, as he ruefully noted, '3 weeks from N.Z.' (24 September 1855); he was much more interested in keeping watch and helping sail the ship. When off duty, he spent time reading in the roundhouse, mentioning *Oliver Twist* and Albert Smith's *The Struggles and Adventures of Christopher Tadpole* (1847), a comic picaresque novel heavily influenced by Dickens, which was to become a popular book in the

Brancepeth library. The voyage was in any case full of excitement and instruction. The crew mutinied en route to South Africa, and there was a long negotiation before they agreed to take the ship into the Cape. Then, while at the Cape, Willie met a Māori who was conversing with the Captain.

> The Maori was a most intelligent fellow; the Governor's servant. If he is a sample of those we are to deal with they are certainly much superior to what I had imagined; he seemed to think New Zealand a cold clime. I am not sure if I understood him aright. (12 October 1855)

Willie's father did not approve of him keeping watch and threatened to put a stop it, but Willie found it gave him an appetite for reading and also for physical work, a capacity he would put to good use when the family landed.

The Beethams had originally embarked for the Canterbury settlement where they had friends and connections, but they were sick of the voyage and also very taken with Wellington when they arrived there on 1 December 1855. So, after a number of meetings with locals, and indecisive fits and starts, 'Papa' returned to their temporary lodgings on 12 December to announce he had bought a 'plot of ground with a nice house and buildings thereon known by the dignified title of "Court Lodge"' in Upper Hutt. By the end of January 1856, Richmond and Willie had found work building the Rimutaka Hill road, and an opportunity shortly arose for their father, with J.H.C. Hutton, to take over the leasehold on a run of 10,000 acres at Wainuioru in the eastern Wairarapa. Richmond and George Beetham, along with Jack Hutton, went on a reconnaissance trek to sketch out the boundaries, and an application for a run licence was lodged with the Commissioner for Crown Lands, William Fox, at the end of August 1856. The next year, Jack Hutton left for the Otago goldfields after falling out with the Beetham sons for undisclosed reasons, and the 'Hutton block' became Brancepeth.

While his sons began work on clearing and stocking the land, William Beetham established himself at Te Mako in the Hutt Valley with his wife and the younger children. He began work on his first commissioned portrait, a posthumous painting of a local chief, but it is not clear who this was. There was some irony in William Beetham's return to portraiture. On leaving England, he had intended to 'make a clean sweep of art from my care and devote myself and family to rural pursuits—that utopian snare to many unfitted persons', but his wife had covertly packed up his pictures from the lumber room, along with his easel and 'other accompanying apparatus', and he was able to continue his career as a portraitist, leaving the rural pursuits to his sons. The generational shift from financially shaky, indecisive father-artist to pragmatic, physically capable and fiscally successful sons is not uncommon in colonial fiction of the period, and indeed in Victorian fiction generally. The Beetham family story contains many of the elements of a successful triple-decker like Henry Kingsley's *The Recollections of Geoffrey Hamlyn* (1859), Mrs Henry Wood's *The Channings* (1862) or Wilkie Collins's *Hide and Seek* (1856)—all popular at Brancepeth and all novels in which characters have the daring to move across the world and establish a new imperial elite, which is morally justified by hard work and the display of typically Victorian virtues such as fortitude, persistence, piety and liberality. New Zealand versions of such adventure-romances appeared a few decades later, like W.B. Churchward's *Jem Peterkin's Daughter* (1892) or F.E. Maning's famous *Old New Zealand, by a Pakeha Maori* (1884), which were heavily read by Brancepeth library subscribers.

Like a number of early colonists in New Zealand, especially those who went to the Canterbury settlement (many of whom later featured in Burke's 1891 *History of the Colonial Gentry*), the Beethams took with them to New Zealand a strong sense of their familial and class destiny.[14] The family originated from Westmoreland, where there is a river called Betha, the village of Beetham and a fourteenth-century fortified house, Beetham Hall. They claimed an illustrious descent from a Ralph de Betham who 'was in enjoyment of the Manor of Betham in the time of Henry 11'.[15] Hugh Horsley Beetham, William and Mary's fourth son and eventually the sole owner of Brancepeth, named his children Ralph, Thyra Talvase, Weva and Orengard, venerable family names that occur among the immediate descendants of Ralph de Betham. This memorialisation of the ancestral lineage was deliberate, as suggested by handwritten annotations in the Beetham family copy of Burke's *Colonial Gentry*, which note that 'Thyra was the daughter of Edward the Elder, King of England' and Weva was the name of her daughter with 'Gorma the old, third King of Denmark'.[16] The smoking-room library at Brancepeth holds a number of books about heraldry and some commissioned genealogies that elaborate the family ancestry. The family coat of arms is a popular motif: it appears on the Beetham bookplate with the motto *per ardua surgam*, and is emblazoned on the front of the house, and on a shield (carved by Thyra) still displayed in the smoking room. In the latter part of the nineteenth and early twentieth century, the motto was painted on the family buggy, which was driven by a groom in livery. Ruth Bidwill Beetham, Hugh's wife (and daughter of C.R. Bidwill, one of those whom A.G. Bagnall refers to as the 'founding quintet' of Wairarapa runholders[17]), kept a scrapbook of press cuttings,[18] some of them from the British papers, which record Beetham family events in New Zealand—funerals, weddings—alongside items about Doncaster, Beetham village and church, Brancepeth Castle and members of the family in Britain. Clearly, the New Zealand Beethams prized their extended family networks and well-documented history.

A major part of the inheritance of the Beetham family, reflected both in William's choice of profession and his son Willie's anxieties about failing to live up to the family's expectations ('I wish I could draw' he wrote on 19 January 1855), was its literary and artistic prowess. William Beetham's fifth cousin was the poet and portraitist Matilda Betham. Born in 1776, eldest of the fifteen children of Mary Damant and the Reverend William Betham, Matilda was a friend of Samuel Taylor Coleridge, Robert Southey, and Charles and Mary Lamb. In August 1905, Hugh Horsley Beetham bought a copy of Ernest Betham's *A House of Letters*, an edited collection of letters written to Matilda Betham by Coleridge, Southey, Lamb and others, plus excerpts from her diaries, and 'notes of some phases in the evolution of an English family'. The Brancepeth copy contains shopping lists ('8 stiff collars, 12 handkerchiefs') memos ('Ring Cockburn') and pencilled lines marking particular passages, such as, in reference to an attempted seizure of estates in Cumberland and Westmoreland by James I:

> . . . the holders replied that they had retained the land by the right of their swords, and that they were still prepared to do so. (22)

Another marked passage is interesting in view of the role taken by various Beethams in settler politics—like other runholders and early settlers they were active members of the Wairarapa militia in the 1860s:

> [T]he main need, in the days of military tenure, was that there should be able limbs and steady hearts when it came to talking to the enemy at the gate, especially if it chanced to be at his gate. (26)

But the bulk of the book is less to do with the Beethams' history of defending their lands than the broad range of talent and success exhibited by Ralph de Betham's descendants. Over the generations, various Beethams built and endowed schools, gave an endowment to the Botanical Gardens at Cambridge, and made their mark as preachers, scholars, soldiers, actors, playwrights, poets and painters. Isabella Robinson Beetham was a famous late eighteenth-century silhouettist, and her husband Edward wrote plays and invented an improved method for gilding glass.[19] Their son William was a distinguished botanist and Fellow of the Linnaean Society. Threads of family stories are woven into the larger patterns of history. Ernest Betham mentions that Elizabeth Betham, daughter of the Collector of Customs on the Isle of Man and a scholar who was said to be a friend of Adam Smith and the Scottish Enlightenment philosopher David Hume, was a 'woman of superior attainments'. She married William Bligh, 'Vice-Admiral of the Blue and Governor of New South Wales, better known as the unfortunate Captain of the "Bounty"' (21). Jane Beetham, Matilda's first cousin, was taught by John Opie the portrait painter, exhibited at the Royal Academy and painted miniatures professionally. Matilda Betham's father, William (the botanist) was known as 'the poplar-planter' to distinguish him from the many other William Beethams, and 'was given to painting and exhibited skill at portraiture' (27). He also wrote two genealogical histories. Ernest Betham includes excerpts from Matilda's diary, in which she wrote,

> In our quiet and unorganized household sometimes the arts were all in all—sometimes learning unlocked her abstruse stores and people talked, albeit without pedantry, as if in the house of a philosopher. Sometimes plays were read and listened to with enthusiasm, or poems, followed in succession by the criticism of admiration . . . We had loads of books in my father's library, and new ones, with reviews, etc., from the book-club every month. (29)

Matilda Betham herself seems to have led a literary life that is almost novelistic in its wealth of colourful incidents and exemplary talents. When she was eighteen she recorded in her diary the development of a friendship with Charlotte Jerningham, later Lady Bedingfield and daughter of Lady Frances Dillon Jerningham,[20] who showed Matilda a poem by one 'Benedict' that had been found fixed to a tree in the grounds of her home, Cossey Park. She asked Matilda to write a reply to it 'that we might find out who it was written by'. The poem 'An Answer to Some Lines in Cossey Park' opens

> Fly Benedict! And in this dangerous way,
> No more, allur'd by thy ill genius stray[21]

The diary does not record whether the girls unveiled the author (who must have had Shakepearean ambitions), but this poem, written in 1794, was the precursor to *Elegies, and Other Smaller Poems,* a collection of poems published by Matilda in 1797, which was widely and enthusiastically reviewed.[22]

Around the turn of the century, Matilda settled in London hoping to earn a living with her pen. She taught herself to paint miniatures, and caught the attention of Coleridge, who wrote a poem addressed 'To Matilda Betham, from a Stranger, Keswick, Sept 9, 1802. S.T.C.', which opens:

> Matilda! I have heard a sweet tune play'd
> On a sweet instrument—thy Poesie—
> Sent to my soul by Boughton's pleading voice . . .
> . . . And now the fair, wild offspring of thy genius
> Those wanderers, whom thy fancy had sent forth
> To seek their fortunes in this motley world
> Have found a little home within *my* heart . . .[23]

Matilda Betham published three more collections of poetry: *Poems* (1808), *The Lay of Marie* (1816), and *Vignettes: In Verse* (1818), plus a work of historical biography, *A Biographical Dictionary of the Celebrated Women of Every Age and Country* (1804). In 1810, Mary Lamb wrote to Matilda Betham

> We have read your poems many times over with increased interest, and very much wish to see you to tell you how highly we have been pleased with it.[24]

A House of Letters contains transcripts of many affectionate and intimate letters to Matilda Betham from Coleridge and his wife, the Southeys and the Lambs, and reports of presents of miniatures and books she sent them. Mrs Coleridge wrote to Betham in 1810, passing on Coleridge's 'best thanks for the elegant little book; I shall not, however, let it be carried to Grasmere, for *there* it would soon be *soiled*, for the Wordsworths are woeful destroyers of good books, as our poor library will witness' (123–4).

A recent biography of Matilda Betham notes that little more is known about her life;[25] Betham's own niece, goddaughter, and partial namesake Matilda Betham-Edwards published a biography of her aunt in *Six Life Studies of Famous Women and Friendly Faces of Three Nationalities* in 1880, but only fragments of her diaries and letters have survived. What is clear from Ernest Betham's collection of letters written to her is that she wrote copiously. Betham's poetry has recently been reprinted in facsimile, including her best-known work, 'Lay of Marie' (1816) concerning Marie de France, and a number of her portraits survive.[26] She remains a minor, though interesting, figure in Romantic poetry, but as an ancestor she is of considerable stature. Matilda Betham died in 1852, just four years before William and Mary Beetham emigrated to New Zealand.

Matilda Betham-Edwards, niece and biographer of Matilda Betham, was a friend of George Eliot's and is represented in the Brancepeth library by copies of three of her novels. She was of Huguenot descent and wrote a number of books about France and the French aiming to improve relations between France and England. Daughter of a farmer, Betham-Edwards was celebrated for her lyrical descriptions of Suffolk country life, and is described by John Sutherland as Suffolk's most famous novelist along with Richard Cobbold.[27] Among Brancepeth readers, the most popular of Betham-Edwards' novels was *The Sylvestres* (1871), a novel set in Suffolk. It is about a social reformer, Ingaretha Meadowcourt ('Ingaretha' is another name from the Beetham family tree) who allows the Sylvestres, a socialist French couple who are political exiles from Algeria, to develop a utopian 'Phalanstery' on her land. The novel is a comic rebuttal of socialism: the Sylvestres are wildly impractical, turning half an acre of corn-land into a rose garden so that 'young men and maidens shall have garlands during the following summer' (164). M. Sylvestre is comically vain. Delivering a lecture on socialism to the bemused country populace, he gives orders that straw should be laid on the road 'for a hundred paces each way' so the noise of carriage-wheels will not disturb his oratory. Hopeless at farming, the community finishes the summer with all supplies exhausted, thanks to its primary rule that each member should 'only perform the work he had a liking for' (199). Socialist politics were not favoured at Brancepeth, and their comic lampooning in Betham-Edwards' novel is likely to have been well received by the Beetham family, who would not have missed the point that the Sylvestres' social reform was dependent on the generosity, virtue and wealth of old landed aristocracy, in the person of Ingaretha Meadowcourt. They are likely also to have agreed that farming requires practical application. John Vaughan Miller, who shared the political opinions of his employers, also read *The Sylvestres*, and annotated some of the more egregious views expressed by the characters about farming. When one of the characters declares that if 'Daisy the cow gave less milk than usual after last night's draining, who grumbled?', he underlined it and wrote in the margin, 'a very happy idea!' (94).

The New Zealand Beethams are likely also to have agreed

with Trollope's sentence on the opening page of *The Prime Minister*, one of the most heavily read books at Brancepeth:

> It is certainly of service to a man to know who were his grandfathers and who were his grandmothers if he entertain an ambition to move in the upper circles of society . . . (1)

Ruth Beetham's scrapbook, for example, contains many press cuttings relating to the extended family in England, including two announcing Matilda Betham-Edwards' death. The artistic inheritance of the Brancepeth Beethams manifested itself occasionally in later generations of the family (Richmond Beetham had considerable talent as a watercolourist and Annie and T.C. Williams's daughters Maude Burge and Hilda Williams were talented artists), but strongly influenced the ways in which they created and maintained their cultural lives. William Beetham, already well-known as a portrait painter before the family emigrated in 1856, had sent portraits to New Zealand in 1853. According to Willie's diary, on the day the *William and Jane* arrived in Wellington Harbour, his father presented a letter of introduction to a 'Mr. Rodes' [28] who had seen the pictures sent in the *Maori* and who 'wants his wife portrait taking'. It was Rhodes who advised Beetham to buy land in the Hutt and follow his artistic profession, which is what he did, leaving the business and trouble of establishing a sheep run to his sons. Beetham's well-known *Portrait of Dr Isaac Featherston with the Maori chiefs Wi Tako and Te Puni* (1857–8) was painted only two years after arrival, and still excites comment and debate. In 1991, for example, Brian Easton described this portrait as a 'political poster' illustrating Featherston's infamous remark that the job of the 'civilised white' was to 'smooth the pillow of the dying race', but more recently, Roger Blackley has persuasively argued that Beetham's portrait is 'imposing and unprecedented', remarkable for its inclusion of Māori leaders with a colonial leader. Blackley posits that Beetham himself must have had a close relation to his subjects.[29] The circumstances which led to Wi Tako and Te Puni being part of the Beetham portrait are not recorded, nor is what they thought of it, but contemporary whānau of the Te Ātiawa chiefs find the picture revealing in its treatment of Featherston, and reflective of William Beetham's relationship with Wi Tako and Te Puni. He has accurately painted the moko of both chiefs, and their demeanour is a counterpoint to Featherston's. The portraits were also praised in the artist's lifetime: an 1888 obituary notes his 'admirable' portraits of 'Dr Featherston, Mr E.J. Wakefield, Te Rauperaha (the famous chief), Te Puni and Wi Tako'.[30]

William Beetham also wrote poetry which was never published, but was preserved in fair copy in a hardback notebook dated '1869, Brancepeth', the year he turned sixty. His poems are very much in the Romantic mode so powerfully established by Wordsworth and Coleridge's collection *Lyrical Ballads*, published in 1798, eleven years before William Beetham was born. The verses reflect on nature, the death of friends, country characters and places, music, his wife's birthday, his own life. There is a set of sonnets addressed to the seasons, and another about the life of Shakespeare, and towards the end, a number of poems set in New Zealand: 'To Daisies in New Zealand', 'Mountain Phases: A Sketch in the Wairarapa', and a sonnet 'Fame: On reading Mr Domett's Poem "Ranolf and Amohia", written in New Zealand':

> Wide Sphery Fame shall reach Earth's utmost bounds;
> And chaplets weave with honors to invest,
> All gifted ones, where'er they chance to rest;
> Where Genius, bright, assays to weave rhymed rounds
> And seek true glory in celestial sounds;
> Due to the few, who, 'mongst the world's great best
> Shall sing sweet poesy, in Truth's behest;
> Than which, no guerdon gleams in higher grounds!

As these lines show, William Beetham's poetry, which bogs down in conventional expressions of sentiment and rhyme-chasing, is not his strong point—an observation indirectly confirmed on another page in the collection, where a charming pencil sketch of St George's Church, Doncaster eclipses in artistic effect the poem it accompanies, 'On hearing the church bells of my native town after a long absence'. But the effort and persistence of his poetic composition shows itself as a gentlemanly accomplishment, as well as demonstrating deep familiarity with contemporary and historical British literature. Regardless of his change in location from Home to colony, William Beetham maintained the life of a cultured person, an artist who was also a poet and a connoisseur, a landowner who was well educated and liberal in his sympathies and knowledges. He operated under a set of expectations that followed not only from his individual talents, but also from his class and his heritage.

Broadly speaking, these expectations were manifested at Brancepeth and in the Beetham family as a kind of continual self-improvement, perhaps more properly described as keeping up to date. This was a never-ending work of cultural and historical maintenance, in which being British (rather than 'colonial') was the unquestioned norm. The station library for example, was overwhelmingly British in its selection of books. (It also included novels and poems from Australia, Canada, South Africa, and New Zealand, but these were variations on the mainstream rather than separate literatures, distributed to far-flung book markets through the cheap colonial editions of major British publishers). In their pursuit of wealth and standing, the Beethams contributed to the preservation of a way of life that mirrored the tastes and behaviours of upper-class Britain. George Beetham was a Member of Parliament for many years and Senior Whip in the Atkinson Ministry of 1887–1890; he was known as 'Gentleman George'. The

Beetham brothers (William's sons) served on local bodies and took on a variety of roles: Hugh Beetham helped to found the Wairarapa A & P Show and the Wairarapa Jockey Club, while Richmond Beetham established a trout hatchery in Masterton, was a senior Stipendiary Magistrate in a number of places including Christchurch, and was instrumental in establishing the Christchurch Art Gallery.

The effort the Beethams put into becoming founding members of the colonial gentry and good ambassadors of the British Empire was also manifested in their acquisition of te reo Māori and their relationships with Māori people, from their arrival in the 1850s. William purchased Te Mako, his house in Upper Hutt, from Wi Tako Ngatata who became a friend. Part of the agreement was that William and his descendants would look after the beautiful pātaka Nuku Tewhatewha which was on the land, and was later moved to Brancepeth.[31] (The arrangement about the pātaka lends plausibility to Roger Blackley's view that it was probably Beetham's initiative to include the chiefs in the Featherston portrait.[32]) William Beetham undoubtedly held conventional colonial views about 'natives' and 'civilisation', noting that while some Māori 'dress like other people[,] some are worse than dirty gypsies', but he was also fascinated by the Māori he met: 'I couldn't keep my eyes off that dark man, his face was figured all over'.[33]

In the 1840s, pastoral leases in the Wairarapa were negotiated directly between settlers and Māori resulting in a complex social and economic entanglement. One of the earliest leases was between Te Manihera[34] and C.R. Bidwill of 'Pihautea', who was Ruth Beetham's father. A later newspaper account of the history of settlement in the Wairarapa described Bidwill as 'one of Manihera's pakehas'.[35] In the early years, the article claimed, Bidwill was never 'molested' by Māori, but was said to be 'obliged to allow them to quarter themselves upon him pretty much as they chose'. On the early sheep stations, there was a close dependency between Māori as lessors and their Pākehā lessees, and this blurring of the roles of host and guest was still in play at Brancepeth in the 1890s. The station had long-running leasehold arrangements with Māori, especially in relation to a block of land called Waipapa, and the 'Waipapa Rents' are a regular entry in the station ledger.

Jim McAloon has observed that early arrival was the key to pastoral wealth in New Zealand.[36] The Beethams arrived rather late in the Wairarapa landrush, when the rich flat land had already been 'taken up', leaving the hilly eastern land in the 'relatively inaccessible' Wainuioru valley.[37] Matthew Hill had been granted 10,000 acres by Francis Dillon Bell, but failed to take up the run, so an enlarged version of Hill's parcel was subsequently granted to Beetham and Hutton. Over the next forty years, the area of the farm increased five-fold thanks to run licences and leaseholds, with four overseers concentrating on different areas, thus widening the network of relationships in the district and also enormously increasing the profitability of the station. A.G. Bagnall's history of the Wairarapa notes that the station's 1890 tax return 'shows what foresight and labour had put into *Brancepeth* . . . The total assessment of the partnership's improvements was more than three times that of any other Wairarapa station and was exceeded by few others in New Zealand'.[38]

This dramatic expansion of the farm was significantly enabled by the establishment of a partnership with Thomas Coldham Williams, son of the missionary Henry Williams; he married Annie, the oldest Beetham daughter, in 1858. (Annie had previously been unsuccessfully courted by the hapless and irksome Jack Hutton, who not only failed to win her favour, but fell out with her brothers as well, although the details are obscure). T.C. Williams, as he was known, became the leading business partner in the Brancepeth estate, providing most of the finance, and was instrumental in increasing its size and capacity over the next forty years. 'T. C.' was fluent in te reo Māori and deeply involved with Māori politics. He wrote a famous appeal to Gladstone on behalf of Ngāti Raukawa, and when the appeal was heard by William Fox at Otaki in 1868, Fox described Williams as better able to speak the Māori than the English language.[39] While not up to the level of their brother-in-law, some of the Beetham boys were linguistically competent in Māori and most of them made an effort to learn it, taking lessons and practising when they could. In his diary entries for the years 1857–8, Willie began using smatterings of te reo Māori, as in the entry for 18 July 1857: 'Turned out before daylight. Kaied and were ready for a start before dawn . . . discussing the pros and cons of our prospects etc. "te akiahi"' (possibly *ahiahi*, evening or afternoon). Willie recorded Māori words and his ambition to pronounce them correctly (for example, Wairarapa), and sprinkled words like 'pikanga' (perhaps *pikaunga*, burden or load) into his writing. Hugh Horsley Beetham, the Beethams' fourth son, who was running the station by the late 1870s, wrote and received letters in te reo Māori and acted as translator and advisor when asked on Māori business. During the Land Court hearings in Greytown in the 1890s, Hugh Beetham was frequently consulted by Māori he knew and often accompanied them on visits to their lawyer and to Court hearings. The station diary records numerous visits, for example by Mr and Mrs Te Tau of 'Kaumoana' in August 1905, on 'Maori business' at Stronvar.

In the homestead at Brancepeth there are a number of books in Māori, including William Williams' *Dictionary of the New Zealand Language* printed at Paihia in 1844; a copy of the first Māori Bible, *Ko te tahi wahi Te Kawenata Tawhito*, a translation of the Old Testament from Genesis to Joshua printed by Robert Maunsell in 1848 and inscribed

'George Beetham with the love of his affectionate Sister Annie P. Williams Dec 29th 1858'; and several other copies of the New Testament in Māori inscribed to various family members. *Ko te Kawenata Hou* (The New Testament, 1852) has 'Na Hui Pitam' (Hugh Beetham) inside the front cover, and a number of passages in Matiu (Matthew) have been underlined and translated in pencil, which suggests both that the books were read and used, and that learning Māori was taken seriously.

The circumstances by which the Beethams acquired land would have made their ability to speak Māori a critical asset. A sizable chunk of the Brancepeth land was leased from local Māori, and the family maintained amiable and close connections with a number of the lessors, particularly Piripi Iharaira Aporo (Ngāti Kahungunu) and Ihaia Whakamairu (Ngāti Kahungunu) who was also involved in selling land for the site of Masterton after pressure from the Small Farm Association.[40] The Beethams' first encounter with Māori in Wairarapa occurred when Richmond and Willie were camped at Nicol's whare at Taueru in 1856, and were 'very much astonished' by a visit from four Māori, 'Piripi, Matihaha, Tamiti Wiremu and another Maori' who 'brandished weapons' and declared that the whare was built on their land. After 'pacific measures' the Māori explained their land claims and boundaries, and the next day Richmond accompanied them to the adjoining station, Moore's, to discuss the state of affairs.[41] Piripi was Piripi Iharaira Aporo, one of the most important chiefs in Wairarapa, who became a close and long-term friend of the Beetham brothers, and often stayed at Brancepeth in the early years of the station.

Leasehold arrangements were not liked by the Colonial Government, which went to some lengths to abolish them after 1853, when Donald McLean began the process of purchasing Māori Lands for the Crown, during which 'six or seven hundred' Ngāti Kahungunu were coerced to part with 'nearly a million acres of ancestral territory'.[42] The original fifteen stations in Wairarapa were all leased directly from Māori, who saw the value of their lands increase as the annual rents rose. This arrangement produced transactional relationships of mutual advantage that were maintained over long periods of time. Brancepeth began as a run license on land that had been acquired by the Crown, but later added Māori leaseholds, including 4000 acres from Ngāti Kahungunu via Ihaia Whakamairu. The mutual benefits of leasehold are said to be one of the reasons there was no armed conflict in the Wairarapa in the 1860s, though there was certainly a threat of conflict in August 1863, after the invasion of the Waikato by military forces in July.[43] The Beetham sons were members of the Wairarapa militia, and a manual in the family library, *Drill and Rifle Instruction for the Corps of Rifle Volunteers* (1860), has a hand-drawn diagram inside the back cover explaining how to lay out a rifle company for battle. By the 1890s, however, Ngāti Kahungunu had lost most of their land, and the disparity between Māori and settler populations made armed conflict unlikely.

Māori visited Brancepeth constantly—sometimes three or four times a week—to buy stores, borrow money and equipment, sell or buy stock, socialise, and sometimes to seek help with their complex legal affairs. Their financial transactions with the station are recorded painstakingly in the ledgers and diaries, and they often ate or slept on the station. The station diary for the 1890s reveals that there was a large casual Māori workforce, mostly shearers and daggers, and several permanent employees who were Māori. There were also Māori who maintained close personal relationships with Hugh and Ruth Beetham, such as Taiawhio and Pani Te Tau, Henare Maaka and his sister (referred to in the station diary as 'Miss Maaka' when she lunched with John Vaughan Miller), and

Hori and Whitianga Te Huki. Hugh Beetham gave evidence for Taiawhio Te Tau in a libel case he took in 1903 against the local Māori newspaper *Te Puke ki Hikurangi,* which had accused him of evading the dog tax.[44] Hugh Beetham, his sons, and no doubt his brothers too, attended tangi for Māori leaders and friends, such as Piripi Aporo in 1895 and Naera Pita in 1903, and the 'immense' tangi at Papawai Marae for the great chief Tamahau Mahupuku in January 1904. Māori who were personal friends were invited to dinners, dined, visited for tea, stayed in the main house, and were guests at family weddings. Newspaper clippings of Thyra's wedding to Marmaduke Bethell in 1903 all refer to the presence of Hori Te Huki, variously named 'Old Huke', 'Māori Chief Heki' and 'Mr Huke', and describe his gift to the bridal couple:

> The quaintest gift was a *taiaha*, presented by Mr Huke, a Maori chief whose friendship with the family is of long standing. With it he gave a little posy of white dried leaves, bound together with some huia fathers and a spray of maiden-hair. He was a noticeable figure at the dance given the same evening . . .

Another paper reported that during the afternoon 'Old Huke' had given them 'a too brief illustration of his own style of dancing, and some of the younger men had joined in the *haka* with him, with a most successful effect'.[45]

Hori Te Huki (Rongokokako) had come to the Wairarapa from Wairoa as a middle-aged man, to settle eventually near Taueru, adjacent to Brancepeth. He had a considerable political profile, representing 'the East Coast', for example, at the funeral of Richard John Seddon in 1906, where he recited a lament.[46] He and members of his extended family were a constant presence at Brancepeth, and he frequently stayed in the house. The relationship between Te Huki and Hugh Beetham appears to have been close and friendly, though Miller had a more mixed view of him, referring to his 'kleptomania' when he visited the Brancepeth store.[47] In the wider community of the farm, the relationships with Māori were not without tension, but the station diary for 16 March 1900, notes (in red ink) that there is an instruction that 'Maori are to be treated with all kindness'. It is clear from the diaries that Hugh Beetham was always available to Māori who came to see him, and they did so regularly.

The Beetham family's intellectual and cultural engagement with Māori was pragmatic, but also sentimental. They established friendships with Māori they regarded as their equals and were carefully paternalist with others. Their enthusiasm and interest in te reo Māori and Māori culture was also connected to what Thomas Richards calls the 'paper empire',[48] the enormously energetic accumulation of knowledge in the colonial world. The printed word, as Benedict Anderson persuasively established, is a foundational element of nationalism; it is also one of the most important instruments of imperialism, both in the wider context of British expansion, and the local context of particular communities. As D.F. McKenzie has pointed out, a community is shaped and formulated by the many texts it receives, produces or makes its own.[49] As a whole, the Beethams' diaries, letters and book collections reveal the assumption, common to many early settlers who acquired land, that culture and learning is part of what it means to live at all. One of the necessities of a manorial life, and a cultured British world in New Zealand, was a good library; the Beethams brought with them a collection of classical texts and the expectation that colonial life would continue and even enhance their engagement with British cultural and intellectual life. In this sense, the family was part of what J.R. Seeley in 1883 referred to as the 'Expansion of England' or what Charles Dilke meant when he called his travel book 'Greater Britain'.[50] They brought quite a lot of books with them from England: many reference works; poetry, especially Milton, Byron and Tennyson; Hazlitt's edition of Shakespeare; and bound volumes of Dickens' periodicals *Household Words* and *All the Year Round.* Some books were brought by accident—including a couple belonging to the Derby County Library—while others were left behind. In a letter of 1867, William Beetham Sr wrote:

> After twelve years of procrastination I write a few hurried lines to enquire about the box of books left with you. I expect ere this you will have found them a nuisance and most likely have sent them to the winds . . . My son Jos. is just articled to the Law and will require some law books. Could you send me a catalogue of Law Books? Can they be procured at second hand? He wants first 'Blackstone's Commentaries' by Stevens. You might possibly have an opportunity of picking up at second hand such books as he may want from time to time—I remember the London Bookshops.

There was also a specifically local dimension to this determined accumulation of knowledge, visible in the acquisition of volumes in te reo Māori, as noted above, and early New Zealand books such as Charles Hursthouse's *New Zealand: The 'Britain of the South'*(1861), as well as volumes on New Zealand flora and fauna, history and Māoritanga.

The formal creation of a library probably began sometime in the 1860s as the station expanded its area and workforce. In the early years of Brancepeth, Willie's diary is laconic and completely preoccupied with recounting the work of the day. He no longer records what he reads, nor any anxieties about improving himself—the work of improvement was physical and agricultural. But in the 1860s, a periodical-lending circle was begun among Wairarapa families. Copies of *The Quarterly Review* (October 1863) and the *Edinburgh Review* (October 1862) have lists of names pasted inside the front cover with 'received', 'dispatched' and 'forwarded' dates beside them, and the instruction 'To be kept one week only/Fine for keeping over time/ and not entering dates 3d a day'. The list of names covers the eastern side of Wairarapa and includes names from South Wairarapa (Riddiford) and also Masterton (Sellar), which raises the question of how the journals were distributed. The answer is probably by coach, but the list offers an intriguing glimpse of early Wairarapa networks. It is also an illustration of how determined settlers were to maintain their reading habits and keep up to date.

In contrast to the station library, the Beetham family's personal collection is dominated by non-fiction, much of it on the subjects of farming and settlement. There are books about guns and horses, a copy of *The Complete Grazier*, a book about sheep and shepherding. Many are Christmas presents, including a copy of *The Poems of Byron*, in a handmade case embroidered with the Beetham coat of arms, and inscribed 'Ralph with love from Mother'. Ralph's school prizes, mostly imperial books for boys like *Famous Frontiersmen* and *Deeds That Won the Empire*, share the shelves with the usual mix of useful and recreational books that characterise many family libraries. Brett's *Colonist's Guide & Cyclopaedia of Useful Knowledge* is filled with clippings with handwritten titles like 'A Durable Whitewash' and 'How to Burn Stumps', and an apparently unread copy of Sir Walter Scott's *Tales of a Grandfather* is inscribed with Ralph's name and the date, 'November 29th, 99'.

When Ruth Bidwill married Hugh Beetham in 1879, instructive books given to her by her father were added to the family collection, notably *Good Words for the Young* for 1871 and 1872, which both show signs of considerable use. There are loose pages someone has scribbled on and dried ferns tucked between the leaves. Ruth was a devout woman who came from a religious family—her mother's obituary, clipped and pasted in the family press cuttings book, noted the 'conscious rectitude of her private life, her fortitude and her faith' (10 July 1894). Ruth gave her children prayer books, and Anglicanism is a distinct subject category in the family library, like heraldry and agricultural knowledge. The smoking-room library also contains a number of works on British military history, science, moral philosophy, and art, including *The Imperial Gallery of British Art* bought by Hugh in 1899. There are copies of Horace, Herodotus, Virgil and Homer; useful reference books, classical texts, major works of the English canon, history and religion, and personal books. In short, the Beetham library is an expression of an upper-class colonial family's interests, made up of books that reflect their education, their needs, and their cultural and intellectual ambitions.

Surprisingly, there is not a lot of nineteenth-century fiction in the Beetham family library. There is a well-read copy of *Middlemarch* (1874), some Dickens, Sir Walter Scott, several books by H. Rider Haggard (one of which, *Cleopatra*, was given to Ruth by Ralph in 1895), a few titles by Smollett, and a complete set of the novels of S.R. Crockett, a minister of the Church of Scotland who became a successful novelist of Scottish vernacular fictions mostly set in Galloway. But if the station library collection began to grow in the late 1860s or early 1870s, its first acquisitions may well have come from, or doubled as, the family collection, constituting a sort of fiction annex to the reference collection in the smoking-room library. The station library's numbering sequence begins with titles by Scott, Fielding, Trollope, Thackeray, Eliot and Dickens, many of which show signs of heavy use. It is not until the 1880s that acquisitions began to pick up in number, which probably reflects not only the boom in British publishing (and therefore far wider choice of new titles and authors) but the station's own development: at this point, it had greater prosperity, more employees and therefore more family leisure time. By the early 1890s, Brancepeth boasted a substantial station library, a formal institution with its own set of procedures and regulations.

From the 1880s on, there is a split between the two collections, with more personal, expensive and antiquarian books kept in the house, and cheaper recreational reading relegated to the outside library building. What is perhaps most interesting is that all but a handful of the books about New Zealand, or produced in New Zealand, were kept in the homestead, perhaps as a recognition of their value as expensive objects (Featon's 1889 *The Art Album of New Zealand Flora,* for example), but also an indication of their significance as cultural capital. There are a few New Zealand novels in the station library, but the useful (and now rare) early New Zealand books, which are all non-fiction, such as William Williams' *Dictionary of the New Zealand Language,* are kept in the house. These books express a sense of being at home in New Zealand, whereas the station library offers a broader, more nostalgic context of 'Home' and many more diversions from the work of being a settler.

By the 1890s, the station had developed other accoutrements of gentility, including a fern conservatory, expansive ornamental gardens, and a tennis court. There were also three vineyards: a small plot next to Willie Beetham's house in Masterton, three acres at Lansdowne and another at Brancepeth. The vineyard employed a winemaker and was overseen by Willie Beetham's French wife, Hermanze Frere,[51] who helped with the harvest along with 'Gentleman George' Beetham and his wife. The vineyard used a wine press imported from France, and had a substantial underground cellar, described in the *Wairarapa Daily Times* in 1897 as being sixty-six feet long and eighteen feet wide. (A photograph of the harvest of 1897 is now a much-reproduced picture in Wairarapa wine publicity.) There is still a collection of late nineteenth-century hock and claret in the cellar at the Brancepeth homestead. The vineyard also produced a sparkling wine and some bottles remain, although they no longer sparkle.

The Beethams supplied wine to the Wellington Club, of which they were members; their strong political connections gave them access to the colonial elite based in Wellington, which supplemented their active social life in the district. In this they were typical of their class—James Belich notes that it was a 'rare genteel family who had no-one on the inside of colonial politics'.[52] The Beethams maintained networks across the country, enhanced by marriages with other New Zealand pastoral families, particularly in Canterbury and Hawkes Bay. They were active in viceregal social circles and invited to parties at Government House. Anyone of importance visiting Wairarapa tended to call at Brancepeth: the station diary records invitations and visits from Lords Glasgow, Ranfurly and Plunket, and Bishop Selwyn may have been an early visitor, as the homestead library still holds a copy of George Grey's *Journals of two expeditions of discovery in the North-West and Western Australia* (1841) with Selwyn's signature inside the front cover.[53] Both Beetham daughters 'came out' at balls in the Wairarapa, and weddings were held in Wellington at houses owned by members of the family in Thorndon. Their social lives were also enlivened by dances, hunts, race meetings, shows, trips to the theatre, visits to relatives and friends in other parts of New Zealand, and trips abroad.

Amid the bustle and activity of an affluent colonial life, why was there such sustained commitment to the station library? They could, after all, have chosen simply to maintain it as a private collection: the Beethams read widely in the Brancepeth library and were among the most dedicated of its users, and although the library charged a solid subscription fee, overheads and other costs were significantly subsidised by the station. That they chose not to buy books only for themselves probably reflects a sense of social responsibility for the recreational and literacy needs of the community they lived in. Matilda Betham-Edwards's *The Sylvestres* is one of a multitude of Victorian novels to make the point that wealth and class bring obligations as well as privileges, a view that must have been reinforced by Ruth Beetham's Anglicanism. But the other reason is connected to more personal tastes—readers like to read, and surely the family wished to encourage the love of reading more generally on the station. Certainly the selection of books in the Brancepeth station library reflects a pleasure in reading for its own sake that was shared by the family. In addition, the Beethams' powerful sense of a familial cultural inheritance no doubt made them want to be in the know, as up-to-date with the literary times as their family and friends still living in England. The choice of books for the station library, for example, shows awareness of the ways in which new social movements were generated and represented in literature, such as the significant holding of New Woman novels.

The 1890s was a decade of intense modernisation at Brancepeth as elsewhere. The station diary records that in 1896 Hugh Beetham learned to ride a bicycle, one of the last of the family to do so, and cycle trips in and out of Masterton were not unusual. The early 1900s saw the advent of the telephone (which was used to place orders at the Masterton shops, always backed up by a written order), and in February 1907, the Beethams bought their first motorcar, which was quickly taken control of by their younger son, Oren, described by Miller as being an 'uncommonly' good driver, with 'nerve and quickness' (2 February). Before long he was taking his friends and the governess, Miss Westall, on excursions. Modernity in the form of car transport and telephones seems to have occurred to most runholders, European and Māori, at roughly the same moment. Miller also noted (4 April 1907) that the Beethams were visited by the Martins, pastoralists from Martinborough, in a motor with a chauffeur, and by Mr and Mrs Te Tau in their new car; reportedly Mrs Te Tau left her sunshade behind and it had to be sent to her the next day. The relationship between the Beethams and the Te Taus seems to have been based on shared tastes as well as social class, notably royalism, politics, horse-racing and print media. Taiawhio Te Tau (Ngāi Tumapuhiarangi) who was brought up at Papawai, farmed family land at Kaumoana, near Masterton. He also owned and operated a horse stud, and bred a number of successful gallopers and trotters. In 1897 he travelled to London to take part in Queen Victoria's diamond jubilee. He was one of the proprietors of the Māori newspaper *Matuhi*, which was edited by his second wife, Pani Parata (Ngāi Tahu).[54] The Te Taus were sufficiently close friends of Hugh and Ruth Beetham to have their photographs preserved in the family album, and to send them studio portraits of themselves, in traditional dress, as a Christmas greeting, fondly inscribed 'from Pani Te Tau' (20 December 1910).

Along with other dramatic changes in the reach and accessibility of life on the farm, the Brancepeth library signaled the advent of a new era, one in which the territorial, social and cultural ambitions of the runholders had been achieved. The proliferation of published titles and cheap editions of old favourites is reflected in the library holdings, which show a deliberate choice to keep abreast of the changing times—new and sometimes daring authors, such as Sarah Grand, Marie Corelli, or Emile Zola were included in the collection. The scale of the Brancepeth library, which was bigger than the Masterton Library in the 1890s, is also a demonstration of modernity—this was not a collection for a handful of bookworms, but an expansive gesture of contemporaneity. The continuing growth of the collection into the new century was an expression of forward tempo, cultural depth and wealth.

However, Brancepeth changed dramatically after the turn of the century, when the build-up of great estates—and by implication of a landed gentry who held most of the pastoral land—was blocked by the government. In 1903 the Williams–Beetham partnership (known to them as 'the Firm') was dissolved as a result of the Land Reform Bill introduced by Richard Seddon, who was determined to break up the large stations in favour of what was known as 'closer settlement'—smaller, more affordable landholdings. The work of valuation continued until 1905, at which point Brancepeth was partitioned into several separate holdings. To Miller's relief, Hugh Beetham decided not to split up the Brancepeth library but to buy it outright from the partnership. In effect it had always been a perquisite of the Beethams rather than T.C. Williams and his family at Te Parae, housed as it was across the yard from the Beethams' back door, with Hugh as President of the Library Committee. A separate library collection was established at Te Parae, and the Brancepeth library remained in active use and continued to expand its holdings, although after 1905 it was perhaps past its heyday. As an expression of culture on a gentleman's estate, the library marked Beetham family tastes and values, but it comes most vividly to life in its role as a community asset, used by a cross-section of the farm society. As John Vaughan Miller's entries in the station diary make plain, the library was embedded in the life of the station. Miller's account of the wider context and contrasts of the social world of the farm recreates the daily world of the station clerk and his fellow readers as they prop a new book against the salt cellar to read over dinner, scribble sarcastic asides in the margins, or play noughts and crosses on the endpapers.

CHAPTER THREE

The Clerk's Tale

In January 1900, John Vaughan Miller, station clerk at Brancepeth, went on a two-week holiday to visit his family at Motueka. When he arrived, he wrote to his employer describing his journey:

> Te Kohanga
> Motueka, Nelson
> Monday 22 Jan, 1900.
>
> My dear Mr Beetham
>
> I did not have a very pleasant drive in the mail buggy. We no sooner got to your bridge tha[n] we picked up Mrs McRae and 2 boys—and a trifle of luggage. At the Parae a hunch-back got in—so the 2 boys were put over into the front with the driver and myself—I need not say it was the reverse of enjoyable. At the Taueru we stopped some time, because Mrs Stronvar was expected, and was welcomed by the McIntosh family with great effusion—a considerable infusion must have followed, for, when the lady reappeared, there was an apoplectic suffusion of her extremely beautiful countenance, and, as I thought, some confusion of ideas—If what she had thankfully partaken of was only tea, it must have been a capital T, and far and away the strongest letter of the alphabet.
>
> But worse was to come—when we got opposite to Tuhua's house, out came a double-peonied faced thing calling itself a woman—and I need scarcely say her name was Mrs Parsons.

> The driver looked at me, and I was far from smiling—Mrs P. came smirking to the front where self, driver, & 2 boys were already stowed, besides luggage, and she lifted a fearful thing (which may possibly have been a leg) to mount—I merely remarked to the driver, ' I shall not allow this; put me down at once with my luggage'—He only smiled and whipped up his horses, and said 'thank you, Mr Miller: I was hoping you would speak'—Mrs P was simply left in the middle of the road, like Lot's wife—and not one of us had the manners to express a word of regret.

This vignette gives a taste of why, a century after the fact, the years during which Miller was the clerk and record keeper at Brancepeth spring off the page with humour and energy. Not only was he a marvellously pungent writer, with literary turns of phrase, Dickensian pacing and joking, vivid characterisation and evocation of scene, but a constant reader, too: opinionated, informed, and aware of the genre in which he was writing, in this case, the comic anecdote. This letter, preserved at Brancepeth among the family papers (presumably because it was so amusing), suggests the place he held on the farm: intimate enough to share frank opinions with his employers and to expect their appreciation of his satirical sense of humour. He writes like Dickens, or G.A. Sala, whose comic articles about journeys in New Zealand and Australia were widely syndicated and enjoyed by local readers, and who also depended on a kind of London club snobbishness for effect. But the letter also reveals many of the conditions of local life that dominate Miller's running narrative of his life on the farm and the life *of* the farm. There was the continuous difficulty of movement—irregular and unpunctual transport, dependence on road conditions, the pressure of passengers and luggage. Drinking was a constant problem on the farm as it disrupted work patterns and social relations. And, too, there was the woman question. Miller had variable attitudes to women and in that respect reflected the Victorian novels he read, where women either conformed to the 'angel in the house' stereotype made so popular by Coventry Patmore's poem, or its opposite, as in the figure of Mrs Parsons, who personifies disruptive, unreliable and unattractive femininity. Miller also fervently disagreed with—and disapproved of—the politically active New Women of the era. But what is perhaps most striking and unusual about the letter, and even more so about Miller's writing in the station diaries, is his vigorous delight in narrative for its own sake.

Miller's letter to Hugh Beetham, relying as it does upon a tacit set of agreed attitudes, conveys something of the nuanced class hierarchy of the farm, and the complicated position of the station clerk, on paper the social and intellectual equal of his bosses, but in practice very much an employee. When Miller retired from the farm in 1908 due to ill health, he was replaced by Frank Garnett, a much younger man who began the job of clearing out a 'great accumulation of dust and old documents and papers of all sorts'—this, on the day Miller left, which also happened to be his 69th birthday (13 January 1908). The insensitive timing may say something about how Miller was regarded by other people on the farm, an impression made even stronger by a subsequent quarrel about money that Miller thought was owed to him. Miller sent two forceful and no doubt intemperate letters to Garnett, which, Garnett records in the station diary, 'really should have been sent to Mr Beetham'. He adds piously 'I make no remark' (Miller himself would not have been so reticent). A few days later, Garnett noted the payment of backdated bonuses to Miller, accompanied by a receipt which 'Mr Miller must sign before he receives the cheque', adding that Mr Beetham is 'heartily sick of the whole business owing to Mr Miller's unseemly behaviour'.[1] This off-stage exchange (none of the letters have survived, only Garnett's record of the correspondence) is no doubt related to Miller's perception that he was overworked and underpaid at Brancepeth. But it also hints at a personality that, while always intractable, had become more quarrelsome and unhappy in his later years. A 'Personal Memo' in the station diary on 23 November 1907 expresses his gratitude to Mrs Beetham for arranging that his daughter Queenie, who was passing through Masterton on her way to visit her brother Basil, should make a surprise stop at Brancepeth to see her father. Miller's heartfelt account of Ruth Beetham's 'gracious and thoughtful act' concludes: 'The pleasure is all the greater to me, as I have not known the meaning of the word for many a long day'. Miller was ill (which must have prompted Ruth Beetham's approach to Queenie) and deeply anxious about his future, which was probably what drove him to write hot-headed letters to Garnett after he left the farm. In a society where the Old Age Pension was not automatically awarded, but depended on the testimony of your employer, retirement was a deeply troubling prospect. He would have another 17 years to live through; perhaps it was just as well for him he didn't know it at the time.

Some people on the station, possibly including his employers, may have been glad to see him go, but for the reader of the Brancepeth station diary, the matter of Miller's departure is a serious loss. From the day Garnett takes over, the diary is colourless. It records only intermittent facts, and on some days, entries amount to just a couple of lines. Long blank stretches occur. Apart from Garnett's aside about Miller, he offers no opinions, no carefully noted prices, no lists of stores required, nor memos in red ink: 'Wind Whare Clock', 'SHEARING'. And least of all is there anything personal. No gossip, no phrases in Latin, French or transliterated Greek, no mention of what he thinks about world events, or who was found drunk at the Taueru pub, or outbursts of complaint about the food.

John Vaughan Miller was a man who could not prevent

himself from creating a narrative of daily life. Seen from his point of view, the farm is an intricate mesh of life stories, economic and social changes, intellectual history, world events, literary debate and novels. In Miller's hands, events on the farm echo the literary world in which its readers delighted—there are unexpected legacies, false identities, sudden death, scandal, social upheaval, shadowy pasts, unfair employers, glamorous lifestyles, drunken cooks, missing brothers, beggars, rogues and beautiful and talented young women. These correspondences between life on the farm and the fiction stocked in the library are only visible because Miller kept diaries that travelled freely between his own life, farm business and the lives of others. He wasn't obliged to do this. He could simply, as Garnett did after him, have noted the details of farm life that were necessary to its operations and required for the record (financial transactions, for example); but probably because he was himself a great reader, highly educated and fluent with his pen, he wrote as if his life depended on it, which perhaps it did.

Miller was born at Bexley in Kent in 1839. On the birth record, his father is described as a clerk, but on Miller's marriage certificate, his father is a 'clerk in holy orders', and in a later newspaper article, Miller described him as having had a city parish. Certainly Miller held strong religious views and was deeply familiar with church politics; the importance of faith and the state of the church are frequent topics in his newspaper articles. He must have received a good classical education, as he falls into Latin, Greek, French, German and occasionally Italian, at the drop of a hat, and he may have gone to theological college himself, as on one occasion he writes a phrase in Hebrew (29 April 1900). It seems likely he attended the Grammar School at Birmingham: in December 1902, he notes a report in the London *Times* of the death of his 'old school chum', Sir Alexander McKenzie, 'late Lieut.

Governor of Bengal'.[2] Miller married Mary Ann Boydel in 1865, and together they had nine children. In London, he was a clerk at the Admiralty, where he worked for a number of years. Perhaps he ran into trouble at work, stopped advancing in his career, or simply wanted a different life, but his previous career remained important to him in his New Zealand life. All through his years at Brancepeth he noted items of Admiralty news and retained interest in people associated with it. On a spring Saturday in 1897, he records having a 'long talk with Mrs Richmond Beetham yesterday about her half brother E.N. Swainson, of Admiralty notoriety'.[3] His death certificate registers his occupation as 'Retired from Admiralty'.

It is not clear why John Vaughan Miller migrated to New Zealand with his wife and nine children in 1880. Part of Miller's reason for emigrating is likely to have been the usual one—to acquire land, with the unstated but customarily related social objective of turning himself into landed gentry. On most of the documents in the public record, he describes himself as a gentleman, and at one point in the diaries claims his birthday is recorded in 'the Peerage', though this is probably a touch of his sardonic sense of humour.[4] The level of his education certainly suggests that gentility was a more legitimate self-description for him than it was for many immigrants. At first, Miller grew hops at Kaiteriteri. In the 1893 electoral roll, his occupation is described as 'farm labourer', but in January that year, the Nelson papers carried a notice that John Vaughan Miller described as a farmer, or a hop grower of Kaiteriteri, was bankrupt.[5] He applied for his bankruptcy to be discharged in June, and this appears to have happened in August. The circumstances of his bankruptcy were probably related to drinking, for in April 1893 the *Colonist* reported that a prohibition order had been granted against John Vaughan Miller, 'to extend over the Nelson, Motueka and Moutere licensing districts'.[6]

It is not clear from the station diary how Miller came to be employed at Brancepeth, but he may have had some contact who helped him to the job.[7] His arrival at Brancepeth in late 1893, alone and far from his wife and children, on the verge of turning fifty-five, suggests a man in self-imposed exile, but as a bankrupt he must also have been grateful for any offers of work. During the thirteen years he was farm clerk, Miller sent regular remittances to his wife and younger children, but was lucky if he saw them in a year. He wrote to his wife every week without fail, always on Sunday and sometimes during the week as well, particularly if he was sending her money. 'M.M.', as she appears in the diaries, wrote at least once but often twice a week. He and his wife had photographs specially taken for each other, and he often sent her books, dress lengths and other small gifts, such as a lace fichu and a necklace. Miller took care of his wife's health, noting in 1897 that while on leave in Nelson he took her to the dentist. She 'had 8 teeth out, & he is to make her the best set obtainable' (21 September 1897). The next month he asked an optician to send her a pair of gold spectacles. Every year he noted the anniversary of their wedding, and he was perhaps the person who ticked this sentence in the Brancepeth copy of M.E. Braddon's *Lady Audley's Secret*, a hugely popular novel: 'My pretty little wife! My gentle, innocent, loving little wife' (18).

He kept in close contact with a number of his nine children via the post,[8] and jotted down their movements and addresses in the station diary, where he also noted their birthdays and weddings. Three of his five sons and one of his daughters visited him at Brancepeth and each stayed for a few days, but his visits home were not regular. In his later years on the farm he does not seem to have taken any holidays, and he was at the farm for almost three years before he went home for the first time (perhaps out of embarrassment at his bankruptcy). In 1901, his youngest son Tony died aged 20 of consumption (tuberculosis). Miller had been to see him in February, but when the telegram came at the beginning of June, he was unable to travel south because 'Tomorrow is Sunday & no trains—so that getting over for the funeral is hopeless' (1 June 1901). After Tony's death, Miller's second son Hubert went to South Africa in the 7th Contingent, and he had to endure further fear and anxiety distant from 'those dearest to me', as he said in a letter to Hugh Beetham in January 1900. Sad personal events must always have been made worse by his inability to be present. When he received news on 14 October 1906 that his son Basil's first-born child had been a stillbirth, he wrote 'Got note from Basil. His first-born son was still-born (I wish I had been the same)'. It was perhaps this event and the remembered grief of Tony's death that prompted him to write two days later, on the blotter in the station diary, these lines from Longfellow:

> There is no flock, however watch'd and tended,
> But one dead lamb is there:
> There is no fireside, howso'er defended
> But has one vacant chair.
>
> Keble's Xth Year[9]
> (16 October 1906)

Miller also maintained a large and regular correspondence with his extended family in Britain, and meticulously records the reception of letters and dates of his replies. In his first three years at Brancepeth his niece, a missionary in China, was murdered, his nephew died fighting in South Africa, and his mother died. In an inevitable consequence of colonial life, each of these events was news to him considerably after the fact. Miller leafed back through the diary and recorded his mother's death on the day it happened (noting also the day he heard about it); clearly, the station diary functioned as a chronologically accurate history of his own life, as well as of the farm. These events also reveal something of his family typology—religious, imperial, adventurous. Perhaps, too, the far-flung English family was driven by financial need, like Miller himself.

Miller had arrived at Brancepeth at the peak of the 1890s depression, which saw a huge rise in unemployment in Australia and New Zealand.[10] Henry Lawson is the best known of the many Australians who travelled to New Zealand in search of work, but the farm diary at Brancepeth records very large numbers of swaggers, reaching a peak in 1895–6, when the farm received visits from 925 needy men. By 1907, Miller's last full year on the farm, the annual number of swaggers was still high. In the meantime, his family seem to have moved to Motueka, but still to have had some crops: he noted helping with the harvest when he visited in later years, and in the Brancepeth diary he frequently referred to hop prices and the state of the crops and the weather in Motueka. Although these entries from his personal life are minimal, they run through the business of his job like a thread of worry glimpsed intermittently. Explicit references to his state of mind relate to his work circumstances, but the bankruptcy and drinking must have remained a dark background to his working life and perhaps explain the tone of some of his remarks, such as wishing he had been still-born. Miller's older children went out to work: his sons Arthur, Basil and Hubert worked on farms or in the army, and the girls moved around city addresses in Wellington and Christchurch, suggesting they were employed in households in some capacity. Things improved in the early 1900s, when his daughter Mary Elizabeth Miller married R.J. Prowse, who later received an unexpected legacy, with which they were able to establish their own smallholding, and Miller later records that his son Basil took on a farm at Urenui.

When he left Brancepeth in 1908, suffering from what he called 'eruptions' on his legs and barely able to walk, Miller was beset with anxiety about what would happen to him. On

7 January, in one of his last entries in the station diary, he wrote:

> I got a pot of ointment this evening from Mr Ralph which Archer Hosking [Doctor] promised on Friday last, to dress the foolish eruption on my left leg—so the medicus couldn't think matters very pressing—the place is healing very well without anything being put to it—and merely keeping the leg up.
>
> I await the issue of events with some anxiety as my next place of abode will be the workhouse, if there is such a place.

His daughter Queenie, summoned by Ruth Beetham, arrived to fetch him, and no more is known about him till his death certificate, which shows he died in Nelson in 1925, at the age of 86, after 44 years in New Zealand, of 'apoplexy and exhaustion'. His death certificate is unspecific about the whereabouts of the faithful M.M., declaring in the space for 'age of widow', 'not known if widow'. In fact she had predeceased him by two years.

Like the histories of many of the farm workers, Miller's own tale ends with a Dickensian note of doom, and vanishes into silence.[10] But through his scribal presence, the life of the farm becomes visible. Part of his drive to record events is connected to his ambivalence about his own status on the farm, and part is no doubt an expression of what Miles Fairburn has described in relation to the diary kept by James Cox, an itinerant labourer who lived and traveled in the Wairarapa and was one of those who arrived as a swagger at Brancepeth. In Fairburn's view, Cox's diary

> was an extension of his mind and body . . . where he could develop and demonstrate his self-discipline and self-control . . . He did everything that could be done with cheap writing paper and a pencil to achieve mastery over a small area of reality.[11]

Miller's diary, like Cox's, was a means of achieving control over his situation, but the whole of his corpus of work on the farm speaks of his determination to hang on to his identity as a gentleman and a scholar. Miller's circumstances must have been painful. Reduced to working in a job well below his educational capacity, under someone he is likely to have regarded as his social equal, and no doubt continually reminded of his own failures, he nevertheless actively engaged in public and professional life, demonstrating the virtues of self-reliance, learning, taste and moral probity so important in Victorian culture. As his letter to Hugh Beetham suggests, Miller regarded himself as a gentleman among gentlemen, sharing attitudes and behaviour, even though he was an employee, and the diary reveals a number of ways in which he implicitly asserted himself across this gap. His frequent asides in French, Latin, German or Greek emphasise an education that was considerably more 'classical' than that possessed by anyone else in the farm community, as well as allowing him to keep some observations and bits of information safe from prying eyes. He made a point of ordering a Greek lexicon and other scholarly books through the bookseller used by the farm to supply the library, and often exchanged books and recommendations with Ruth Beetham or the few other similarly inclined readers on the farm. The station diary makes many comparisons between his own customs and behaviour and those of other farm workers, from their table manners and education to personal and public hygiene. In 1906 he noted in the diary a repulsive incident, one that had happened before, men soiling the path to the outside WC:

> *Die Weg nach das Closet ist nicht sicher*
> *Ich Habe den Herrn Ralph gesprechen*
> *Die Vōr damnten Schweinen haben es gethan*
> [The path to the WC is not safe. I have spoken to Mr Ralph about it. Those damned pigs have done it]
> (24 July 1906)

It is not immediately obvious why Miller wrote this in German, but it was probably both the indelicacy of the subject matter and a means of preventing those he was accusing from reading about it in the diary. He was alert to station politics, and telling Mr Ralph who soiled the path to the WC was no doubt a breach of class loyalty, though one of Miller's salient characteristics over his years as a diary-keeper is that his own loyalties were always divided. An interesting question is *why* he noted such events in the station diary. There is an argument for keeping track of episodes that affected the health and safety of Brancepeth workers, but writing about it in German does not fit with the idea of a public hygiene record. It seems likely Miller's note was prompted by disgust and dislike, and using German was a way of distancing himself, both from the perpetrators and more generally other station workers, as well as from what he was describing.

Miller's sense of propriety was always strong. When he recorded the sad news that the daughter of the vicar of Motueka had died a year after her marriage, the phrase 'in childbirth' has been crossed out (21 October 1906). There can only have been personal reasons for Miller to record the death of someone who was a complete stranger to everyone else on the station and perhaps it felt like a posthumous betrayal of friendship and her privacy to explain why. But it is exactly these complex reflections of Miller's world and personality, the crossover between the diary as a public station record and as the private diary and self-portrait of the record-keeper, that make it so fascinating. Miller's asides and in-jokes, and his aggrieved descriptions of the job, his circumstances, his employers and fellow employees, are deeply personal and often injudicious. But they build an intricate, though partial, picture of the emotional, intellectual, social and literary life of the Brancepeth community. Interestingly, while forthcoming about everyone else's business, he only obliquely referred to his own circumstances. His bankruptcy and the reasons for it are never mentioned. Miller's diary-keeping was not, in any personal sense, confessional.

However, the station diary reveals how outward-looking Miller was. He noted many significant international events in the diary, including British and European politics, battles in the Crimean and Boer Wars, and general world affairs. The entry for 21 September 1906 is typical:

> There is a shocking accident to a King's & Scotch express—and an eruption in Mediterrn—and a terrible typhoon in Hong Kong & Manila—and the papers are full of horrors.

Along with assiduously reading the news, Miller kept up a steady flow of pseudonymous articles, poems and letters to the local paper, the *Wairarapa Daily Times*, and occasionally sent pieces to Wellington's *Evening Post*, Nelson's *Colonist*, and once to *The Times* of London. He had pronounced political and religious opinions, which reflect both his entrenched conservatism and a liberalism that came from witnessing how the other half lived and was perhaps deepened by his own adversities. One of his most firmly held beliefs was that the labourer is worthy of his hire, a phrase he used as a title for one of his articles. He demonstrated this conviction in his opinions of men on the farm, many of whom he believed *not* to be worthy of hire, such as the 'little Cockney coal-trimmer' who, according to Miller, did his hardest work with his knife and fork,[12] while others he thought should be remunerated more generously. He never explicitly included himself in the latter group, but his descriptions of his working day over the years make that clear.

Interspersed with ordering stores, stock returns, paying off dismissed men and making out accounts, Miller noted some telling details of his daily life. He was a bit of a dandy and had enough money to treat himself to clothes, ordered from the Wellington department store, Kirkcaldie and Stains. He favoured garments that were dressy as well as warm, specifying their quality—tweed suits for example—and returning those which didn't match his expectations, like a cap sent to him which was a 'hideous shape' (25 April 1904). Summer clothes were ordered from David Jones in Sydney. He had a dinner suit and bought fine dress-boots, including some described as glacé Kangaretto (7 October 1904), which he wore when dining in the homestead, an event always recorded in the diary as 'I dined with the family'. When Pat Hamill, a local hawker, visited the farm, Miller bought shirts, waistcoats, socks and dress lengths for his wife and daughters on credit, noting the amount owed in the diary. On 8 July 1905 he noted:

> Hamill here—I owe him for today shirt 6/3, shirt 7/6. Silk handchf 4/6 & 4 pr cashmere socks on 12 Aug 6/- & post 3d.

Miller's comments about the table manners, general condition, and dress of many other employees on the farm—'Old Taplin is never sober and has not changed his shirt for a month' (6 June 1905)—reflect a class-driven fastidiousness and separateness. Dressing appropriately marked the gentleman, just as other kinds of behaviour delineated those who were not 'well-bred'. A comment made in French referring to Hugh Wilson, the head shepherd at the time and one of the men with whom Miller had longstanding friction, gives the flavour:

> HW et moi sont 'deux' depuis le jeudi-passé—je crois que Mr H.H.B a lui parlé au sujêt de la coupe des ongles dans le bureau le Dimanche après-midi 25th inst. Il m'a donné mal-de-mer.
> [HW and I are 'two' since last Thursday—I think Mr HHB has spoken to him about cutting his nails in the office last Sunday, 25th. It made me seasick.][13] (29 July 1897)

Much of Miller's attention was focused on the Beetham family, or 'the house', and he meticulously recorded occasions when other farm employees dined with the family (not nearly as often as he did), as well as which of them was received by Hugh Beetham in the house and how long they stayed. The Beethams' social life was noted with great precision—who the house visitors were, the length of their visits, and the occasions on which they paid him 'the courtesy of a call' in the office. The movements of family members and visitors on the farm and in and out of the station are documented down to the minute. Miller took most of his meals in the 'saloon', a separate dining room in the main cookhouse where the men ate. The saloon was for senior staff like the station manager and the head shepherd, and the table might be shared at breakfast with Ralph and Oren Beetham (after they left school and began to work on the farm), and professional short-term employees such as the surveyor and the wool-classer. When Māori guests came, their welcome was also finely calibrated. The most senior visitors were received in the house—Hori Te Huki (also known as Tuhua) and Mr and Mrs Te Tau, for example, dined or lunched with the family. Others, like 'Miss Maaka', lunched with Miller in the saloon (although sometimes this was because the Beethams were away). Māori who worked on the farm ate in the cookhouse, where there was a large dining room which sometimes fed more than 40 people at a sitting.

Miller was very sensitive to table manners and the quality of the food. He had a private supply of such things as biscuits, Spanish olives, nuts and tins of fish, and in later years when his teeth were bad he was very fond of Lazenby's concentrated soup lozenges which he ordered on his personal account. He seems to have been one of the few men who used a toothbrush, noting in 1905, 'Lambert uses a toothbrush—in consideration of which I gave him some camphorated chalk (private store)' (23 October 1905). Despite his dental hygiene, Miller had immense trouble with his teeth, as did many of the men on the farm, and performed his own extractions: 'I extracted, with great difficulty, last night a double tooth which has annoyed me horribly for a long time' (7 August 1904).

Miller was certainly one of the few who washed regularly and kept his linen and clothes clean, sending what he always referred to as his '*linge sale*' [dirty linen] out for laundering. On arrival at the farm he ordered, on his own account, a set of green bed linen from Kirkcaldies, which was later paid for by the station. Most farm workers slept only in blankets, and many of them in rough tent camps. His comment on 'Young Byon' is not unusual: 'quite unfit to mix with any other people. His face is horribly broken out & he stinks beyond all endurance' (27 August 1896).

Unsurprisingly, Miller had firm opinions on behaviour. Dr Spratt, a visitor to the station at the end of October 1894, behaved improperly on a number of counts: having a case of whisky and a parcel of tobacco dropped off in the library porch; consorting with the servant (the female house cook) till late at night; 'bothering' and overstaying his welcome; and then:

> Dr Spratt had 4 chops for breakfast & then left—he 'sneaked' a cake of scented soap & some bootlaces. What else is uncertain. Mr B spoke severely to him last night about his proceedings. (26 October 1894)

Miller saw himself as standing for some of the qualities of civilisation and gentility that had been eroded, or never existed, in members of the farm community. His commentary on the life of the farm is a constant reminder of the pressures and irritations of living in a community of mostly single men, distant from your own family, and with little control over events. There is a regular thread of anxious self-assertion about the kind of life he would choose to live, or felt himself entitled to, mixed with the description of what was, on anyone's terms, a demanding occupation.

Miller's job was not an easy one. He arrived at Brancepeth

on foot on Boxing Day 1893 and stayed as a guest of the Beetham family until he commenced work on 30 December. He soon discovered that 'there is no proper check' on bills, and that a number of accounting systems needed to be overhauled. He kept the accounts, paid the bills, made out the Sheep Returns and insurance claims, and dealt with the often very large mailbag. In 1903, Brancepeth posted 40,000 letters; there is no total record of how many were received, but it must have been at least equivalent.[14] In addition, he did the ordering of stores both for the homestead and the station generally; ran the farm store, which included helping to load and unload the wagons; dealt with the complex financial and supply relationships with the large Māori community connected to Brancepeth; selected, ordered and organised the library; convened the Library Committee and acted as its Secretary (an office he was elected to three weeks after starting his job); supplied the poison and rabbiting gangs; organised shearing, crutching and dagging; and did numerous small jobs around the homestead. He had some skill in calligraphy and painting, and decorated household objects such as vases; he made photo frames, copied out music for Ruth and Thyra Beetham and wrote labels for the jam pots. Most of the professional photographs still in the house have captions in his distinctive handwriting. He also wrote most of the letters for his employer and acted as a scribe for other employees, including writing love letters, though he drew a comic line under his obligations when Garratt, the overseer, reported that one of the out-stations, Oruatamore, complained they hadn't had 'a male (sic) for a fortnight'. Miller expostulated, 'This is wholly untrue. Are we to write letters to them as well as send them?' (5 February 1897). He gave out advice, dispensed minor medicines, and submitted to having his office used as a point of contact for anyone with a complaint, request, or appointment to see Hugh Beetham—or anyone just wanting a chat. Unsurprisingly, given the extent of his workload, Miller resented the numbers of people who drifted in and spent the morning 'jawing', something that happened particularly when it was wet, or on a Sunday like this one:

> The office door wasn't shut for 5 minutes together from 10.30am to 8pm. Motete and other Maoris, Armstrong, McDiarmid &c & Gibson worrying for 4 cheques for his men to pay small bills to Crawford the hawker, who is here again waiting for his money. (17 September 1905)

The hours were long, demanding and not highly paid, a point that recurs through Miller's fifteen years on the farm, tempered with expressions of gratitude that at least he had a 'billet'.

> I have now worked 7 days a week for 3 ¼ years with 5 days off, 2 of which were spent in travelling, and have not had an hour's illness ever. Attendance in office 14 ½ hours per diem, wages 4/- a day. (14 March 1897)

He was not always so sanguine, or at least uncomplaining, about how much he worked, and towards the end of his time at Brancepeth his hours became extreme. In 1907 he started work in the office at 3.30 or 4.00am and sometimes did not finish till midnight. These hours were always recorded, suggesting perhaps that he wanted his employer to take notice of them, and raising the interesting question of who he thought he was writing for. His explanation in the diary for such early rises was about his state of health and consequent inability to sleep rather than the demands of the job—though he noted with exasperation that there was always a 'great deal of nothing' to do. Miller's long work hours and the way in which his office was used generally as a pivot for station business exacerbated the fluidities of his social and professional status and the contradictions between his instinctive class sympathy with his employers and the position he occupied as their underpaid factotum. Miller's straddle between being a gentleman and being an employee was the fulcrum on which much of his effortful life rested, especially those activities that amounted to self-assertion as a cultivated professional man, and which produced outbursts like the following. On Saturday 21 December 1895, when he had been working at the station almost a year, Miller wrote:

> Mr B annoyed that Brenchley should ask whether a beast should be killed. It seemed to Garrett and me a rare and reasonable question—I am also 'in disgrace' because Mr B did not see Tioi Waaka yesterday afn as I tried 3 times to find Mr B (who was playing tennis) and put a memo on his table, and told him personally at 6 o'clock that Tioi was going to stop for the night I do[n't] see exactly where the blame comes in & considering the work I had to do yesterday from 7.20am to 9.30 pm the fairness of this treatment is not very apparent. There were 63 cheques—Guest's row going on—the Cook's discharge—several men for stores—and a lot of stores for Te Ao—In fact it is simply white slavery and abuse for payment.

The sheer variety of Miller's duties and their incessant nature is apparent here—he was the hub for most of the farm business as well as the person who did all the paperwork—and his overworked state is given a particular piquancy by the reference to Mr B's leisurely tennis game. Over his years at Brancepeth, Miller's loyalty to, and genuine affection for, members of the Beetham family, and his identification as a gentleman with their social class and attitudes, is also shot through with bitter comparisons between their situation and that of the men who worked for them.

Some of the tensions of Miller's position, along with many of his opinions and much of his current reading, was converted into newspaper articles, most of which were published in the *Wairarapa Daily Times*, a paper owned by Joseph Payton. Like Payton, Miller had conservative political and social views that mostly reflected those of Brancepeth and its owners. A year after Miller arrived at the farm, he intervened in a spat between the *Wairarapa Daily Times* and its rival the *Wairarapa Star*, which had published an article alleging that the Beethams exploited their work force. Under the pseudonym 'Nemo', Miller roundly attacked the style, learning and morals of the *Star* editor, quoting Fielding, Carlyle, Theodore Hook and the Bible, and finishing with a passionate endorsement of his employer, from whom, he said,

> I received most generous and considerate help at a critical moment, and when I was a total stranger to him: kindness which altered the current of my life. Thank God! I fell into such hands and not into those of a man who for merely business purposes can indite such ungenerous and gratuitous insults as appeared in the *Star*.

The generous help at a 'critical moment' must be a rare reference to the circumstances of his bankruptcy, events that underlie his complex and only partially visible attitudes to the Beethams. Miller was always grateful for what he referred to as his 'billet', and he expressed considerable affection for the Beetham family, particularly Ruth Beetham and her children Ralph, Thyra, Weva and Oren. Even so, he was always punctilious about keeping a 'polite' social distance, referring to the boys, after they left school, as 'Mr Ralph' and 'Mr Oren', and to Thyra as 'Miss Beetham' until she married, when that title was taken by Weva. Hugh Beetham is unfailingly referred to in the station diary as Mr Beetham or Mr B. The amount of time devoted to the Beethams and their doings in the station diary reveals their importance, both in Miller's personal life and in the social environment, though some of the intensity of his gaze might have been generated by a sense of having fallen from grace and needing to make up for it. But the nature of Miller's job meant he was also very aware of the difficulties experienced by working men during a time of economic depression. The diary reflects a potent mix of Anglican fortitude, liberalism, sympathy, disgust and righteousness. He execrated the ruffians, blackguards and scoundrels who turned up on the farm, like the 'tall, swivel-eyed' insurance 'drummer' who invited himself for dinner and bed and the next day was given a 'regular dressing' by Mr Beetham (8 April 1895). He had no time for those he identified as fools, mischief-makers and drunkards who flowed through the farm and its business, but swaggers who arrived 'starving and naked', or were 'decent' looking men willing to do a few days' work, were always accommodated, and he was very conscious of his own closeness to their situation.

In 1898, with the depression still in ascendancy and waves of unemployed single men arriving at the farm, Miller wrote a letter to the *Wairarapa Daily Times* in response to 'a controversy now being carried on in one of your Wellington contemporaries, about the work of Mr Hall, a city missionary' (17 August). In the course of arguing that 'spiritual warfare' may be successfully carried out by 'irregulars' with a 'Christ-like endeavour' like Mr Hall, Miller gives a glimpse of his own early life, a window onto many of the attitudes driving his behaviour at Brancepeth.

> I saw a great deal, in my younger days, of the work of Curates, District Visitors, Scripture Readers and City Missionaries; and I have had much to do with Ragged Schools, Shoe-Black Brigades, and Working-Men's Associations; and I can bear witness that in my father's parish, which was one of the largest town parishes in England—although the four Curates did excellent work—the four Scripture Readers, who were in fact the City Missionaries, were his right hand in dealing with sickness, want, sorrow, suffering and sin.[15]

The ring of the pulpit heard here, which often appears in his published articles and is one of the distinctive modes of Victorian fiction, was accompanied by acts of considerable kindness to distressed 'travellers'—he lent them money, gave them blankets and clothes (quite often his own, but usually clothes from the Brancepeth store with Hugh Beetham's permission) and instituted a system for dealing with them fairly. At the same time, he applied strict standards of behaviour to all the people he worked with, including his employers.

In 1901, Miller published an article in the Nelson *Colonist*, his hometown newspaper, which, because it was published in Nelson, was unlikely to be read by Hugh Beetham or anyone on the farm. Called 'The Hire of the Labourers', it is a stern disquisition on the Biblical text 'the labourer is worthy of his hire', and a return to Miller's furious point about white slavery, made in 1895. By 1901 the depression was starting to lift, and Brancepeth was losing skilled workers to better-paying jobs elsewhere. Miller wrote that men were still being paid wages that 'just rise them above the condition of beggars':

> The kindness of these people [employers] (who are on excellent terms with themselves) is the kindness of persons who consider themselves raised above the mass of mankind; who are accustomed to be addressed with at least outward deference, and to see all who approach them either mortified and depressed by their coldness or difference, or elated by their approving smiles. (31 May 1901)

The article goes on to ask a number of hard questions about what these labourers receive for their £1 a week, which was the standard wage at Brancepeth. How are they housed? How are they off for holidays? What chance have they of ever attending church or chapel? What amusements have they? What chance have they of promotion? How many of them are condemned to forced celibacy? What have they to look forward to as the result of hard work?

> 'but', says the employer irritably, 'all this is no business of mine, how can I help it? What is the good of making a fuss, and putting mischievous ideas into the men's heads?

> I'm all right: I have every comfort about me, I have my wife and children, my good table, my wine and beer, and spirits *ad libitum*; and the men are all right too—without these things. I dare say it seems a bit hard, and it may be rather monotonous; but they get their mutton and decoction of ti-tree regularly, and £1 a week . . .'

Miller's portrait of an employer (probably his own employer) reflects a spectrum of views that describe a quintessentially Victorian state of mind. Politically conservative, religious, highly educated, a gentleman, Miller was at once loyal to the class he felt he belonged to, and critical of the way it operated. He was an ardent royalist and imperialist, but also conscious, like Gladstone or Disraeli, that the world is not a just or equitable one, and in 'The Hire of the Labourers' he gave voice to an uncharacteristically direct class attack. In his published articles, Miller usually wrote as someone whose cultural and intellectual credentials were British, European and metropolitan. His article for the *Colonist,* on the other hand, was driven by more personal and local interests, and—despite his unrelenting opposition to socialism and anything that smacked of it—a strong critique of social inequity. The complexities of Miller's situation and the range of attitudes he expressed across the diary, articles, letters and marginalia in the library books, illustrate at a personal level what Tony Ballantyne has more broadly described as 'webs of empire': the dynamic and overlapping (but also fragile) linkages between constantly fluctuating metropolitan and colonial interests.[16] How to be both British gentleman and New Zealand employee, engaged with world affairs but living in a small hierarchical colonial community? Miller's writing, in its various forms, reveals the intricate tangle of what Eric Wolf has called the 'bundles of relationships' that lie at the heart of history.[17]

Most of Miller's articles were not about local matters, though clearly he believed, with Payton, the editor of the

Wairarapa Daily Times, that his topics would be of interest to the local readership. This in itself says something about the expectations of readers in a tiny rural town, about their level of education, and the extent to which they wanted to be informed about the world by their local newspaper. The difficulty of getting good copy was likely also an issue. On several occasions when Payton was ill, Miller stepped up his supply of leaders and was thanked for filling the breach, once with the presentation of a copy of Tennyson. He wrote about the closing of the Indian Mints, banking, sugar duties, unrest in the Transvaal, British enterprise in China, and women's rights (he advocated separate spheres and had much to say about mothers). He published opinion pieces on large abstract questions—humanity, priests and people, the decay of the Latin Races, what is education; translated letters in French that had been published in British newspapers; summarised the state of British foreign policy, and attacked Cecil Rhodes. He sailed blithely into French and German, assuming his reader was as well-educated and informed as he was himself, and he used the station library as a source of quotation and opinion. His leaders were well read. On 24 May 1903 he noted, with a mixture of sarcasm and pleasure, that his leader of 19 May on the Victorian strike in the *Wairarapa Daily Times* had been copied to the *Manawatu Daily Times*: 'This is glory! honour! and renown!'. Most of these articles were written on Sundays, which, while not a day of rest—he recorded various duties most Sundays—had a higher percentage of time devoted to his own pursuits.

A constant reader, Miller was heavily involved in the management and affairs of the library almost from the day of his arrival. In 1906 Miller sent a library return to the Brancepeth accountant and noted that the library had been in existence 'about 25 years ('81)'. The years in which he was involved in its administration saw a big increase in stock. Bookish habits were not unusual in nineteenth century New Zealand. Indeed, many travelers commented on the availability and currency of private libraries. When the historian J.A. Froude visited Sir George Grey at his house on Kawau, he remarked on the

> Quarterlies, Edinburghs, magazines, weeklies—all the floating literature of London, only a month or two behindhand. Every important movement in domestic, foreign, or colonial politics could be studied as exhaustively at Kawau as in the reading room at the Athenaeum.[18]

A number of large sheep stations had libraries that were available for staff to use,[19] but what was unusual at Brancepeth was the size of the library (2000 volumes) and the predominance of fiction, which made up 88% of the collection.[20] The selection of illustrated papers, reviews and periodicals, and English and Scottish newspapers, was similar to Grey's reading matter, and was replicated in many large houses.

Once Miller had been elected Secretary of the Library Committee ('against my desire', he noted in the diary on 21 January 1894), he set about improving it. Although the committee included the post of Librarian, which for a long time was filled by the carpenter, W.R. Richards, who was paid a small annual honorarium, Miller was clearly the man behind the scenes. He made himself responsible for everything to do with the collection: the selection of books (for which he established a 'Committee of Taste' in 1895), ordering, reviewing (sometimes he published short pieces in the newspaper on books he had read), covering and labeling the books, producing the catalogue, writing and administering the rules and collecting subscriptions. In 1895 he invited Ruth Beetham and Miss Liddle, the first of a stream of governesses, to join the Committee, which had previously been all male. That same year, he substantially increased the volume of book ordering, in collaboration with Ruth Beetham, whose influence on the collection became more pronounced. Sometimes as many as 70 books were ordered in one batch. The library also grew physically in his first years at Brancepeth, with the building enlarged and special shelving put in place. Particularly in Miller's early years as clerk, the diary is filled with notes about library work—covering and labelling new books, 'putting books in circulation', developing the library rules, updating the catalogue. Some of this work was generated by his twin passions for books and for order; the library underwent a significant professionalisation under his care, work that was recognised on 8 June 1897 when Mrs Beetham 'on behalf of the Library, presented me with a beautiful edition of Tennyson'. In December that year, Tennyson was the subject of a comic article Miller published in the *Wairarapa Daily Times*, 'Tennyson Spoiled'. This was a humorous tirade against 'Any More' who had written, in Miller's view, a bad pastiche of Tennyson's poem 'In Memoriam':

> The punctuation which 'Any More' revels in, is worthy of the curate, who notified, before the 'General Supplication', that 'A man going to *sea his wife* desires the prayers of this congregation'. Again, the *pause* (marked –) should not be abused. The abuse of the pause reminds one of the story of the cook whose husband had become a millionaire: as she sat at the head of her grand dinner-table the conversation flagged: one of her guests, who habitually shortened the word 'gentlemen' by two syllables, exclaimed 'horrid pause,' on whom the good lady retorted indignantly as she snatched her honest hands from the snowy damask, 'So would yours be, if you'd cooked as many dinners as I have'.[21]

Miller actively encouraged others to join the library, on one occasion writing a 'private note' to W. Armstrong, one of the shepherds, suggesting he become a member. The library was run by subscription at £1 per year, though many seasonal or temporary workers joined at a quarterly rate of 5/-. These were not insubstantial sums for men earning £1 a week, and unsurprisingly it tended to be the higher paid, semi-professional workers at the upper end of the farm's social scale—the head shepherd, the overseer—who were the long-term subscribers. The library operated as a sort of club and social space, where 'the men' gathered, and it hosted occasional events. In the winter of 1897 Miller noted that he made a lectern and the men came to hear the Reverend Yorke give a 'reading' on a Saturday evening of 1 and 3/4 hours: 'slow and poor but the men were fairly pleased' (10 July).

Miller was not the only keen reader. Ruth Beetham lent him books, and he exchanged books and opinions with various governesses, but particularly Miss Liddle. Both women frequently called into the library to discuss purchases and other business. Visitors to the farm were shown the library, the best-known among them the flower painter Ellis Rowan, and visiting friends and family liked to look over the new books.[22] In August 1897, during a busy work time when the ewes were lambing, the cook spitting blood, large groups of swaggers were passing through and the usual list of daily chores had to be done, Miller noted caustically that Wilson, the head shepherd, was

> . . . apparently hors-de-combat with an inflamed eyelid—he can read as usual
> (7 August 1897)

The most sought-after items in the Brancepeth library were not the books but the newspapers. In the first weeks after he arrived on the farm, Miller was caught up in a dispute about how many newspapers should go to which group on the farm. This dispute recurred in 1898, and both times resulted in resignations from the Library Committee. Brancepeth received several copies of both the local papers, the *Wairarapa Daily Times* and the *Wairarapa Star*, which broadly represented the political and class divisions in the wider community. The dispute that broke out in 1898 was about how many copies of newspapers should be supplied to which gangs, and it suggests something about the politics of the Library Committee and how it operated as a small elite, asserting some control over farm affairs. Charles Brenchley, a general hand and a member of the Library Committee, wrote to Hugh Beetham to resign, explaining that he had done so because a

> Proposition that had not been placed before the members of the Committee, was forwarded to the President [Beetham] for his sanction, thereby ignoring the feelings and opinions of those members of the Committee who were most directly concerned. I make this explanation because I find myself credited with selfish and unreasonable ideas. (10 May 1898)

Miller responded the next day with a memo to the 'President of the Library', declaring that 'Brenchley's letter is not quite such an artless document as it seems', and describing the battle lines which had been drawn up, with at least four members of the Committee resigning. He suggested:

> Why 3 men at the Parae[23] should get 2 papers from Library funds, and none of the others anything may be settled at the next meeting. 15 of the Rabbiters are members and they are not represented on the Committee. There was not the slightest intention on my part to do anything irregular or offensive but I thought it was quite time somebody moved in the matter. (11 May 1898)

The distribution of newspapers was one of many issues on the station in which Miller expressed his sense of natural justice, which was connected no doubt to his Anglicanism and to his upbringing in a hard city parish. His offer to resign from the Secretaryship was not taken up and the matter was resolved by a further resolution in September, but these heated disputes are eloquent about the role the library played in the community dynamic. In a memo later that year, which returned to the vexed question of who was supplied with newspapers, Miller made two important points. He noted that there are 'at least 5 men' at the Parae 'who can read the papers without being subscribers', and expanded this inequity by noting:

> The men in the Gangs get very few of the benefits of the Library, and if their welfare is not consulted in some way, they will be disposed very naturally to withdraw their subscriptions—They are called upon to pay the same as the men on the In-station who enjoy the full benefits of the Library. (23 September 1898)

To Miller's mind, the library (and its supply of newspapers and books) was a privilege as well as an investment, but it also demanded equity, especially as it was not simply a facility for men working at the in-station. Out-whare members, which meant men working in gangs or on other parts of the station, were allowed to have two volumes at a time, which had to be returned in fourteen days. The books were sent out with the stores, and though there is no record of this, were presumably requested at the same time as the stores list was sent in. Newspapers were supplied daily to men in the out-station.

The newspaper, as Benedict Anderson has argued, is an 'extreme form' of the book, a book sold on a colossal scale, but of ephemeral popularity; he calls them 'one day best-sellers,' and says of their function:

> . . . the newspaper reader, observing exact replicas of his own paper being consumed by his subway, barbershop or residential neighbours, is continually reassured that the imagined world is visibly rooted in everyday life.[24]

Anderson's point, that readers share a set of interests that connect them locally and internationally with other readers, is amply supported by the place of the newspaper in the daily life of Brancepeth. The politics surrounding library use and newspaper supply illustrate the value of the library not just as a recreational space but as the primary mechanism by which the farm workers retained and maintained their connections to a world outside the farm. It was also a way to assert their social standing, though for many there was a fine balance between the benefits of being a library subscriber and the cost to their own households of £1 per annum. When one of the subscribers was recorded as having resigned from the library on his wife's orders, the entry for the next quarter noted that he had been charged again as he continued to withdraw books as usual. Reading, evidently, was not an easy habit to break.

The library was open all days of the week, but working on a Sunday was a thorny issue for Miller right from the start of his employment at Brancepeth. The main part of his Sunday job was dealing with the mail, and when Sunday mail deliveries were abolished early in 1897, he greeted the announcement with Latin joy: '*Bulga Sabbatica mortua est—Laus Deo*! [The Sunday mail is dead—thank God!] Mr B has received official notice that the Sunday Mail is abolished' (11 March 1897). Five years later, when it looked as though the Sunday mail work would be reinstated, Miller wrote a letter of resignation:

> My dear Mr Beetham
>
> The new arrangements for the mail oblige me, to my very great regret, to give up my billet here, as I will not again work on a Sunday at the bidding of any man; and the avowed object of the change is that the work of Monday may be done on Sunday . . . . This termination of my 9 years service is as unlooked for as it is unpleasant; but I hope it may present itself to you as the only feature of my connexion with you which calls for regret; I, certainly am unconscious of any other. You will easily fill my place; but it will probably be difficult for me, after being so long out of the world, to find anything to do, But, at whatever sacrifice, I can only do what seems to me right,—you yourself would not wish me

to do otherwise,—and I am sure my wife and children will endorse my action.

I am, at the same time, quite conscious that you may possibly be glad to make a change. No one knows better than I do how little a man is missed, and how soon he is forgotten.

Yours very sincerely
J. Vaughan Miller
(29 November 1902)

An unstated subtext of this letter is religious—Miller's objection to working on Sundays seems likely to have its origin in belief that Sunday is the day for God's work, but there is also a broader question implied: the employee's right to a day off, which is never fully stated, but implicit perhaps in the amount of moral blackmail Miller brought to his letter, with its talk of sacrifice, change and forgetting. He did not record this dispute directly in the diary, no doubt because the diary was an official record and the property of his employer, but referred to it by noting a telegram in French he sent to M.M.: '*Il faudra retenir ce billet de banque jusqu'à la reception de ma lettre de dimanche*' [You must hang on to the bank note until you get my letter of Sunday] (29 November 1902). On 1 December he wrote that 'McRae wanted to know if Mr B would agree [to the change of coach day]—I told him I could not answer for Mr B but that I believed the arrangemt proposed would be quite satisfactory to him'. But later that day, he wrote to Hugh Beetham retracting his resignation after a 'short conversation with Mr Ralph' revealed to him some misapprehension:

> If nothing more has to be done, as Mr Ralph says, than to open a Brancepeth bag, and bring you in your letters, and if the business letters are to be dealt with on Monday morning, I have no wish to make any difficulty.

Two days later he wrote 'a line' to M.M.: '*In statu quo*

ante bellum' [in the state in which things were before the war], i.e. things had returned to normal. But they were never quite the same. Although Miller lunched with the Beethams on Christmas Day that year, he glossed his invitation in the diary as 'Lest the blind Fury with the Abhorrèd shears/ should split the thin-spun life', referring to the fact that without him there would be the unlucky number of thirteen people present at the table. His relationship with Mr B did not seem to be as cordial in later years. He frequently complained in the latter years of the diary that 'Mr B and Mr Ralph' had left for Masterton without having told him of their departure, and noted that he was not aware of their business. During the years when the estate was being valued and partitioned, from 1903–1905, there was continual work of surveying and valuing being done, and visits to lawyers that required many trips to Wellington, often at short notice. Miller's exclusion from the arrangements was a palpable contraction of earlier times on the farm, when nothing stirred without his knowledge.

A large part of how Miller sustained himself at Brancepeth (and probably also before and after his years there) was the continuation of cultural interests and activities. He had access to many of the facilities of the homestead throughout his employment. When the household left for the Masterton Show in February 1899, he noted that 'Mrs B' gave him permission to use the pianos indoors as much as he liked. He also had access to the smoking room, and when his son Basil visited him they spent their evenings smoking with Hugh and Ralph Beetham. His similarities to the Beethams, in most ways more striking than his differences, show themselves in his taste for painting watercolours, writing poetry and expressing opinions. He treated himself to a long fulmination about Impressionism in the diary in June 1906, describing a particular picture of cattle in a harvest field and opining that:

Front and side of original Brancepeth homestead. Unknown photographer, caption written by John Vaughan Miller. Private Collection.

1898 view of Tempest Paddock in front of homestead. Caption written by John Vaughan Miller. Private Collection.

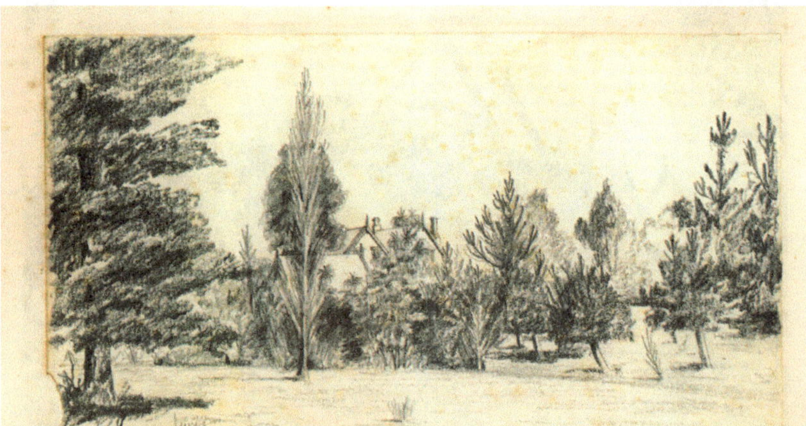

Pencil sketch 'Brancepeth from Tempest Paddock' by the schoolmaster, Joseph Guest 6 September, 1896. Private Collection.

H.H. Beetham and his sons Ralph and Oren, on their mounts, 1898. Unknown photographer, caption written by John Vaughan Miller. Private Collection.

'The Fernery, Brancepeth' showing Thyra Beetham in foreground and her mother Ruth Beetham at the back. Undated. Unknown photographer, caption written by John Vaughan Miller. Private Collection.

Brancepeth 1905 homestead which replaced the original building. Unknown photographer, date 1950s? Private Collection.

Brancepeth Station Library in 1966 before the collection was taken to Victoria University of Wellington. Unknown photographer, Private Collection.

Back of 1905 Homestead, showing station store on left and station office on right. The library was at the other end of the office building. Unknown photographer, date 1950s? Private Collection.

The 1897 grape harvest at the Lansdowne vineyard. William Beetham and his wife Hermanze are on the right. Wairarapa Archive 05-89/3.

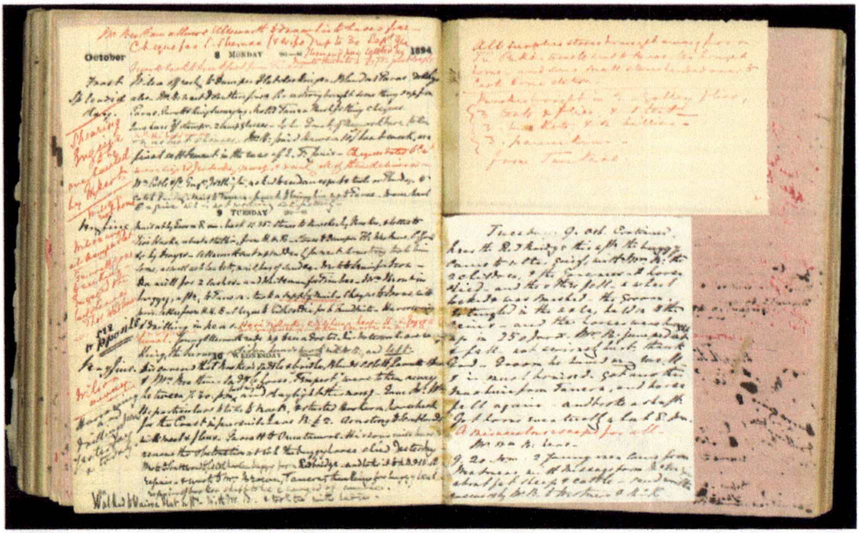

Page from the Station Diary for October 8 1894, in John Vaughan Miller's hand.

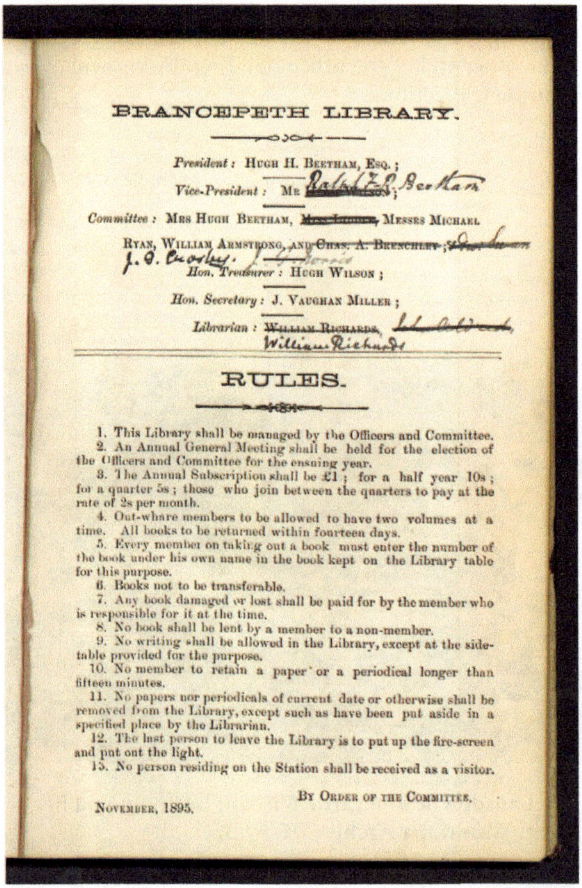

BRANCEPETH LIBRARY.

President: Hugh H. Beetham, Esq.;

Vice-President: Mr [illegible];

Committee: Mrs Hugh Beetham, Mrs Lowes, Messrs Michael Ryan, William Armstrong, and Chas. A. Brenchley;

Hon. Treasurer: Hugh Wilson;

Hon. Secretary: J. Vaughan Miller;

Librarian: William Richards.

RULES.

1. This Library shall be managed by the Officers and Committee.
2. An Annual General Meeting shall be held for the election of the Officers and Committee for the ensuing year.
3. The Annual Subscription shall be £1; for a half year 10s; for a quarter 5s; those who join between the quarters to pay at the rate of 2s per month.
4. Out-whare members to be allowed to have two volumes at a time. All books to be returned within fourteen days.
5. Every member on taking out a book must enter the number of the book under his own name in the book kept on the Library table for this purpose.
6. Books not to be transferable.
7. Any book damaged or lost shall be paid for by the member who is responsible for it at the time.
8. No book shall be lent by a member to a non-member.
9. No writing shall be allowed in the Library, except at the side-table provided for the purpose.
10. No member to retain a paper or a periodical longer than fifteen minutes.
11. No papers nor periodicals of current date or otherwise shall be removed from the Library, except such as have been put aside in a specified place by the Librarian.
12. The last person to leave the Library is to put up the fire-screen and put out the light.
13. No person residing on the Station shall be received as a visitor.

By Order of the Committee.

November, 1895.

Page of Brancepeth Library Catalogue, 1895, showing corrections in John Vaughan Miller's hand. Printed by the *Wairarapa Daily Times*. Private Collection.

Photograph which may be John Vaughan Miller. Miller recorded Weva Beetham taking his photograph in the office in 1904. This photograph has been labelled 'Frank Roberts 1920' but may be misidentified. It is clearly home-developed and the clothes suggest an earlier date than 1920.

A photograph of the office at Brancepeth taken in 2010 showing the clerk's desk. Property of R.E. Beetham.

Brancepeth homestead from the back, showing the library at centre with a white roof. Watercolour by J.J. Guest, 1896. Private collection.

William Beetham, *Portrait of Dr Featherston and the Maori Chiefs, Wi Tako and Te Puni* (1857–58). Collection of Te Papa Tongarewa Museum of New Zealand.

> 'Impressionist' pictures are so called because the painter (do not call him an artist) is under the impression that he has painted a picture.

Later the same year he described buying a 'marine painting' from a disabled swagger: 'sort of "pavement artist"—it is a curiosity—it is enough to give anyone a fit—"realistic impressionist" is the school' (31 August 1906).

He also cared for his environment, painting the fire-surround black, training a passion-flower vine over the porch and making sure the office windows were washed and that his room, which was next to the office, was kept clean. Miller's attention to domestic detail was part of the struggle he maintained in every dimension of his life to live like the gentleman he was. It is impossible not to see his ceaseless effort to order, describe and correct the world he lived in, an effort which extended to the novels he read, as an essential assertion of his identity, which had become vulnerable. Under far more arduous circumstances than the Beethams, shadowed by past failure, and under considerable financial constraint, Miller undertook the same colonial work that they did, a work of cultural and social maintenance, the articulation of what it meant to be British, a gentleman and a citizen of the civil world. It is as if he continually policed the borders of self-definition that distinguished him from an encroaching and coarser environment. He was helped in his situation by a lively and sardonic sense of humour. The station diary is full of comic asides, satirical descriptions and, Miller's favourite form of humour, puns, which take the edge off his moral indignation and what was perhaps an agonising inside knowledge of his fall in the world. The slide from Admiralty clerk and landowner to an impecunious station clerk at everyone's beck and call was not a pleasant history. When he joked about 'Fletcher in here this evening on his way back to Kaiwhata—he has been under the doctor's hands—extremely loquacious—says he was brought up at Eton—but he looks more as though he had been eaten and brought up' (September 1905), he was able to put the world he lived in, with all its inequities and disappointments, in its place. He was given to outrageous puns, as in this account of the weather during shearing:

> When this sort of wether is rammed down an owner's throat, it is hard to take it like a lamb—it makes one right Down Cross. (13 December 1906)

He could take a kind of textual revenge for what seems to have been a vicious snub by recording, on 12 August 1896:

> Rutherford, the poisoner and ex bank clerk and prospective runholder, here to lunch—he would not have lunched with a clerk only that he had a disgusting cold in his bald head. He was very sorry for the ladies disappointment.

And it seems as though the Beethams, for much of his time at Brancepeth, recognised his ambiguous social situation: they regularly invited him to dinner, including at Christmas; brought their guests to the office to meet him, invited him to Thyra's wedding and welcomed his family members in the house. Miller, however, trod a fine line. He did not accept the invitation to Thyra's wedding (though he did attend another wedding held in the homestead) and he was always careful to preserve lines of distinction between himself and his employers. It is because Miller inhabited such an equivocal position on the station, and also such a central one, that his diary-keeping is so revealing. It is revealing about his personality, his intellectual life and the life of the community, particularly its social dynamics. The diary, as a portrait of the social world of Brancepeth, helps us respond to Robert Darnton's request for book historians to pay more attention to the 'where' of reading. As Miller worked his way through the Victorian novels in the Brancepeth library, the place in which he lived and worked also clamoured for his attention. Vividly described in his writing, life at Brancepeth with all its social tensions, squabbles, and practical demands affected him deeply, and was the inescapable daily context in which the library books and their readers came together.

CHAPTER FOUR

The Social World of the Reader

The social world in which the Brancepeth readers lived bore many similarities to the much loved and often melodramatic narratives of Victorian fiction that stocked the library shelves: there were scandals, sudden death, attempted murder, false identities and unexpected legacies. The world of the farm was also distinctively part of a specific colonial society at a particular time, itself a dynamic narrative of diaspora and mobility, class ambition, gender and race relations, and rural economies. As Miles Fairburn has said of James Cox, an itinerant labourer who kept a detailed autobiographical diary from 1880–1925 and was one of the swaggers who visited Brancepeth, the Brancepeth workers were men (and a few women) of 'no historical importance'.[1] But the records kept by John Vaughan Miller of who was on the station, what they did and how they did it, open an unusually wide and detailed view of the daily lives of ordinary people—most of whom were living away from their families and subject to the pressures, demands, and occasional pleasures of a collective working life. The library building was a crucial part of the emotional and social landscape for these station workers. It gave them a means of maintaining cultural connections and some intellectual company; there, they could keep abreast of current affairs and what was happening in the world of literature. For many, it was also a social space away from the overcrowded whares and men's quarters, a place where a lonely male reader might pick up *David Copperfield* and imagine future domestic comfort, or turn to H. Rider Haggard for a more adventurous and glamorous life than the one he was living.[2] It was also a place where he could enjoy the company of other readers: Miller grumbled in the diary one day in September 1894 that the library had become uninhabitable, what with 'a fire, a Rochester and four men smoking' (the 'Rochester' was a notoriously smoky oil lamp).

Readers bring to their books a number of motives for reading, including the age-old wish to escape, but the circumstances of their life are still present in the room. Indeed, it is these material circumstances—the everyday life and social world of the reader—that not only constitute the 'where' of reading[3] but often part of the 'why'. A list of the supplies sent out from the station store on 27 October 1896 to one of the working camps is evocative about the unremarkable yet vital movement of library books about the farm: 'Cart came up from Parae. Sent back curry powder, Library books, Dungarees, trousers and jumpers, black slippers, saddle tweeds towels brown and white, pipes &c'. Books, it is clear, were as matter-of-factly essential as any of the other goods that circulated on the station.

The chapter that follows is a portrait of the everyday working life of the station, as seen through the station diary over the 14 years of Miller's tenure as clerk (1894–1908). It is a life characterised by transience, hardships and privations, difficult relationships, complex motivations and personal emotions, poverty, mess and dirt. The station diary inevitably gives John Vaughan Miller's view of Brancepeth. His job was to be a record-keeper, so he provided factual detail: timetables, statistics, accounts, orders, daily tasks. But as James Belich reminds us, statistics and 'cold analysis' can never tell the whole story.[4] Belich is talking about migration, which is a large part of the history of the Brancepeth community, but his point—that facts by themselves are not history—is vividly illustrated by Miller's station diary and ledgers. Gossip and events are not merely reported, they are selected and coloured by Miller's own opinions and values. It was a material and personal history he kept, and also an intellectual one: the diary is full of notes about the library, and his reading and critical analysis are reflected in the frequent newspaper articles he wrote, some of which lampoon or critique the community in which he lived.

Miller wrote copiously. Each day he covered a folio page with his clerk's hand, which got loopy when he was rushed. During the day, or sometimes several days later, he returned to his earlier notes and revised them, noting for example when guests were expected and then returning later to add the actual time of arrival. When the page space ran out, he wrote in the margin. Important events or reminders were written in red ink and sometimes capitalised. Occasionally, he added emphasis by scrawling a headline across the page or carefully drawing one in red ink, such as SHEARING. Miller's prose is full of clerical abbreviations and, like a clerk in a novel by Fielding or Richardson, he used the long s (*ſ*) of the eighteenth century. Each page of the diary is the image of a man pressed for time—his sentences are full of shortcuts, abbreviations, and dashes—with numerous tasks, duties and interruptions cascading in on him, but all are strongly marked with his personality. Miller loved puns and often made sardonic jokes at his own or other people's expense. When he had something deeply-felt to say (often generated by irritation), he delivered a long and perfectly shaped paragraph, complete with reported speech and literary turns of phrase. His frequent sorties into other languages (French, Latin, Greek, German, Italian and Hebrew) combine with learned asides on literature, politics and foreign affairs. The result is an abundant, exuberant text that records the world as well as the station, giving a highly personal and unique view into the complex brew of work, recreation, emotions and relationships.

The depression of the 1890s, which resulted in large numbers of itinerant unemployed men in New Zealand, Australia and North America, began in the 1880s with a deep agricultural crisis in the American South, and spread to Wall Street and world financial markets in the form of the 'financial panics' of the early 1890s, around the time John Vaughan Miller started work at Brancepeth. By the beginning of 1894 the depression was well established; it was exacerbated in Australia by drought, which resulted in large numbers of Australians, among them the writer and journalist Henry Lawson, crossing the Tasman in search of work.[5] In New Zealand, 1890 began with an election won by the Liberals under the leadership of John Ballance, introducing what has been called the 'Liberal Era', a period that ended in 1914 with the start of the Great War, and was dominated by the figure of Richard John Seddon, Premier from 1893 to 1906. The Liberals came to power facing the problems of a depressed world economy, mass unemployment, and significant national debt. They proposed to address the depression by 'bursting up' the great estates, like Brancepeth, and freeing up land for smallholdings, advancing the policy of 'closer settlement'.[6]

These political and social currents underlie the diary narrative at Brancepeth from 1894 to 1908. From the turn of the century, Hugh Beetham made more frequent trips to Wellington to discuss with lawyers the complex business of dividing the estate. Meanwhile, the local papers were full of articles for and against close settlement, and a number of men working on the station aspired to own land, including the overseer, George Garratt, who went on to develop a farm of 150 acres at Taueru. The desire to 'better oneself' has been described by Belich as the 'universal motive' for migration to New Zealand,[7] and part of the anguish of the 1890s was the wreckage of that hope for many people, including Miller, whose drinking may have been exacerbated by his looming bankruptcy (or vice versa). But the most immediately visible effect on Brancepeth of the 1890s depression was the huge and constant flow of swaggers through the station.

Only four months into the job, Miller noted that eight or nine swaggers arrived each night. One of them told him, on 23 April 1894, that the Te Ata station, near Napier, had seen 2000 swaggers inside 12 months. A week later, Miller underlined in the diary that during April there were 111 swaggers at the Parae (where T.C. Williams's homestead was), and at Brancepeth, 114 in the last fortnight. Miller's beliefs and almost certainly his own circumstances made him quite sympathetic to swaggers, many of whom he saw as desperate men. The numbers arriving were so large that a system of numbered tickets was introduced, which was intended to provide a record, for tax purposes, of the actual number of men who received help from the station—and also to discourage repeat visits. At the end of the first year, Miller wrote:

> Last night completed 12 months since numbered tickets were issued to 'swaggers' properly so called. The number of the last ticket was 925. Everyone of these men has had a bed, and at least 2 meals—many of them have had more & many of them have had clothes, boots, tobacco, or medicines & a few have had money given them. Old men have been allowed to stop for 2 or 3 days rest whenever it seemed required. (28 March 1896)

Miller humanised the anonymous social disaster of unemployment in the 1890s by intermittently noting details of individual swaggers. On 30 June 1900, he wrote in the station diary:

> Gave a swagger boots & socks because he has a fine bass voice, and was dancing on the grass at 6am this morning—'It's a poor heart that can't sometimes b—y well rejoice'.

He recorded names and nationalities, commented on appearance and occasionally on individual circumstances, noted those who came more than once, and always took note of the men who had been employed on the station and later returned as swaggers after, as Miller never failed to observe, 'foolishly' throwing up their billet. Swaggers covered a wide range of nationalities. Miller recorded Scandinavians—'young Scandinavian saw Mr B in office and after a good cry was set to help Brenchley at wood chopping' (15 June 1898); a 'Creole' or 'coloured' (West Indian) cook; a Japanese cook; a 'Brummagem' youth, i.e. from Birmingham; a 'Silesian'; Australians, including 'Sydney-side loafers'; Canadians, Americans, Germans, French and the usual range of Welshmen, Cornishmen, Irish and Scots. A number of the swaggers were 'run' sailors, which is perhaps not unconnected to the fact that *Kidnapped* was one of the most heavily read novels in the Brancepeth library. Belich has stressed the importance of overseas sailors in the floating labour market of nineteenth-century New Zealand.[8] By the 1890s, when they formed part of the patchwork tide of unemployed who arrived at the station, their presence on the station was simply a reflection of the times, but sailors are an especially visible subgroup because Miller, perhaps because of his previous career at the Admiralty, always recorded their presence and was usually kind to them, often ensuring they received a few days' work. Miller's sympathy for the plight of many of the men who arrived at Brancepeth destitute and, as he often remarked, 'naked',[9] depended on their circumstances. The majority of swaggers in the 1890s were men in evident need, but Miller had no time for 'rascally' swaggers, or those whose sense of entitlement he thought outstripped their deserts, and he was critical of many repeat visitors, whom he thought were 'loafers' and 'town men'. He noted caustically on 3 July 1894 that 'every swagger now thinks he's fully entitled to a pair of boots', and later that he had refused to issue blankets to a swagger who told him he had deliberately not brought any from Wellington so as to get some from the station. As Miller noted in the diary, the station did supply boots to many men, also socks, trousers, drawers, blankets, food, shelter and occasionally money, and in a month where it was not unusual to have 18 swaggers arrive on a single day, or find that two or three returned three times within a few days, demand exceeded willing supply by a considerable margin. Miller was always able to find clothing or some petty cash for those he considered genuinely needy and 'decent' men, but others he ordered off for insolence or laziness.

In 1900, at the beginning of the new financial year, Miller set out a table (in red ink) of swagger numbers, a table he updated every April first until he left the station.

1895–6, 925	1896–7, 730	1897–8, 620
1898–9, 660	1899–1900, 520	

The annual number remained high, between 350–550, until he left Brancepeth in 1908—the figures for his last three years (1905–7) were 533, 486, 450.

Swaggers were a considerable cost to the station, and formal social and economic distinctions were maintained between swaggers and employees. An order was issued in February 1896, for example, instructing the cook to feed the men before the swaggers, as the men did not like to eat with them. A long-running saga about the use of butter dated from 1896. Butter was not issued to swaggers, but the consumption of butter exceeded what was thought reasonable by both Miller and Hugh Beetham, resulting in successive whare cooks being shown 'Mr Beetham's Minute of Feb: 1896: "Butter is not to be given to the swaggers under any circumstances".' Few swaggers, though, were sent away without a meal and a night's shelter, and when they were, it was generally because the station had had previous (and negative) experience of them. Most swaggers were treated with humanity, or humanity mixed with expediency, as in the case of E.T. Louis, a swagger who travelled through the station periodically, was briefly employed, then sacked and sent on his way. A month later, in October 1894, he turned up again, ill and destitute. Louis was a Tasmanian. He was given a suit of clothes and £1 and told to turn up at the Wellington office of G.M. Hewson, Agent, for a one-way ticket to Hobart on the next ship sailing, with a promise of a further £2 on landing.

Not all such cases could be dispatched to another country. Ernest McGlashan, son of an acquaintance of Hugh Beetham's, also drifted in and out of the farm community, working for a few days here and there before being paid off (and refunded his library subscription). Eventually, turning up very ill and in 'utter distress', he appealed directly to Hugh Beetham:

> Brancepeth
> April 17th, 1896
> Mr Hugh Beetham
>
> Dear Sir
>
> I trust you will excuse the liberty, I take in writing you, as I am fairly cornered, & don't know what to do; I have tramped round the country looking for work in vain, & have suffered such privations that my constitution has completely broken down—I have hardly made sufficient money this last twelve months to keep myself in clothes.
>
> If I could only get sufficient money to take me back to the South Island, instead of tramping about living in misery & having to associate with all classes of men. I could at least have a comfortable home with my sister, Mrs Henry Orbell

who has a Station at the River Waikouaiti near Dunedin, & who, I am sure would repay for me, any kindness done here in my distress.

My only hope is that you knowing my late Father, Edward McGlashan will save me from leading a life of misery & degradation & enable me to get back, to my relations, who will I know give me a helping hand.

Trusting you will assist me, as I really am anxious to make a fresh start in life, anxiously awaiting your reply—

I remain
Yours obd
Ernest McGlashan[10]

McGlashan may have had a family connection with the Beethams, as Ruth Beetham's mother was an Orbell. There is no record of what happened to him, but it is likely he was assisted, as Hugh Beetham was said to be openhanded to many who asked him directly for money or help. The visible human cost of the depression was a constant Dickensian backdrop to daily life at Brancepeth in the 1890s. Like Mr Micawber, Miller was very aware of his own relative good fortune in having a job at all. On 21 February 1896, just one of numerous such occasions, Miller noted that he had given 5/- to a penniless man who was 'just too late for a job and was grievously disappointed'. Even if all the swaggers had wanted to work in exchange for the charity offered by the station, it would not have been possible to find employment for them. It was relatively few who were kept on for a few days of chopping wood or working in the garden. The flow of the unlucky included professional men, like the ex-Sanitary Inspector who arrived on foot in July 1901, and on one occasion a married couple, of whom Miller said

I gave the woman swagger a pair of canvas shoes—and 5/- as she and her husband are destitute—they have walked from Wellington. (12 August 1901)

In other words, they had travelled about 120 km of rough roads on foot. A woman swagger was unique; there is no other recorded, just an endless trail of homeless single men, many of whom were elderly, ill or 'lunatics', to use Miller's word, for whom there was no welfare provision. Attitudes about these harbingers of despair who struggled to the station gates were reflected in the way regular station workers maintained a safe distance from the less fortunate by having separate meal times.

Mixed in with the indigent was a more general outflow from towns and cities, the people Belich refers to as 'shifters' and Fairburn as 'vagrants',[11] which included various kinds of rogues and opportunists. Miller described these men variously as gentlemanly swaggers, impostors, 'cool hands' and gaolbirds. A steady run of thefts accompanied the swaggers (though a number may also have been the work of farm hands) especially spoons and plates from the men's whare, where the swaggers and station workers were fed; goods from the store, especially tobacco and boots; meat from the meat safe; and once an entire treeload of yellow plums. One night Miller woke to hear the door handle of his room being stealthily turned, and on another occasion

> . . . on going to the letter box yesterday morning for letters for mail, I found a bent wire hook, well made for fishing up letters thro' the slit—but it had slipped from the operator's hand into the box, and could not be withdrawn as the box was locked. (2 October 1897)

The mail frequently carried money or cheques and its security was a matter of great concern. The bag was only supposed to be opened by the station clerk or the owner's family, and on the few occasions when someone else opened it, Miller issued stern notices and reprimands. When he sent remittances to his family in Motueka, which he did most weeks, he noted the fact in the diary in transliterated

Greek, presumably to hide it from casual readers: 'Wrote MM ενκλοπινγ φινε πουνδς' [enclosing five pounds] (14 April 1901).

At the beginning of 1894, in Miller's first month on the station, the *Wairarapa Daily Times*, a conservative paper friendly to the large runholders, published a leader about Brancepeth. Entitled 'A Big Local Industry', it praised 'large settlers' for 'yielding such excellent returns and distributing so much money in labour'. The editor claimed:

> We never met a swagger yet who had not a good word for Brancepeth or a resident workman employed on the station who did not praise the management for the liberal treatment and consideration which was extended to one and all.

The following week the *Wairarapa Star*, a rival left-wing paper, published a rebuttal alleging that the Brancepeth workforce was underpaid and exploited, 'black in the face' from their exertions. This elicited a long and passionate response from John Vaughan Miller in early February. Miller began by asserting that the *Star* editor was engaged in poisoning the minds of his readers just as he had once poisoned rabbits at Brancepeth, and continued:

> Ask, sir, any of the men employed at Brancepeth, ask those who have at different times worked there, ask the men who have gone there to look for work, how they have been treated. The answer will be tolerably unanimous . . . I have talked with a great many men in the last few years in the South Island, as well as in the North, who have spoken in terms of warm gratitude of kindness received, and I have never heard a contrary opinion expressed.
> (*Wairarapa Daily Times* 9 February 1894)

Although Miller's view of the generosity of his employers shifted over time, culminating in a highly critical article he published in Nelson in 1901 ('The Hire of the Labourers,' discussed in the previous chapter),[12] the station diary recorded many acts of generosity towards the indigent, including his own; he sometimes gave his own boots or spare clothing to needy men. The sheer size of the swagger numbers suggests that Brancepeth's generosity was well known to the itinerant population of the Wairarapa, and for some it was obviously a regular circuit stop which they made for years.

Alongside the continuous stream of swaggers, a flow of employees, opportunists and hopeful contenders for highly sought-after jobs flooded through the station office weekly. A 'Professor Cotching' turned up in March 1895 with a phonograph.

> Prof Cotching gave his entertmt 8pm lasting 1hr 25min. Very 3rd rate charge 2/- a head gave him a cheque for £4.12.0

A week later Miller indignantly records that 'Mr B had private letter from Cotching (ex-Professor) yesterday asking for some billet—apparently mine' (16 March 1895). Despite the scarcity of good jobs, the turnover on the farm was high, though not amongst the employees who held senior positions. Miller, along with Wilson, the head shepherd and Garratt, the overseer, stayed for many years, and William Armstrong, a shepherd who was there when Miller began work at Brancepeth in 1894, was one of the station hands who carried Hugh Beetham's coffin at his funeral in 1923. In June 1895 Miller recorded that there were 68 men working on the station, which didn't include Michael Ryan and Charles Rehall, the roadmen who were employed by the Road Board but worked and took their meals at Brancepeth, the overseer George Garratt's three sons, the temporary hands working in the garden, or the women working in the house. The number of workers fluctuated considerably during the year, as shearing, dagging and crutching gangs were all brought in for the season. During shearing there could be as many as 50 sitting down for dinner.

The long-term employees, Wilson, Garratt and Miller (the

most recent arrival), had frequent feuds, which seem to have been both territorial and hierarchical. Garratt often accused Miller of not doing his job properly, particularly in stocking the store.

> Garratt was very offensive last night about there being no potatoes in store. He doesn't care a damn about the expenses and nobody does anything right except himself. He will only have been here 2 days this week to look after his own dept. (22 March 1895)

Miller kept a sharp eye on everyone who came in and out—the office was and still is the natural gateway to the back of the homestead—and was particularly conscious of Wilson's and Garratt's appointments with Hugh Beetham, logging how long they spent, and their business, if he knew it. (If he didn't know their business, he noted that too, implying that he should have.) All three men exercised influence over the hiring and firing of staff, though they operated in distinct spheres. Miller hired cooks and temporary employees, made arrangements for the family to hire household servants, and supervised the shearing, crutching and dagging invitations. A large part of the station clerk's job in the second half of the year was getting ready for, and managing, the shearing. Professional men like the wool classer (who was given free use of the library) and the shepherds were hired by Hugh Beetham, who also made the final decisions on the white shearers, which may have been because many of them returned over many years.

Shearing was a 'crew culture' as Belich and others have described: one of the male-dominated groups who did often dangerous manual work such as bushfelling, lived rough and constituted a floating rural working class.[13] In the late nineteenth and early twentieth centuries, shearers followed a climatic and geographical cycle that began in Queensland and ended in Southland, and they developed their own argot and an often disreputable way of life. Edward Wakefield's description of shearers in 1889 records them 'spinning yarns' totally unfit for polite ears.[14] Miller frequently notes furious rows and fights at the shearing shed, and long weather-induced delays in the shearing schedule inevitably caused trouble, with shearers disappearing without leave, to drink. Shearing was also a spectacle—the Beethams invited parties of friends to visit the shed and watch the shearing, and the household servants were escorted down each year to see the action. In 1899, an election year, candidates from both sides of the political fence held electioneering meetings at the shed and the shearers were taken to the polling booth in Taueru.

There were two shearing boards in the woolshed—a Māori board and a 'white men's board'. The Māori board was organised by Motete, a regular employee at Brancepeth, who simply gave Miller a list of the crew. White shearers applied individually and got their jobs on reputation or performance. Shearing stands were highly sought after, particularly during the 1890s when jobs were scarce. When the economy began to lift, the station was less able to pick and choose, and lost good men when they could earn more elsewhere. In the early 1900s, Māori shearers were allocated stands on the white men's board. This may have been a reflection of the shift in labour conditions that meant there were fewer men competing for jobs, though Miller implies in the station diary that Māori shearers were better performers:

> Some steps must be taken to find out what Maoris are coming—as it may be well not to refuse all applcns from white men. (18 June 1903)

By Miller's last years, when good workers were in demand, Brancepeth had become uncompetitive in its rates of pay for some sought-after occupations, like cooks and shepherds, and it took considerably more time to organise the shearing crew.

The shepherds, who were disproportionately Scots at Brancepeth as in most of New Zealand,[15] were under the charge of Hugh Wilson and his successors as head shepherd. They formed a distinct group within the social world of the station, even demanding special meal schedules, which was a point of some annoyance for Miller:

> Shepherds breakfast now at ¼ to 7 in order to annoy the cook—as nothing else is gained—if they were to spend the ¼ hour in saddling and getting their horses out they could breakfast at 7 & not lose a moment. When they do start they crawl 2 ½ miles an hour—No cook will stand such selfish want of consideration and it affects the comfort of the whole whare. (7 February 1895)

The other large group was the rabbiters, who operated in gangs and had a fairly high turnover. From the late 1860s, rabbit control had become a significant industry, with exports of 100 million rabbit skins in the 1880s.[16] The calculation of the value of a rabbiter's skins was one of the recurring tasks of the station clerk, who also administered the supply of food and goods to the gangs, including their library requests. Rabbiting was not well-regarded as a profession. Miller noted that he gave two references to Trigge, one of the longer-term rabbiters: one as a rabbiter and one as a station hand to use in places where 'rabbiters are regarded as the off-scouring of the nation' (8 April 1905). George Garratt, the overseer, was in charge of the rabbiting, fencing and grass-seeding gangs, as well as the general business of the station. Each gang had its own boss and the gang was referred to by his name; for a long time, the predominant gang was Charles Gibson's, and Gibson answered to Garratt. In Miller's view, some of the tension between the uneasy triumvirate of Miller, Garratt, and head shepherd Wilson, was about unequal workload and habits. In August 1897, he remarked sarcastically that Garratt had left to shoot 'two mythical dogs and this will be his mythical day's work', this, on the same day that Wilson was 'hors de combat' with an infected eye but had no trouble reading (7 August 1897). But some of it seems to have been caused by the play of ascendancy, which depended on a variety of factors—closeness to the station owner, seniority, and differing spheres of influence, power and expertise. The station hierarchies are both subtly and overtly reflected in Miller's record-keeping. He noted, for example, writing a 'friendly' note to N.C. Davidson, described in the ledger as a labourer, 'advising him in his own interest' not to deal directly with 'Mr B', but to 'do everything thro' Garratt who is his superior officer' (16 February 1895). Miller's highly developed sense of propriety had no doubt been honed by working in the Admiralty, but social distinctions operated keenly on the station, which was, as the *Wairarapa Age* noted in Hugh Beetham's obituary on 4 January 1923, run in an 'almost manorial style'. The bad blood that surfaced between Miller, Garratt and Wilson reflected their implicit and explicit competition for favour and influence, and was accentuated by Miller's acute sensitivity to his social environment, evident in his frequent descriptions of manners and behaviour.

Miller was clearly a fastidious man, but his fulminations against the way other employees ate and behaved, like the close attention he paid to the activities of the Beethams and every shade and nuance of Hugh Beetham's interactions with his employees, were also a fairly direct expression of his feelings of social displacement and superiority. In his early years at the farm, Miller regularly noted each occasion on which he 'dined with the family'—usually once a week. Later these social encounters became less frequent, though they continued throughout his time on the station. He was always acutely aware of any transactions that took place inside or around the homestead, and made sure they were written down. Miller's self-appointed role as gatekeeper was implicitly also a kind of social policing and says a great deal about his status anxiety and the accompanying competitiveness.

In March 1897, Miller had a row with Summers, the Brancepeth gardener. Summers had sent his son to get some butter from Miller, which Miller refused, since 'strict orders have been given this week about butter & I will not ask Mr B to order more, unless I know it is his wish'. Summers accused Miller of swearing at children. Referring to 'Summers and his area-sneak of a boy', Miller wrote angrily '[I] never swore at a child in my life till now—Damn Tom Summers and all other crawlers' (7 March 1896). Miller's sense of himself as a gentleman—cultivated, literate, exemplary—was frequently in friction with the community in which he lived. His clash with Summers and his son was the product of working at the inevitably tense point of supply for the wider community, acting as broker between his employer's orders and other people's needs. Miller recounts the incident in language that situates Summers and himself in different social spheres, despite that fact that Summers was an employee of some distinction. Summers had worked at Kew and had great expertise as a plantsman; he discovered a variegated flax in the Wainuioru gorge after a storm and developed an important cultivar from it.[17] He left Brancepeth the following year to set up a nursery in Masterton and later Lower Hutt, and by the time he returned temporarily to help re-establish the gardens after the 1904 earthquake that necessitated the rebuilding of the homestead, Miller finally behaved towards him as a coeval. Similarly, Miller's relationship with Garratt moderated over the years. After Garratt left Brancepeth and retired to Hastings, his periodic returns to help out were greeted by Miller with enthusiasm.

Miller's fastidiousness was most pointedly expressed around questions of personal hygiene (other people's hygiene), social behaviour and table manners. Making common cause with Garratt about Wilson, he wrote:

> Garratt and I have made up our minds that we cannot much longer put up with W's filthy and disgusting habits and behaviour at table. I never met a man so wanting in all sense of what is due to his fellow men—his manners would disgrace the Old Men's Home. (25 March 1898)

When Wilson was succeeded by McLeod, another Scot, Miller's disgust was transferred to McLeod's eating habits, which he claimed were synonymous with his Scottishness:

> Mcleod away 7.15 am leaving the breakfast table in such a filthy mess as is only to be achieved by a Scotch shepherd: his predecessor was quite as good in this respect, but he added hawking to his other accomplishments. (23 February 1901)

McLeod never arrived at favour with Miller. In the station diary he is referred to as 'Chef de Bergers'—the Francophone nickname was not a compliment. When he had been at Brancepeth only six days Miller wrote darkly: 'McLeod back 4pm. *Je crois que le berger si renommé est sot*' [I think that the famous shepherd is an idiot] (12 January 1901). Part of the tension around food and eating was that Miller, McLeod and Garratt shared a dining room; another part of it was the constant difficulty in finding and retaining decent cooks. The whare cook was always a man (as opposed to the house cook who was always a woman), often inexperienced though usually claiming experience, and very frequently a drunkard. It was a hard job, cooking for as many as 40 some nights, making the bread and providing food on a strict timetable. According to Miller, not many of the incumbents were up to the task.

> Wright, the whare cook, came over to know if I wasn't well, as I ate nothing—and there is nothing fit to eat but 10th rate confectionary—The plain cooking has never been so bad since the station was born—told him every man thinks so. (22 July 1899)

Miller was even more forthright about B. Goff and W.A. Smith, the whare cook and his mate, whom he described in a 1906 ledger note as debauched ruffians. Goff was characterised as 'utterly brutal and vile. This man is not fit to cook for a kennel of hounds'. Even a good cook would have faced the problem that station food was monotonous—mutton with occasional episodes of beef. Miller frequently noted that the meat was rotten or uneatable, but the principal hardship, recorded again and again, was the combination of tedium and bad cooking. In the station library's very dirty, heavily read copy of Steele Rudd's *On Our Selection,* a remark about food must have found a feeling echo at Brancepeth: ' that old familiar repast, hot meat and pumpkin' (208).

On 2 February 1906 Miller wrote

> I have never fared so badly, during the chances and changes of 12 years, as I have since Xmas. 2 slices of cold mutton, cut the wrong way, have formed my luncheon every day since Xmas—except when I have bought something for myself.

Miller suffered from bad teeth, as did many of the men on the station—the diary records numerous episodes of workers being sent to the dentist in great pain. Miller performed his own extractions, but was also driven to visit the dentist at considerable expense to have his teeth seen to after a period of prolonged abscesses. Because of the state of his teeth and the unpleasantness of station food, he ordered, on a private account, supplies from town—Spanish olives, soup squares, biscuits, nuts, tins of fish. Sometimes he would share these with fellow sufferers or those he particularly liked. But Miller was also the food police. He kept the store and was responsible for issuing tea, sugar and cheese to the cooks, including those from the outlying camps. The diary often expostulates that station workers, along with their other spoiled habits, eat too much.

> H Ross here fooling round after clothes and boots but nothing is good enough for him—he has a no 9 boot and grumbles because 7s pinch him—ends by having nothing. He is a stolid conceited ass—eats too much—more matter than mind, a good deal. (19 September 1896)

Station workers were profligate with tea ('9 lbs a week in the whare', 23 July 1900), sugar ('shamefully wasted—piled on an inch thick on the top of jam . . . it takes three dessert spoonfuls to sweeten a "drink o' tea"', 8 September 1900), and mustard (Miller refused to send mustard to the camps because they had no supplies of beef—he thought the men should not be allowed mustard with their mutton).[18] Regulations were posted in the whare about how culinary matters were to be conducted. Miller recorded them in the diary, and they give a good idea of the strict paternalism that operated on the farm, and Miller's role in enforcing it.

> Whare Regulations: Cook informed that butter is only to be put on the table at breakfast. Tea is to be emptied out after tea, sugared by cook & 2 pannikins left available—1 lamp to be turned out after tea—the other lamp to be turned up by one of the senior men at 9.30. [in red] Card playing on Sundays is forbidden. (8 September 1896)

Butter was a continual sore point and Miller also thought the consumption of cheese was extravagant:

> I told the cook yesterday not to put it on the table at 6 o'clock dinner—it is used always at breakfast and lunch. At 6 o'clock yesterday there was good soup, usual hot meat, and pudding—there is always a pudding in the men's dining room. But there were loud complaints of the cheese being stopped. In my opinion it is mere wanton waste to use it as the men have got into the habit of doing. They cannot possibly require it. It is not as if they had no butter. I have no more cheese in store as supply has already been used this winter. It is about three cheeses a month for our whare only. Neither Garratt, Wilson nor myself eats cheese more than once a day. (23 August 1898)

The continual references to the quality of the food and the behaviour of the cook in the station diary testify to the importance that food assumed in a society with few opportunities for relaxation, very few women and little chance of domestic comfort. There was also the question of the nutritional needs of men doing hard physical work. Brancepeth maintained a huge kitchen garden to supply the station and the food appears to have been plentiful, but it was a poignant reflection of the tedious repetition and deficiencies of station cuisine when Miller noted an extremely rare highlight in the diary. He had 'two native trout for breakfast this morning—small but quite delicious they are beautifully delicate' and 'some lovely silver eels this evening—they proved perfectly delicious' (3 March 1907). The eels and fresh trout were caught for Miller by his '2 boys': Wilfrid Saxby, the head shepherd at the time, and Wilfrid Horsley, a cadet who was friendly with the Beetham sons. Miller had the luck to share the dining saloon with Saxby and Horsley who evidently developed an affectionate friendship with him and were familiar with his culinary complaints.

Getting rid of bad cooks and retaining good ones were problems of equal magnitude. After the whare cook who provided '2 shoulders of small shrunken mutton on my table every day without a break' (8 January 1907) was dispatched, an angel descended in the person of a cook named Reinhardt, but he proved susceptible to the enticements and higher pay of another station owner, which Miller was unable to match. His description of the offer made to Reinhardt is revealing about a cook's life, what he might expect to earn and the lengths the men would go to retain a good one:

> Reinhardt the cook has given notice. This is a terrible loss to us all—he is the very best cook in N.Zealand for a large station. He has seemed happy & contented—and we all like him—But he has an offer of 35/-—and will get the fat, which is the cook's usual perquisite—and where men are boarded

> 2/- a week a head is added to the ordinary charge of 10/- and this 2/- is handed to the Cook—a Cook's work is 7 days a week and the Sunday the hardest day of all. If such a thing were allowable I could easily make his pay up to £2 a week, or more, amongst ourselves. (1 July 1907)

Cooks were notorious drunkards, and their frequent turnover on the farm was often due to being dismissed for drinking. In February 1898 Miller noted caustically that the cook had a sprained wrist and arm caused by falling from his bunk: 'it is not too far to fall and as he has damaged himself so much he may possibly be sober'. Drinking on the station was an endemic problem tied to the pay cycles of station workers, though the phenomenon was an old one, linked to the crew cultures of whalers, sawyers, navvies, goldminers and other groups paid in lump sums after a period of hard and lonely work.[19] The usual pattern was to cash the pay cheque, go straight to the pub at Taueru or into Masterton, and 'knock it down'—drink until it had all been spent. Men were forbidden to bring drink onto the station or to be drunk when they were there, on pain of instant dismissal. Still, the diary is full of references to drunkenness, and to illicit supplies of alcohol being brought on to the farm. There are descriptions of chronic alcoholics, like James Campbell, who had 'D.T. hanging about him' (8 December 1900), and John Maltby, who, 'ill from drink', said he must make a fresh start somewhere else. Miller paid Maltby what was due and noted that he 'says he shall come back later on and do some draining—at present he is draining the flaming bowl with disastrous consequences to himself' (3 January 1901). A favourite novel at Brancepeth, Amelia Barr's *Jan Vedder's Wife* is a moral tale about a fisherman in the Shetlands whose drinking causes the loss of his marriage and family life. Even more popular was Wilkie Collins's *Hide and Seek* whose hero, Zack Thorpe, undergoes the painful effects of a 'thick night'. As Dorothy L. Sayers remarked, Collins's detailed description of a hangover suggests 'the stamp of agonising inside knowledge' (107), and the popularity of both novels with readers might reflect a familiarity of experience in the social world of Brancepeth.

Miller was not entirely unsympathetic to these troubled alcoholics, which hints at his familiarity with the demon drink in his own past, as does the acute attention the diary displays towards drinking and drunkards. In his article 'The Hire of the Labourers', he made the point that employers had at their 'good table . . . wine and beer and spirits *ad libitum*' but the men had none of these things.[20] Miller remarked sourly on 22 October 1905 that 'everyone was supposed to be drunk in honour of Nelson and Trafalgar, except the men on Brancepeth'. He also recognised that for men in the grip of alcoholism the fury to obtain it could be fatal, and complete prohibition not always the answer:

> Mr Ralph rode to x [the Cross, which was the intersection at Wainuioru] before breakfast and on his way back he met Fletcher and tried to persuade him to come back—if F. could have had a whisky last night it might have kept him straight. Fletcher . . . has gone off again mad for drink . . . (25 January 1905)

When the cook dobbed in Richards (the carpenter who was also the librarian) to Garratt for having a supply of whisky and wanted Garratt to pass it on, Miller 'declined to hear a word on the subject' (19 April 1901). As far as it is possible to tell, Miller did not drink at all while at Brancepeth, a question on which there was little room to move, as drunkenness would have meant instant dismissal. However, he took a great deal of interest in the Brancepeth vineyard and the much larger vineyard managed by William Beetham at Lansdowne in Masterton, noting visits from wine experts and commenting on the size of the harvest—the first in April 1896 was 'a fine crop for 1st year'. He also noted when wine supplies were received at the homestead and recorded that Dry Monopole (a French champagne) was drunk at a wedding breakfast hosted by the Beethams for Lucy Miller, a wedding which had to be 'absolutely quiet' as it took place shortly after the death of Queen Victoria in January 1901. But Miller was one of the few station employees who never visited the pub at Taueru or went into Masterton on a binge, something that distinguished him from the culture that dominated the men's whare. It seems likely that the prohibition order taken out against Miller in 1893 marked the end of his drinking, at least until 1908 when he left Brancepeth—although dining with the Beethams or joining Hugh Beetham in the smoking room, where he was sometimes invited, must have exposed him to temptation. But on drink as on many other subjects, the diary reveals Miller as someone whose tastes and attitudes ranged across a spectrum of sympathies and had more to do with his beliefs about what constituted decency and equity than fixed positions on social issues.

After his initial and deeply felt defence of the Beethams in 1894, Miller's views about the station are reflected in three pieces he wrote for the paper from 1897 to 1901. They describe an increasingly critical trajectory, and also provide a sardonic description of station society as Miller saw it. In 1897 he wrote a letter to the editor in response to the publication of something he called '"The Makers of New Zealand" (or whatever it is called)' in 'six (only six) volumes, price only ten guineas'. The letter made fun of what is probably the entry on Brancepeth in the *Cyclopaedia of New Zealand* published in six volumes between 1897 and 1908. Miller dubbed Brancepeth 'the Nulli Secundus' Station. He satirised the one employee whose photograph is featured, George Garratt, as one 'who is styled officially "Chief Rabbi and Fencing-master" (it seems a curious title)'. Miller wrote from the collective persona of 'our fellows' and their view of the book:

> Sir, we think it is hard lines, because on this station there is what the police vulgarly call a 'Rogues' Gallery', which contains portraits, instantaneous photographs, etc, of an immense number of men, besides the Chief Rabbi, who have helped during the past thirty five years to make the station what it is. (*Wairarapa Daily Times*, 29 June 1897)

But the letter has a serious and partisan point to make. It is not 'Messrs Lincoln and Downs, the run-holders' (both breeds of sheep that the Beethams bred) who have been the 'real makers of New Zealand', but the 'gallery of rogues' whom Miller described as follows:

> . . . some 1897 Rabbiters, say 100 odd Shepherds, whisky and weather-proof; (the Head Shepherd's likeness has gone 'missing' having been stolen by a little French milliner;) a noble band of Teetotallers—all Station Cooks—with little angelic wings sprouting from their heels, indicating that they are birds of passage; several yoke of Ploughmen; a good team of Bullock-drivers; some Married Couples—(no copies of these are attainable);—some Artificers who have obeyed too literally the Apostle's instructions to 'try the spirits'; some aged but otherwise not very extraordinary Butchers; Grooms amatory and bland; Gardeners who have looked after the flowers and frosts of our prolific summers; groups of Poisoners—these form a chamber of horrors);—Grass-seeding Gangs all wearing No.10; an Instructor of Youth, very clever with his hands, and whose delicate feeling for his fellow creatures may be guessed from his portrait (not yet hung); a 'fellow-feeling makes one wondrous kind,' as David Garrick said; a liberal percentage of Lunatics, including a Storekeeper who has not gone to bed in his boots for several years; and, to crown all, some 75,000 Swaggers. There is also a curious collection of Maori daggers. The 'gallery' contains only a few Fencers because the office is hereditary, and the present holder is now immortal.

The letter is signed 'Huki Waaka, Nulli Secundus Station, June, 1897'. The letter is full of in-jokes, including puns on the names of a number of station employees—Summers the gardener, Fred Bland, the groom who was about to be married, and the schoolteacher, Joseph Guest,[21] who earlier that year had failed all his examinations and about whom Miller seems to be hinting at another story which the diary does not record. Guest left later that year and was part of the ongoing feud Miller conducted with Summers. Miller noted in the diary, at the end of 1896:

> The schoolmaster's aim, since he received notice to quit, has been to induce Summers, who is the father of 2/3 of his pupils, to give notice to leave, in order that Guest may be able to say he left because the school was broken up—he knows he could only get a very qualified recommendation from station. He got Summers into the right frame of mind yesterday by plying him with whisky since Friday. This is my opinion. (21 December 1896)

The article also made jokes about Garratt, whose sons were fencers, and Miller poked fun at himself as the storekeeper. His choice of pseudonym was pointed. 'Huki' was the surname of the most frequent Māori visitor to the station, Hori te Huki, and also the nickname of the Beetham's younger son, Orengard. Waaka was the surname of some prominent Māori stationhands. Miller here seems to be suggesting something about the importance of the Māori presence on the station, and perhaps registering another category of 'makers of New Zealand', but the name is counterpointed by his other double entendre, 'the curious collection of Maori daggers'. The dagging gang, like the crutchers and shearers, was Māori, but the hint of curios and museums is also linked by association to the homestead, which displayed a number of objects given to the Beethams by local Māori. Miller was pleased with his letter and sent a copy of the paper to his son Basil. Others on the farm were aware that Miller published articles in the paper, though he always published them under pseudonyms and leaders were published anonymously. Someone must have told Hugh Beetham about the 'Makers of New Zealand', as Miller noted that on 15 July 1897, 'Mr B' asked to see the letter 'Makers of New Zealand', though he does not record his employer's response.

In 1899 Miller noticed an article about station life in New Zealand written by the Rev A.C. Yorke, the vicar who gave services at Brancepeth. Yorke had published an article in *Nineteenth Century* entitled 'The Jackeroo' which Miller picked up from a review in the London *Spectator* (6 May 1899). Yorke's article advised that 'the fate of the educated youngster newly arrived in Australia is usually a melancholy one'. Miller's response in the *Wairarapa Daily Times* took the same title and extended the argument into the New Zealand context, noting that 'if a young fellow has a little money', he should not be allowed to invest it until he has had a 'couple of years hard work, and has met with older men who thoroughly know the country'; and that if he has no money 'let him seriously consider this hint, viz:, as a rule, gentlemen on a station are a nuisance. If he spends five or seven years in good practical hard work, and gets his £1 a week, where is he at the end of his time? Too often he is "no forrader".' This hard-nosed observation reflected Miller's experience of many young men working on Brancepeth whose rate of pay and way of life would not allow them to save enough to establish themselves, and was perhaps also a bitter reflection on his own pay and conditions. When Fred Bland, the groom, got married, Miller—employed as a single man and with no prospect of his wife's being able to join him—remarked 'I suppose [Fred Bland] will be on married scale of pay—I wish I was' (2 July 1897). He ended his opinion piece on a bitterly cautionary note.

> Shall we be thought very absurd and offensive if we say that parents and guardians at home would do well to bear in mind that, in most cases in which a young man gets on to a station, this is his 'environment' (to use the hideous slang of the day): utter and absolute irreligion; a total disregard of Sabbath observance; not a thought or chance of any religious observances; in case of illness, get him up to the Hospital, where he may die like a dog, and be buried with the burial of an ass; a system of white slavery worse and harder than that of negroes; entire confinement to the station for many months on end, the only relaxation recognized being a few days' trip to the nearest town where a cheque may be knocked down; in fact, it is the understood arrangement, that a fellow should go and have a 'burst', and have done with it. Is it wonderful that so many go to the bad?
> (*Wairarapa Daily Times* 28 June 1899)

Miller's triple mention of the lack of religion on the station underlines what was a particular point of tension for him. Miller reported some interest in religious questions among the station employees, noting sardonically on 14 November 1896 'I left Mr Johnson at the breakfast table misquoting texts to Garratt & proving that the Ch. of Rome is not Xt' [Christian], but he was very critical of the local clergy. Religious services were held on a monthly basis, though they were not entirely regular and Miller had a low opinion of them anyway. His references to the Reverend Yorke in the station diary were, without exception, unflattering. Yorke 'misconducts' divine service in April 1897, and on 19 January 1896, 'within five minutes' of conducting divine service at 11am, Miller notes, the reverend's 'surplice was off and he was reading the "Sporting and Dramatic" and making a pipe'. Of the Reverend D.H. Hampton, he observed, after hearing him preach, that it was 'no wonder he has emptied St Matthews', the church in Masterton (24 April 1904).

The clergyman with whom Miller did have a convivial

relationship, Wyndham Earée, became involved in a very public scandal and left the parish. Miller's absences at Divine Service were a form of protest, entered in the diary as 'Divine Service. Self absent.' Few of the station hands attended in any case. When the Reverend Spencer administered Divine Service on 11 December 1904, Miller noted that there were only three men present besides himself, and no women except the ladies of the house. Regular church attendance was lower in New Zealand than in Britain and in the Australian colonies, which Belich has suggested may partly be due to 'hints of a correlation' between migration to New Zealand and low-church-going districts in England.[22] But the quality of the clergymen may also have had something to do with it. Miller held strong views on religious issues and was a committed Anglican, as his published articles show, but he despised pious affectation and was not disposed to overlook the deficiencies of the clergymen, even the high-ranking ones, who visited the flock at Brancepeth. Most clergymen, he insinuated, had pastoral ambitions of a different kind:

> 18 Mar 98
>
> There was a very good congregation to hear the Bp [Bishop] last night—and they were all grievously disappointed. He is by no means a second Chrysostom. He wore a 6' t [cross]on the pit of his stomach. I don't believe in 't-bred' bishops and pastors. They bring their flock to the 'well of living water' and then 'they have nothing to draw with,—and the well is deep'—any intelligent child of 10 years old could have preached as good a sermon and many a better one—All the parsons now seem to keep a private 'Wolsely shearing machine'.[23]

A week after his comments on 'The Jackeroo' were published, he noted that he had 'had some talk with Mr B about "the Jackeroo" art: he agrees with it: but Nevins objects' (6 July 1899). Tom Nevins, who had come to Brancepeth in the 1880s and become manager of Annedale, the northern bush block of the station purchased in 1883, was socially integrated with the Beetham family. His photograph appears in the family album and he was married in the homestead. Miller's critique of station owners for not taking responsibility for the conditions under which jackeroos and other employees worked must have struck a nerve with Nevins, though a couple of days later he recorded having a 'long chat' with Nevins in the afternoon.

In any case, many of the points Miller made were irrefutable. The station encouraged the workers to take out a subscription to the cottage hospital in Masterton, which at least ensured that when they became too ill to work to they could be looked after professionally. Those who did not have a 'hospital ticket' had to rely on what Miller could dispense from the store, or retreat to their families. Usually this meant they lost their pay and sometimes their jobs, though if the sick person was a long-time employee, or a particularly satisfactory one, Hugh Beetham would issue orders that their pay was not to be stopped. When he wrote his paragraph about a sick man dying like a dog, Miller may have been thinking of an incident on the station two years before. Henry Miles, a young rabbiter, appeared at the homestead in the middle of the grape harvest of 1897. As Miller was noting the news in the diary—the grape tally (10 tons at Lansdowne and 37 casks at Brancepeth), the selection of 70 new books by the library committee, and that William McIntosh had an inflamed axe wound on his foot—'Henry Miles came in—very ill—will go to Mast by coach. He looks as though he has had an epileptic fit—his tongue is in a shocking state' (12 April 1897). Three days later Miller noted briefly 'H. Miles has been received in Mastn Hosp. with supposed typhoid'. Miller was working on the station balance sheet, irritated by 'incessant petty interruptions' and 'utterly unbearable' flies, and dealing with various staff problems, like Edward Sherwood, who wanted to leave because 'the Irishman in the ditch with him asked him how he liked working in irons' (22 April 1897). (Sherwood turned out to have had just such an 'unfortunate episode' in his past, after a forgery conviction and an escape attempt; Miller gave the man a reference at Hugh Beetham's request). Through the habitual turbulence of daily station life runs a thread of notes on Miles's condition: his parents have been told he is sick, he was reported so ill as to be unable to speak, slightly better, and then on 26 April, two and half weeks after appearing at the office, a telegram came to say he had died. The funeral was held the next day and Garratt deputed to attend. Miller wrote a 'letter to the father, or any relative, signed by Mr B, explaining circs and speaking v. kindly of the youth', and sent it to an address in East Oxford, Canterbury. No relative was present at the funeral, and the telegram from the hospital to East Oxford was returned 'not known'. Miles's swag was brought in to the office and Miller commented 'it had better have been burnt'; nevertheless he wrote to the Public Trust about the swag and Miles's share of the rabbit skins waiting to be sold. A few days later a paid-off station hand rode Miles's mare down to the Public Trust and all his things were sold at auction.

The sad tale of Henry Miles's death, almost completely unremarked except in the station diary, is a clear example of what Miles Fairburn has called 'social atomisation',[24] the isolation produced when colonists who had severed connections in their metropolitan society had not been in the colony long enough to replace them. These primary effects of migration were exacerbated in the 1890s by economic hardships, which increased transience and the dispersal of families as soon as children were old enough to work (Miller's own family is a case in point). Brancepeth's working population was principally made up of men whose families were somewhere else and whose kinship ties were distant or weak. Henry Miles may have been cast off from his family, or his family was in such dire straits they were unable to maintain contact with him, and the pitiful collection and distribution of his goods speaks of a life, like many others recorded in the diary, without resources or affiliations of any kind. However it is a measure of the social cohesion that did exist at Brancepeth that the station responded to his illness and death in the way it did. It is also emblematic of Miller's own engagement with the people around him and his sense of community that he recorded so much detail about what happened to Miles, and indeed other desperate people who were not even employees. As a father of sons about Miles's age, the loneliness of the young man's sudden death may have struck him particularly hard.

With such a diasporic and mobile workforce, informing relatives of sudden deaths was always protracted and difficult. When Charles Prophit, the cook at the Brocken, one of the out-stations, died of a heart attack in October 1901, Miller informed the police, as he was required to do, and later put a notice in the *Inverness Courier*, where Prophit had come from. Some months later he received a shocked letter from Prophit's sister, Mrs Isabella Ross, who had seen 'the detailed letter I wrote to the Editor—needless to say she asks for more'. Mrs Ross wrote again several times and became demanding, and eventually, almost two years after Prophit's death, Miller put an end to the correspondence:

> Have written again to Mrs Isabella P.R. [Prophit Ross] particulars of her brother's death & told her that Mr B sees with regret the morbid and exaggerated expressions she uses in her letter of 3 March. (28 April 1903)

Prophit had been one of the station's notorious drunken cooks, something Miller probably did not reveal to Mrs Ross. His death also illustrated the difficulties of providing any kind of medical aid on the station. The news of his illness was brought in by Con Nyhane, a rabbiter, who arrived at 6.40pm on a Sunday to say that Prophit had been taken very ill at 5pm, and 'looked like a dead man'. Nyhane rode to Masterton and returned with the doctor to the out-station at the Brocken at 2am, but Prophit had died half an hour after Nyhane left the first time. His body was put into a shell made by the carpenter to await the arrival of the undertakers and a proper coffin, but the undertakers were delayed: 'Garratt says decay is very far advanced'. Again, Prophit's effects were sent to the Public Trust, and Miller noted a sad little list: 'small silk handf: spectacles & case—Notes £4 Gold 10/- Silver 10/6 and cheque for pay to day of death £15.3.2' (22 October 1901). Prophit's death was a much more dramatic event than Miles's. He was better known than Miles and had been an employee on the station for several years. Miller recorded the entire narrative in great detail, including a sardonic and disapproving note on the head shepherd's overly zealous behaviour, which Miller saw as a dereliction of duty as well as unseemly self-aggrandisement—McLeod spent Sunday, Monday and Tuesday in 'representing the Station'. However the 'funeral went off quite decently yesterday'.

The deaths of Miles and Prophit, as captured in the station diary, evoke the threadbare and socially exiguous lives endured by many of the station workers. Miles Fairburn has argued that the high percentage of transience in the New Zealand population (he estimates a mean of 57.5% of the population were transient from 1850–80) was produced by high rates of immigration which disrupted extended family networks, followed by isolation and lack of bonding, especially amongst single men.[25] While generally agreeing that the theory of social atomism in nineteenth century New Zealand is a powerful one, Belich has pointed out that not only single men but whole households had a high rate of transience in New Zealand. Two studies using alternative measures of transience estimate that 50–76% of households were no longer in place 10 to 15 years later,[26] which suggests a late nineteenth-century transiency rate of 73–77%. This high percentage must reflect the reduced social cohesion that resulted from the 1890s depression as much as the 'demographic shock' of migration, but Brancepeth station itself is not a simple picture. New Zealand was not the only country to experience divided families and large numbers of men out of work, and as Miller noted, many of the swaggers came from abroad. Brancepeth employees moved on to countries which seemed to offer more promising prospects, with a kind of restless optimism. This may have been an effect of relentless nineteenth century propaganda about self-improvement and the countless narratives of economic and social betterment that circulated in fiction. Picaresque novels, such as Albert Smith's *The Struggles and Adventures of Christopher Tadpole* and Mark Twain's *Tom Sawyer* and *Huckleberry Finn* were heavily-read Brancepeth library books, and the romance of travel and adventure was everywhere in the print press. H. Rider Haggard's *King Solomon's Mines* was a favourite book, and the gold rushes of the 1860s were a relatively recent event. Driven no doubt by many reasons, a number of men left Brancepeth to work in Australian and South African mines, but the attraction of imagined worlds and heroic adventure may have been as strong in real life as it was in the book market.[27] Brancepeth men also left to enlist in the South African war. The core staff, including the rabbiting gangs, remained fairly stable over the years that Miller was station clerk, and his comments about events on the station, arrivals and departures, and the way he kept in touch with ex-employees, suggests the presence of a loose but functioning social network amongst the men who worked there.

As a community dominated by single men, the station

hands depended on the sympathy of their fellow workers for emotional or physical assistance. Despite the high turnover of manual labourers and the isolation many of the men experienced, the diary records affiliative networks of some strength. When ex-employees returned as swaggers they were assisted, often with temporary work, and many of the men who left Brancepeth stayed in touch with the station and with Miller for years after their departure, often from distant parts of the world. Charles Brenchley, a general hand who had been at odds with Miller over library business when he first arrived, wrote to him regularly from Aden, and George Mallory, the cowman, not only kept in frequent contact after his return to England but also presented the station with his family Bible when he left. Some close friendships developed, such as Miller's affection for his 'boys', Saxby and Horsley, towards the end of his time at Brancepeth. But the station diary also offers a graphic picture of the extent of family dispersal. Miller received numerous letters from relatives of men who had worked on the station in the past seeking news of them. He forwarded mail around the globe, and recorded a ceaseless mobility in the lives of station workers, who moved on from Brancepeth to Coolgardie, Aden, the Poseidon Mine near Melbourne, Sydney, the Transvaal, the Argentine, or back to Sweden, Scotland, Ireland and England. Several ended up in the Lunatic Asylum; others wrote desperate letters seeking confirmation about their employment and character references from Hugh Beetham so they could qualify for the Old Age Pension. Most of the restless movement recorded in the diary was both economically and socially driven. Men who thought they had a chance of making more than the wages offered for station work took the risk of leaving, and as the economy improved, they became more adventurous. Young men went off to the Boer War, or the South African War as Miller called it, including one of his sons and one of the governesses, who left to work in the concentration camps in the Transvaal. Only a handful left to establish themselves with a new family of their own, but that was another reason for moving on: the near impossibility of establishing a heterosexual or domestic life when you lived and worked as a rabbiter in an outlying camp. As Miller pointed out in his article in the *Colonist*, men working on stations, unlike their employers, lived in enforced celibacy.

The relative absence of women on Brancepeth is representative of station life throughout New Zealand in the nineteenth and early twentieth centuries. Single women were employed in the house (which had a servants' wing) as cook, parlourmaid, nursemaid, sewing maid and laundress, and there was also a governess who lived in. Some of the longstanding families on the station—the family of Fred Bland for example, who worked at Brancepeth for forty years—had daughters who worked on the station, and there was a sprinkling of women in the district, but female company was scarce and highly sought-after. New female arrivals were always noted in the diary (25 October 1896: 'There is apparently 5'10" of new laundry maid here at work') and Miller was alert to romantic and sexual escapades in the world around him. When he discovered 'FB and SM <u>on the</u> <u>table in the laundry</u> 10pm Sunday night in very questionable position' he recorded it in the station diary.[28] Aside from the underlining, he didn't express any views, but the amorous affairs of station hands were not regarded with tolerance by everyone. The whare cook in 1895, Warren, 'has heard disquieting rumours as to his tenure of office—I suppose what is at the bottom of it is that he is "spooning" the cook in the house'. And the scarcity of young women inevitably caused rows and competition as Miller noted in 1896:

> There is a row at Westmere—the old story 'cherchez la femme'—S.S. versus Polly P. and J. Henderson—the latter

> is a poor measly scrub to commit the scarlet letter with. (10 January 1896)

A number of the men asked Miller to write letters for them, including love letters. Miller wrote a love letter to Miss Jane Jones, Lansdowne, for Charles Rebeck, a scrubcutter: 'He wanted to send her £2 but I told him it was indecent' (9 September 1900). Miller could never resist the pun on male/mail, and could be quite risqué about it.

> Sleeman in 4pm. He wants a cheque for £6 sent to his lady at the Occidental by Friday's mail. I did not ask him how many males per week his lady received as he might not quite have liked it. (26 January 1901)

Miller's hints of prostitution may have been more than an idle joke: according to Belich, prostitution was carried on in most New Zealand towns and often in the hotel.[29] Perhaps because of his location at the centre of station business, Miller knew a lot about what was going on in the broader community, and recorded a great deal of it. When Samuel Wilson, a young shepherd (and nephew of the head shepherd, Hugh Wilson), left the station in July 1900 after receiving 'a nasty letter from his uncle', Miller noted wryly that he was 'supposed to be the fiancé of Parke Bland—and will undoubtedly be the father of her first child' (28 July 1900).

Life on the station was not easy for women. Even if you were widely admired, like Alice Odlin, the parlourmaid in 1899 whom Miller dubbed a 'household Venus', the turnover of servants in the homestead was high, especially of cooks. The work was demanding, there was little to do in the way of recreation and the pay was moderate. In 1908, the ledger recorded the following rates of pay for Brancepeth's domestic servants:

Cook	Wages £52	Board £26	Total £78
Parlour Maid	£39	£26	£65
House Maid	£39	£26	£65
Laundry Maid	£45/10/-	£26	£71/10/-
Sewing Maid	£6/7/6	4/5d	£10/12/6

Some female servants arrived only to leave again the next day. Sometimes there were evening 'entertainments' at Taueru, such as the one attended by four girls from the house in March 1899; when the family went away, the household staff took holidays, but most of the time entertainment consisted of walking to the shed to see the shearing, or occasional excursions to different bits of the station. Eligible girls, both those who worked as servants and those who occupied a more socially mobile world—the governesses for example—were married relatively quickly. Miller recorded a number of weddings during his time at Brancepeth, such as the Lucy Miller wedding. As the social hub of the station, he took it on himself to organise wedding presents to which stationhands subscribed, including one for Thyra Beetham at her wedding in 1904.

Miller's own attitudes to women mixed admiration and affection with paternalism, snobbery and sexism in a way that reflected broader Victorian attitudes; they were later thrown into sharp relief by the New Woman debate, as discussed in the next chapter. Deeply loyal to his wife and daughters, with whom he kept in constant touch, he was also full of imprecations and judgements about women. There was the house cook who arrived on a Friday evening in October 1900, and left again the following week: 'she looks like a convict—and not a first class one'; and Rose Richards, the parlourmaid, who was 'surly, ugly and low-bred' (5 August 1901). In 1900, he remarked sourly that a man 'here traveling who used to be here 16 years ago—became schoolmaster up North £150—Is a Cambridge man—made his property to his wife with the usual result—is now homeless' (4 June 1900). He frequently commented on the appearance of the women in the house or those who lived in the district, though it is hard to imagine how he came by some of his information. When a Mr and Mrs Herepath visited the station in October 1899, Miller noted in the diary that 'Mrs Herepath weighs 17 stone 6 lbs'—perhaps she weighed herself on the postal scales. Levels of literacy were noted ('Nelly Bland spells pyjamas "bejambes"—a great improvement', 4 December 1900) as well as habits and behaviour. When Mrs Parsons, in Miller's eyes an infamous resident of Taueru, was told that her request that 'Mr B buy 11 of her husband's dogs' could not be complied with, Miller added in parentheses, 'she pleads her daughter's ill health but her daughter was at two picnics last week, and goes to everything she can hear of—like her disreputable mother' (30 January 1901). But Miller approved of Mary Prendergast, the kindly cook who cleaned his office for him, including the windows; and he was appreciative of the succession of women he paid to do his laundry (wives of other station employees), sometimes sending little treats of nuts or Spanish olives for their children. When Mrs Bartholomew, the wife of one of the shepherds, came to the station in August 1903, he thought she was 'such a lovely lady that the males will find their way to her of their own accord', and he thought that Mrs Holmes Warren, who was Ruth Beetham's sister, had such a 'kind good face' he recorded it in the diary. He also commented on clothes that he thought were becoming, like 'Miss Burke's serge dress', and expostulated against the bad-mannered (and possibly dangerous) treatment of the laundry maid Rose Jacobs and two other women from the house who came back alone after dark from a visit to Rose Jacobs's fiancé.

> Greenbank (being engaged to Rose Jacobs) ought to be kicked for letting the 3 women from the house leave the Brocken at dusk, to come home alone. (11 August 1906)

Rose Jacobs left three months later to get married and Miller joked that a 'year hence the Green-banks will probably show a Rose-bud' (30 November 1906).

Miller's closest friendships on the station were perhaps also with women. He forged a bond with Ruth Beetham who, like Miller, was a strong Anglican, and had a major involvement in the library. When friends of Weva and Thyra Beetham stayed on the station, the 'young ladies' would visit Miller in his office. His particular affection for Thyra Beetham was demonstrated at the time of her wedding to Marmaduke Bethell. Thyra made a point of visiting Miller in the office to tell him of her engagement, and he was invited to the wedding, although, unlike a number of the other senior staff, he declined the invitation, perhaps because the event would pose too many temptations to a reformed drinker. When Thyra left the station for Wellington a week before her wedding, Miller wrote, in an observation that brings to mind the darker fates of many fictional heroines in the Brancepeth library:

> When one sees a happy & innocent girl leaving her old home, one may well thank God she is going to marry such a good fellow as Bethell. (24 November 1904)

After Thyra left, he saw more of Weva, who developed an interest in photography and took photographs of Miller in the office and at Christmas dinner, which he sent to his wife. His ability as a handyman led him to make photo frames for her, and for other photographs given him by the family.

Unsurprisingly perhaps, given Miller's literary preoccupations, the person he was closest to at Brancepeth was Miss Liddle, the governess during his first four years at the station. Shortly after he arrived, Miller suggested that both Ruth Beetham and Miss Liddle join the library committee, and the diary is full of references to Miss Liddle's participation in library matters. She was a member of the Committee of Taste that Miller set up to select the acquisitions, and they frequently exchanged books and bookish information. Miller wrote in Miss Liddle's autograph book, noted her movements, saw her frequently, swapped books and opinions with her and visited her when she was ill in Wellington. He also made his favourite male/mail pun about Miss Liddle:

> Break left 9.30 for Taueru with Miss Liddle to catch the mail (the male she catches will be a very lucky one). (16 December 1896)

Miss Liddle left the station in 1897, 'to the great regret of everybody', after a period of serious illness. On leaving she presented a 'book of views' to the library; Miller wrote her a valedictory letter from the committee, and she paid him a farewell visit in his office. On 27 May 1902, Miller recorded that Miss Liddle was to be married that day, 'to Mr Kebble'. The tenor of Miller's friendship with Miss Liddle is clearly marked by his notes about her in the diary: he lent her books, including Stevenson's 1881 collection of essays and stories *Virginibus Puerisque* (9 April 1895), and they both assisted the station schoolteacher, Mr Guest, with his examinations, Miss Liddle providing information on Hindu Deities (22 April 1896). Behind these brief but continuous references to Miss Liddle lies a level of socialisation and intellectual exchange that is not as visible in Miller's other interactions on the farm, though he did at one point mention a long conversation with Joe Akel, an 'Assyrian' [Lebanese] hawker who visited regularly, and whom he found to be a very intelligent man.

While Miller did not seem to develop such closeness with

subsequent governesses, they were always natural allies, selected for their educational qualifications and interested in the library for their own use and that of their pupils. Miss Okey, whose tenure at Brancepeth also lasted several years, became a friend, and Miller noted her doings in the diary. He commented in 1907 that the then-governess, Miss Westall, was 'fairly read' (he exchanged books with her from time to time) and regretted that she was leaving for another post. Miller's intellectual snobbery was always to the fore in his descriptions of station employees, but towards the governesses, partly also because they were young women of a similar class, he displayed considerable good will. None of these women were listed in the ledger as subscribers to the library, though the library was clearly used by the women in the household, and must have been a perk of the governess's job. Thyra and Weva wrote their names in a number of books, and their mother and the governesses were engaged in book selection. None of the women who worked in the house were listed as members, nor the wives of men on the station, but it is hard to imagine that books weren't shared once they were taken home. It is clear the library did not function as a social space for women in the way that it did for men—when Garratt left for example, there was a 'presentation' to him (for which Miller wrote the speech) in the library one Friday evening (March 1901). Women were more likely to meet in the office—indeed, when a raffle was drawn on the station, Miller noted ironically that the office had been the scene of 'illegal gatherings'.

Other recreational activities on the station clearly demonstrated the divide between the general workforce and the employer's family, and particularly in relation to the women. Thyra and Weva Beetham were keen horsewomen who competed in showjumping. They also enjoyed deerhunting and often rode out on the station with their father and brothers.

But once they had finished their education with the governess and 'come out' to adult society, their lives were punctuated by picnics, balls, dances, trips to Wellington, going to the races and competing at the Masterton A & P Show, a customary round of pre-marital social life for young women, and part of what Belich has described as the 'leisure ethic' of the runholders and the people with whom they associated.[30] Ralph and Oren Beetham participated in many of these activities, but were also learning how to manage the station by working on it. Everyone else had little free time outside annual leave. John Vaughan Miller worked a seven-day week, as did most of the men on the station, despite Sunday being nominally a day of rest. Such entertainment as there was, beside the library and the pub, tended to be sporadic and occasional. It was sometimes provided by people passing through, like the 'humbug here calling himself Prof Schmidt spouting phrenology etc' noted by Miller on 3 June 1896. When Professor Lichtwark, an American horse trainer, was touring in the early 1890s, he gave lectures on 'educating the horse' and visited stations to provide 'class lessons' on horsemanship. Lichtwark had drawn a certain amount of serious attention for his methods of horse training. The *Wairarapa Daily Times* reported in 1892 that he had been examined by the Joint Stock Committee of the House of Representatives, and the paper reported earlier in January that he had received 'flattering testimonials' from a number of stations including Brancepeth. Lichtwark 'gave an exhibition', in Miller's words, at Brancepeth on 13 January 1895 and turned up again on 24th, when Miller noted 'he has been generally drunk since Sunday week—Mr B did not see him'. The next day he wrote: 'Prof L who is a dirty, drunken sweep, left aftn on a grey buck-jumper which gave him a rare dusting this morning' (25 January 1895).

One of the striking things about the Brancepeth diary is how full of activity each day is and how connected to the world station life was. Miller recorded many world events in the diary: the death of the Queen, the Coronation, key battles in the South African War, the Russo–Japanese War, assassinations and coups. Many of these events were reported by telegraph, and after 1904 by telephone. Telegrams arrived continuously. The Beetham family telegraphed arrivals and departures and sent progress reports and instructions; senior station staff telegraphed their whereabouts when they were off station; significant events were communicated by telegram. Large quantities of mail were sent from and arrived at the station: the mailbag (often several bags) left in the morning and came back in the afternoon and was one of the most important daily tasks. Some idea of the volume of mail is given by the dispatch totals for 1903: 40,000 letters, 140 newspapers, 122 samples (of all kinds of goods) and 102 parcels, books and photos. The volume of inward mail, especially newspapers and parcels, would have been even greater.

Just as important as the mail for connecting the station to the world was transport. From the 1860s New Zealand had one horse for every three people, a 'vastly higher ratio than in Britain',[31] and Brancepeth was well-supplied with horses. For those who could not ride, there was a procession of station carriages—the break, phaeton, dogcart, buggy, pony cart, coach, bullock dray—to take them into Masterton or connect them to the public break that brought the mail. Some employees and members of the family learned to ride bikes in the early 1890s and cycled into Masterton, a bumpy trip over bad roads which took them a full day return. When a motor was purchased in 1907, Miller enjoyed recording its lengthy breakdowns and slow progress. The diary brims with logistical accounts of organising people and goods in and out of the station—and also with anguished notes about the effects of the weather on these movements. During the winter, the roads became impassable with mud, and a distinct note of cabin fever entered the record when the rivers flooded and the bridges were down. Even under ideal conditions, journeys were arduous affairs. When Miller went to Motueka to visit his family, his journey took at least three days, involving starting in the break (a large horse-drawn carriage used for transporting passengers and goods), catching the train from Masterton to Wellington, and then boarding the Nelson steamer, so that he often spent a night or two in hotels in Masterton and Wellington en route. The physical distance of the station from town was not enormous, but the station workers experienced varying degrees of isolation and remoteness, despite the relatively fast delivery of communication from the rest of the world.

One of the consequences of this remoteness was a low-level anxiety about whether people were who they said they were. Nineteenth-century New Zealand novels are full of references to characters who swindle and cheat others by misrepresenting their identity, and Victorian fiction generally is full of fraudsters and con men. Anxiety about identity theft was widespread, enhanced by the grand scandal of the Tichborne claimant, who dominated the press for years and the public imagination for decades. Identity fraud in the nineteenth century was a paradoxical side-effect of colonialism and its social atomisation: you could reinvent yourself in the colonies, and many people did. Most of the cases at Brancepeth were not obviously fraudulent, but it is remarkable how often Miller noted people who used more than one name, sometimes in a minor way. Take, for example, Ellis, the cook at the Parae, said to be the 'biggest liar in the island' which as Miller wryly comments is 'saying a good deal': his given name was Harry but he signed himself James. In 1906, Miller recounts the unfolding story of David Wilson, a 'queer fish' according to Miller, who received a letter addressed to David Salmon. A week later Miller noted that Wilson was allowed to draw £5 to send to his wife who was threatening proceedings: 'she knows him as D. Salmon'. As Wilson had been at Brancepeth for some time working as a rabbiter, his wife had presumably taken a while to track him down. Cases of wife avoidance were not unusual among the men who worked at Brancepeth. The broader problem of whether a prospective employee was who he (or she) said he was, and was trustworthy, was usually resolved by references and other forms of affidavit. Miller wrote literally hundreds of references in his years at Brancepeth, which were signed by Hugh Beetham; they varied considerably in their assurances and recommendations, but were essential documents for employees looking for work elsewhere.

A 'good name' was a currency that could not be taken lightly, when station life seethed with gossip, rumour and scandal. Miller recorded an episode in 1907 when he was given a £1 note by Ryan the roadman. He gave Ryan a receipt, but when the cheque and the note went missing, a rumour circulated that Miller had stolen it. He wrote furiously:

> I lie under a scandalous insinuation. At noon today it was discovered that I had not stolen a £1 note, as it, and the cheque, were safe in the hands of Chennell's [the accountants] joint sec: O. Bagnell, which was the proper place for them. I would rather steal a man's money than his good name and character . . . It seems to have been the infernal blackguard, Abel Kerr, who was slinging mud about the . . . cheque. (20–21 July 1907)

Money was a major source of contention because poverty—or the fear of it—dominated the lives of most of the station hands, both during and after their working careers. In the absence of a universal Old Age Pension and no state aid for illness, many men were left to destitution when they couldn't work any more.[32] Such a fate was a constant anxious preoccupation for Miller, whose hard and unremitting work was not, in his view, justly compensated, and who also thought that station conditions generally were deeply unfair. This became the subject of his most trenchant critique of the station and New Zealand runholders generally. Part of Miller's point in 'The Jackeroo' was that things had been very different in New Zealand forty years before, when people (like the Beethams, he implied) could arrive with some capital and make a lot of money fast. This is a point endorsed by Belich: 'Money made money and it made most for the gentry'.[33] 'The Hire of the Labourers', a polemic against class privilege published in the *Colonist* in 1901 is indirectly about Miller's circumstances, but takes as its target a broader view about how workers should be treated. He asks:

> . . . why should any class of men be allowed to impose on other men conditions of life which they themselves would rather die than accept?

Repudiating the idea of an essential difference between employers and their employees ('in *God's* name how?'), Miller's article spoke of the self-control, self-denial, unselfishness, hardiness, perseverance and power of work shown by 'the men'. This view did not always prevail in his accounts of station life and 'Brancepethmen', but a principle of equity, associated with religious principles, was evident in all his transactions and narratives.

The place of the Brancepeth library in the social world of the station takes on a particular sharpness viewed through this article—both as a concession to the idea of recreation and amusement for station hands, but also as a cost borne by the individual subscribers, supported somehow from their wages of £1 a week. 'The Hire of the Labourers' illustrates how Miller was able to combine his convictions, scholarship, authority, experience and literary skills to speak for the people he worked with. The irony of his article is that he was a natural conservative, and came from a social class and upbringing that meant he felt more like the runholders he worked for than he did most of the men who worked the station. Nevertheless, this did not prevent him taking their side. Miller was not exaggerating the conditions under which most employees worked, and was writing his critique at a time when such social and ethical questions were surfacing in the public sphere, including resistance to the growth of great estates expressed in the push for closer settlement.

The *Colonist* waited several months before publishing Miller's article, no doubt out of concern about its reception. Miller wrote to the editor a number of times and finally cancelled his subscription before it appeared. As discussed in the previous chapter, he wrote the article partly as a response to the proposed reintroduction of Sunday mail at Brancepeth, which meant his one day of leisure would be lost (as already described he had tendered a letter of resignation, but after negotiations with Ralph Beetham, withdrew his notice). Still, the principles of his objections to the conditions of employment on the station remained in place throughout the rest of his time at Brancepeth, and mark a trajectory from his grateful beginnings there to the exhausted and embittered end of his tenure. There is now no way to determine if Hugh Beetham saw 'The Hire of the Labourers', but Miller's gift for narrative and reported dialogue suggests some of the employer's speech came from Beetham's own mouth. It is also likely that some now unknown event provoked his article, but in its essentials, 'The Hire of the Labourers' reflects how social and financial disparity generated neediness and inspired discontent.

In any case, the various tensions of life at Brancepeth were never short of disagreements and rows, and sometimes involved brushes with the law. As depicted in the diary, Brancepeth consisted of a relatively stable core of permanent employees, surrounded by the ebbs and flows of an unsettled labour force that was both necessary and troublesome. The Masterton police were relatively frequent visitors to the station, and Miller recorded their advice, such as the notification about the presence of a 'well-dressed burglar' in the neighbourhood in 1895. He also objected to their manner, like the 'pushing and impudent' police constable on his way back from an investigation nearer the coast who 'came into the saloon without invitation, and into the office where he took off his boots and sat with both feet on the mantelpiece' (3 July 1906). A number of station hands were involved in court cases, which tend to fit the 'bingeing, hitting and suing'[34] syndrome symptomatic of colonial disorder, described by Miles Fairburn and other historians, which was prevalent up to the 1880s and declined slowly thereafter. More serious episodes, including murders and suicides, occurred on the fringes of Brancepeth society and were noted in the diary. In 1900 Miller mentioned that the *Evening Post* had an article about John Deighton, 'our rabbiter . . . murdering child with an intention of murdering wife & self as well' (10 March 1900), although the dreadful event did not take place on the station itself.

An unexplained scandal ran intermittently through the diary in 1903. It concerned allegations about Mr Empson, headmaster of Wanganui Collegiate, the school the Beetham boys attended. Part of the narrative concerned a Rev J.M. Marshall, whose mysterious disappearance in Christchurch was finally solved by the discovery of his body in a deep hole in the river. Miller noted various references in the paper to the search for Marshall, and wrote a leader for the *Wairarapa Daily Times* on what he called the 'Wanganui School Affair' which did not get printed (7 July 1903). On 22 September he quoted an excerpt from the Christchurch *Press*: 'J.M. told Cocks that he had "reserved facts of which Cocks did not know". This is, to my mind, a most unpleasant statement as regards the past history of Mr. Empson, or the boys, or both.' Miller never reveals what the implication was, though a reasonable supposition is that it was sexual, but the sketchy details of the case as woven into Miller's record give a tantalising glimpse of the story, and the gossip, attitudes and networks on the station. Both Ralph and Oren Beetham were involved in an Old Boys' group that established a petition to support Mr Empson and clear his name.

Miller was also quite discreet in the station diary about the other great scandal of that year, the feverishly reported divorce of Wyndham Earée, the Masterton clergyman who held services at Brancepeth. Miller noted that Earée's divorce proceedings had begun on 14 May 1903, and made one or two other comments about him, but perhaps felt that the reports in the *Wairarapa Daily Times* made a complete record in the diary superfluous. It is clear, though, that the divorce was a subject of considerable talk on the station and in the town, Miller reporting that the 'town is full of angry scandal' (12 July 1903), and with its echoes of sensational novels, it is not hard to see why. Percy Wyndham Earée had brought charges of adultery against his wife, Florence Dashwood Earée, and William Harvey Noble, refrigerating engineer on the *Athenic*. Florence countercharged with neglect, desertion and cruelty. Miller must have had some sympathy for her, as he noted approvingly in the diary that two Masterton women had made a point of calling on the 'unfortunate' Mrs Earée. The Earées had married in Suffolk in 1896 and six weeks later emigrated to Palmerston North. They had two children. Florence was said by her husband to have become dissatisfied with life in the colony, and she went 'Home to England' in 1901 and returned in April 1903 to a household that included Miss Mary Boddington, whose role is not entirely clear, and a servant. A few days later Florence announced that she intended to have breakfast in bed, and 'unpleasantness' ensued with her husband 'requiring her to get up and come down to breakfast unless she was unwell'.[35] Florence left for Wellington, and on her return told her husband that she had been at the City Hotel with Mr Noble, an engineer she had met on the ship returning to New Zealand. Wyndham decided on divorce and they reached an agreement that she could stay in the house 'on probation' but he would no longer 'take the place of a husband to her'; the housekeeping would be handed over to Miss Boddington, who was sworn not to disclose the 'secret of their lives'.

In May, Florence left again to join Mr Noble. In the court report, her letter announcing this to Wyndham, in which she asked that her rings and money be given to the children and that her wedding presents, pictures and sewing machine be sent to her, was published in the paper. Poor Florence then changed her mind, and a series of heartbreaking but useless begging letters to Wyndham were published in full. In court, she said that Wyndham had told her the marriage was a mistake after the birth of the first child, and he had refused 'relations of husband and wife' after the birth of the second. Florence accused Wyndham of trying to persuade her to procure an abortion, neglecting to procure assistance prior to the birth of the younger child, forcing her to go to England in 1901, refusing to provide clothing for her and the children, refusing to cohabit with her in January 1900 and remaining out all night on many occasions.

Details of Wyndham's earlier life emerged, one of which Miller noted in the station diary; apparently he was reading the case with some attention. What struck Miller was that Wyndham Earée had been on the stage in England and had played in comic opera at the Prince of Wales theatre for three years, under the name of 'Dore'. Under cross-examination, he admitted having 24 photographs of a well-known actress, Miss Eva Moore, in the nursery. At this point the case starts to sound like the plot of a novel by Wilkie Collins, Mary Elizabeth Braddon or Mrs Henry Wood, all extremely popular with

Brancepeth readers. It was revealed that Florence's parents had objected to Wyndham's suit on the grounds that he was not sufficiently well-off. Before her marriage to Wyndham, Florence had been engaged to an officer in the Imperial Army and broke off the engagement when Wyndham proposed to her. She was nineteen at the time, and said to be under his influence. Wyndham countered these unflattering allegations by suggesting that Florence's mental health was not as sound as it ought to be:

> He had then expressed the opinion to some of his friends that she was suffering from a 'mental kink'. He had regarded her as rather hysterical, but he had never consulted a medical man on the matter.[36]

After an altercation about a servant in 1901, Florence had left the table saying she had a good mind to stick a knife in him. Wyndham went straight to his study and wrote her words in his diary, then showed the page to his wife, and asked her to put her name to it which she did. Wyndham denied he had got the entry for the purpose of Court proceedings. Wyndham Earée was eventually granted a decree nisi provided he paid Florence, 'as long as she remains chaste and unmarried', £2 a week. Nothing was reported about the fate of the children.

Reading the tale of the Earée divorce reminds us that the narrative worlds of Victorian fiction are not as remote as they might seem from colonial life. Like a serialised novel, the drama of the court case occupied double columns in the *Wairarapa Daily Times* over several days; every charge and counter charge was spelled out in full, with detailed descriptions of each allegation, and statements of witnesses reported in direct speech. For readers at Brancepeth, the florid allegations thrown about by each of the parties and the intense interest taken in them by the town and district, would have been familiar territory—the complications of M.E. Braddon's *Lady Audley's Secret* are no more frankly revealed than Florence Earée's relationship with her lover and her husband, and the self-serving caddishness displayed by Wyndham Earée is common fare, both in sensational and New Woman novels. Working life at Brancepeth, too, was reminiscent of nineteenth-century fictional worlds, both Dickens' London full of orphans and debtors, and the plot complications of sensation fiction and Victorian romance, which always involve financial reverses and lucky windfalls. 'Carter sent letters to his people in Petone and to PJ Hollings about some money in Chancery of which he has just got the first intimation –but it is probably some years too late', wrote Miller on 10 November 1905, in a sentence which makes you long for the narrative resolution of a novel so that Carter would eventually find he wasn't too late after all.

It might be tempting to think of the Brancepeth library as functioning primarily to deliver escapist fictions to people oppressed by hard and plain lives, but the station diary suggests a much more colourful and complex social world on the farm, one familiar with real life versions of the seamier sides of the Victorian imagination. Miller's newspaper articles only enhance this overlap between life and the page: whether they directly reflected what he thought about the Brancepeth community, or were drawn from his life as a reader, these worlds intersected and were always part of each other. What Miller wrote in the station diary, along with his letters and newspaper articles, offers that rare and wonderful thing, a glimpse of the reader at work amid the bustle and tedium of his daily life. As he snatched a quiet hour to write a letter to the editor on a Sunday evening, or set to the task of composing the day's entry in the station diary, he committed the narrative of his life and the daily lives of others around him to the page, creating—at least from the perspective of a twenty-first century reader—a vivid and unruly companion to the dog-eared novels on the library shelves.

CHAPTER FIVE

What They Read

> Oh what a beautiful history!
> Think what temptations they passed!
> Each one more cruelly trying,
> More tempting, indeed, than the last.
> And what a lesson it teaches;
> No passion from evil's exempted—
> Whilst admiring the moral it preaches,
> It makes you quite long to be tempted!
>
> Sarah Grand, *Ideala* (83)

Book history often gets stuck on the dry matter of titles, authors and chronologies and ignores what it is that attracted readers in the first place, what made them 'long to be tempted' as in Sarah Grand's verse above. In this chapter, drawing on categories of use and the composition of the library, I give a sense of what was most read at Brancepeth, and why some novels and authors might have been so popular with readers on the farm. Speculative connections between life on a sheep station in rural New Zealand at the turn of the century and reading tastes across the empire are also possible, because the Brancepeth library affords a view of how a particular community, in a specific place, selected and consumed what was on offer in the 1890s book market.

There are three ways to trace reader preferences in the Brancepeth library: the condition of the books, the composition of the library, and the comments of readers themselves. The most obvious source of information, the lending register, has been lost. But books are paper objects that absorb liquid and are easily stained and torn; the spills, dirty edges, broken spines and muddy fingerprints made by careless readers stay with them. In order to clarify the reading preferences of Brancepeth users, I have developed loose categories of heavy, medium and low use based on wear and tear of the books, providing an impressionistic gauge of what readers liked and didn't like. Some books are almost destroyed, while others are so clean and stiff they may never have been read. A related, but harder to interpret category of use, is books that were listed in the 1895 catalogue but have since gone missing. Some of these were bestsellers and likely to have been in the 'heavy use' category, so their absence may be as eloquent about reader preference as visible evidence of heavy use. Because the Brancepeth committee bought cheap editions of popular novels, most of the books had low-quality paper stock and glued bindings, and inevitably their spines became broken and pages abraded in the course of travelling around readers. But the Brancepeth library tended not to throw books out, no matter how tattered, so it is possible that some of these lost and loved novels were appropriated by keen readers.

The composition of the library is also revealing about reader preferences, in that some authors have large numbers of titles, not all of which are heavily read. It is fair to say the Brancepeth library committee had favourite authors whose work they diligently collected (Miller noted looking for cheap novels by M.E. Braddon for example). In the station diary, Miller mentions a Suggestion Book that was kept on the library table; this is also missing, but it suggests some degree of subscriber choice in the selection of books, though the committee did the ordering and had the final say.

Authors and books cluster in particular areas—for example, the New Woman novelists—and in genres, such as historical novels, sensation novels and adventure fiction. There are also regional tastes—Scottish novels and novelists were a focus, for example.

And then there is reader comment. The Brancepeth readers belonged to a Victorian reading culture that actively encouraged readers to discriminate between books and authors. Some did this more than others. John Vaughan Miller wrote about books in the station diary and in the newspaper, and was a heavy annotator, both of books he liked and didn't like. Other readers also made comments or marked certain passages, which will be discussed at length in the next chapter. Implicit and explicit literary hierarchies were described in novels and debated in the press. Some of this discussion is visible at Brancepeth, while some is implicit in the choices readers made.

Book choices for a nineteenth-century reader were more than simply a question of what you were in the mood for; they revealed character and moral predisposition. Victorian fiction, generally, is a broad and running conversation about reading and its impact on emotional, moral, and especially sexual behaviour. In many of the novels of the age, what is on the heroine's bookshelf alerts the reader to the likely direction of the plot and has implications about the reader's own choices and actions. Take Evadne Frayling, the heroine of Sarah Grand's hugely popular novel *The Heavenly Twins* (1893),[1] which sold 40,000 copies within a few weeks of publication. Evadne is an intellectual. Despite her father's view that 'only confusion' comes of women thinking for themselves on 'social subjects', her bookshelf is crammed with works on histology, pathology, anatomy, physiology, botany, 'not to mention the modern writers'. She is particularly keen on higher mathematics. When Major Colquhoun comes calling, a 'fine looking man' in her mother's opinion and 'more Irish than Scots by predilection', she falls in love and marries him, but as they are driving to the station to begin their honeymoon someone thrusts a note into Evadne's hand telling her of the Major's disreputable past. Evadne gives him the slip and flees to her friends, forcing the Major to the humiliating task of searching for her. Evadne's parents are horrified by this turn of events. Her mother tells her that a woman is able to change 'even a reprobate' into a 'worthy man', but Evadne will only yield to the barest of conventions, agreeing to accompany her husband to his garrison in Malta as long as the marriage is not consummated.

A Victorian reader who was keeping up with the literary times would know by this point in the book that Evadne is a New Woman—in particular, one of the heroines of what Gail Cunningham has called the 'purity school' of New Woman novelists.[2] Evadne's strength of character partly comes from, and is shown by, her choice of reading. Grand is careful to note that her heroine was 'never a great reader in the sense of being omnivorous in her choice of books' but she became a 'very good one', always having a 'solid book' in hand and some 'standard work of fiction also' (23). *Tom Jones,* for example, a favourite novel at Brancepeth, is dismissed with contempt by Grand, through her heroine's eyes, as the story of 'another young man steeped in vice' (20). When Evadne's 'very good' reading habits and strength of character triumph over her parents' wishes about her marriage, her mother laments, in a 'broken' voice: 'I never, never thought that she would live to quote books to her parents' (86).

The Heavenly Twins was a heavily-read book at Brancepeth. Dirty, battered, covered with fingerprints, it has done the rounds. Evadne's taste in reading, however, is not reflected in the Brancepeth collection, which held almost nothing in the categories she preferred. Brancepeth was much more conventional in the sense that it endorsed the appetite for 'beautiful history' satirised in the verse from Grand's novel *Ideala* (1893) with which this chapter opens. But the attitudes towards reading expressed by Evadne's tastes are familiar territory for Victorian readers. They were long accustomed to debate about appropriate reading matter, especially for young women, a debate that had become much more pointed with the advent of the New Woman.

When Evadne's father inspects her bookcase, he takes down a work on sociology, reads a few passages that Evadne has marked, and

> solemnly ejaculated 'Good Heavens!' several times. He could not have been more horrified had the books been 'Mademoiselle de Maupin', 'Nana', 'La Terre', 'Madame Bovary' and 'Sapho'. (104)

An avid Victorian reader would not have had much difficulty in discriminating between Mr Frayling's unwarranted suspicion of a 'work on sociology', a choice of reading that signals the intellectualism and social purpose of a New Woman, and the infamous 'yellow back' French novels, believed to encourage sexual license and vice. The latter is something that Evadne, with her distaste for *Tom Jones*, would never have dreamed of reading. The point is rubbed in further when she goes to Malta to join her licentious husband, who, as a surprise, has recreated her room in the image of her bedroom at home, and has a pile of novels waiting for her:

> See, here's Zola and Daudet complete, and George Sand. You'll like them better, I fancy, when you get into them than Herbert Spencer and Francis Galton.[3] (176)

Evadne dutifully reads the books (sure enough, *Nana*, *La Terre*, *Madame Bovary* and *Sapho*), which are a transparent ploy to arouse her sexuality, but when George Colquhoun asks what has struck her most in them, she replies:

> the suffering George ... the awful, needless, suffering! (221)

Next time she goes to her bookshelf, these 'dangerous works of fiction' have disappeared.

The Brancepeth library held no works by Herbert Spencer or Francis Galton, inclining more to George Colquhoun's view of what its readers might like, but it offered only a carefully judged glimpse of 'dangerous' works of fiction. The library held just one novel by George Sand (*La Fadette*), and did not contain *Nana*, *Madame Bovary*, *La Terre* or *Sapho*, though it did hold other novels by Flaubert, Daudet, and Zola, demonstrating simultaneously a recognition of modernity and a sense of discretion that might have done credit to Evadne herself.

It is not hard to see why Brancepeth readers liked *The Heavenly Twins*. The novel is competently written, full of incident and drama, fast-moving and sometimes funny. It is also up with the literary and political play, and has a serious and sensational point to make. Evadne is one of three characters who provide case studies into the social and sexual predicaments of women that the New Woman novelists described. Edith Beale, a bishop's daughter, encouraged by her parents, marries one of Major Colquhoun's fellow officers, Sir Mosley Menteith, who is syphilitic. After discovering the sexual history of her husband, including his abandonment of a young woman (sold to him by her sister) and their child named Mosley, Edith gives birth to a deformed baby, 'speckled like a toad', and dies. The third heroine, Angelica, is one of the heavenly twins of the novel's title. A free spirit, she and her twin brother 'Diavolo' create mayhem wherever they go. Alas, she quickly learns that the transition from a tomboy childhood to a marriageable young woman imposes unbearable restrictions:

> I found a big groove ready and waiting for me when I grew up, and in that I was expected to live whether it suited me or not. It did not suit me. It was deep and narrow, and gave me no room to move. (450)

Angelica marries young, after proposing to an older man who agrees that she shall be free to do as she likes. She develops a friendship with a male singer who comes to live in the village, by cross-dressing as her brother and answering to the name of 'Boy'. The Wildean resonances of these scenes are unmistakable, with 'Boy' dressing in velvet and pelting the 'Tenor' with roses through the open window. After a boating accident in which 'Boy' is narrowly rescued from drowning, the singer discovers who and what 'Boy' really is. Angelica is astonished when the 'Singer' is shocked that she is married, and the erotic potential of the narrative is instantly erased, as in other sensational Victorian novels that only go so far in depicting sexuality.[4]

Despite the shock value of Grand's plots and subject matter, *The Heavenly Twins* is ultimately a conservative novel. New Woman novelists such as Grand were opposed to the aesthetic movement of the 1890s, and the scenes in which Angelica plays a seductive, sexually ambiguous and irresponsible boy make it clear that aestheticism and decadence are not a possible escape route for New Woman heroines. In a complementary triptych of neat narrative resolutions, Angelica realises the importance of her marriage and her love for her long-suffering husband (whose name, Mr Kilroy, suggests his relative absence from the plot) and embarks on charity work; Evadne marries a doctor after the convenient death of her licentious husband from a heart attack; and poor Edith is the sacrificial example of what it means when Angelica says 'It isn't safe to be an exquisite womanly creature in this rotten world.'

As Gail Cunningham has noted, the New Woman had high ideals, and was 'intelligent, individualistic and principled'.[5]

She was typically a bluestocking, who may have outraged her parents and convention, but she had a mind and stuck to her principles. The New Woman's most controversial arguments were about venereal disease and marriage, which is depicted in novels like Grant Allen's *The Woman Who Did* (1895) as social oppression. The New Woman was politically activist and campaigned for female suffrage, but also, as Cunningham points out, was 'essentially middle-class', and unlike Lady Chatterley, observed social proprieties in her choice of lover.

The New Woman debate as it was conducted in literature is reflected in the Brancepeth holdings, with most of the prominent New Woman novelists represented. As well as Iota, Sarah Grand, and Grant Allen, there are novels by Mene Muriel Dowie, George Egerton, Olive Schreiner, Mona Caird, Thomas Hardy and George Gissing. Of these, the most popular with readers were the first three. Iota's *A Yellow Aster* (1894), a huge popular success and well-read at Brancepeth, charts the progress of an experiment in free thought, in which the heroine, Gwen, neglected by her scientific parents and brought up to be free of religion, painfully learns to love her husband. Paris, as usual, is the scene of debauchery and dissolution, but *A Yellow Aster* is not as preoccupied with the sexual exploitation of women as with their religious and emotional needs, which probably went down well at Brancepeth.

Eighteen of Grant Allen's titles were held at Brancepeth, one of which (*The Scallywag* 1894, a detective novel) was presented to the library by the schoolmaster J.J. Guest, perhaps before he was encouraged to resign from his post. Allen's novels adopt a variety of genres, chiefly adventure, romance and detective stories, and are variously set in Jamaica, Algeria, Australia, South Africa, Tibet and the Tyrol as well as 'at home' in England (Allen was born and brought up in Canada). As John Sutherland notes, much of Allen's fiction takes emancipation as its theme.[6] *The British Barbarians* (1895), which is famous for defining the 'purity school' has a number of passages marked by Brancepeth readers. The novel is a futurist fantasy of a twenty-fifth century 'Alien' (with the very English name of Bertram Ingledew) who returns to the 1890s as a kind of anthropologist, and finds England 'hypocritical and puritan'. What particularly offends Bertram Ingledew is the 'system of closely tabooed marriage, founded upon a broad system of prostitution and infanticide' (113). Someone has marked this passage in the text. On page 112, a pencil line draws the reader's attention to a description of Bertram rising from his seat to help Martha the parlourmaid pass the cups:

> He remembered with a checked sigh how infinitely superior they would all at home have considered that wholesome, capable, good-looking Martha to an empty-headed and useless young man like Philip . . . (112)

The question about what the reader intends to remember, or others to notice, in this sentence, or who the reader was, is perhaps made clearer by looking at another marked passage. A pencil mark accompanies Bertram's observations about frock coats:

> . . . though the classes who really did any good in the state, the working men and so forth, seemed exempted from wearing it . . . (52)

These passages seem likely to reflect the views of a Brancepeth worker. *The British Barbarians* is the most marked-up of the Allen novels in the collection, with 14 marginal pencil lines drawing attention to comments on marriage and gender relations, the hypocrisy of the Church, class hierarchies, mercenaries and free speech. As with all anonymous non-verbal marginalia, it is not possible to interpret these marks in any specific way—the point of emphasis might indicate agreement, or be a reminder, or be there to attract the attention of other readers. What is clear, though, is that reader attention to the social critique of *The British Barbarians* was more than cursory. The heroine of the novel, Frida, eventually takes her children and leaves her unhappy marriage to live on the heath with Bertram, but her hard, cold husband, Robert Monteith, follows them and shoots Bertram. His demise ends the novel, as he dissolves into a column of blue flame amid the scent of violets, presumably returning to his own world.

Grant Allen's most famous (or most notorious) novel, the massively successful *The Woman Who Did* (1895), was listed in the 1895 printed catalogue and must have been bought as soon as it was published. *The Woman Who Did* took a more realistic and therefore even more radical stance on marriage than *The British Barbarians.* Allen's heroine, Herminia Barton, refuses to marry her lover legally. She conducts her own version of a 'pure' bridal ceremony as an expression of 'Freedom', although they live together and she bears his child. Herminia comes to a 'stainless' end, killing herself when her adult daughter announces she will take her dead father's name and live with her grandfather on the grounds that 'no right minded girl' could continue associating with 'such a woman' as her mother has been (163). Sixteen of Allen's books have survived, and most are damaged and dirtied by Brancepeth readers, but one of the two missing is *The Woman Who Did.* Was it censored and suppressed, stolen, or read to death? The latter seems most likely.

Kate Flint has argued that the attraction of popular fiction for Victorian readers went beyond the appeal of accumulating cultural capital. Rather, 'becoming excited by these fictions was a means of asserting one's claim to be modern, to be in the know'.[7] In New Zealand—'last, loneliest, loveliest', in Kipling's words[8]—the desire to be modern, to seem to be in the know, may have had even more urgency. Tim Dolin has suggested that reading was a kind of 'contact zone', part of the settlers' 'struggle to stay in touch with the centre, to imagine themselves in some merely outlying province, where news took a little longer to reach'.[9] The substantial library at Brancepeth made a powerful claim about being up-to-date and in touch, a claim supported by visitors such as Ellis Rowan. At Brancepeth, unlike the South Australia Institute library described by Tim Dolin, there is no precise record of who borrowed which book, but the range of wear and tear, the large holdings of particular authors and the concentrations of titles in specific categories and areas, make it possible to understand the Brancepeth collection, as a whole, as a record of reading. The likes and dislikes of individual readers might be 'read' in the condition of the books, and the library collection itself is an expression of what it means to be colonial, caught in the tension between creating a new Britain and remaining part of the old one. In other words, the problem of how to transfer culture to a distant location is partly resolved by reading. If, for example, the New Woman was synonymous with various forms of (often unwelcome) modernity, then the concentration of New Woman novels in the Brancepeth station library may reflect both the urge to keep in touch with contentious issues of the moment in British society, as well as a useful and reflexive context for social changes also happening in New Zealand.

Education and reading were not only key to the New Woman's world view, but were highly valued at Brancepeth. While the conservative Beetham parents would not have felt comfortable with some aspects of the New Woman's free-thinking ways in their colonial daughters, New Zealand in the 1890s was a relatively progressive place. The Matrimonial Property Act of 1884, universal suffrage in 1893, and the Divorce Act of 1898 were a 'real, substantial and internationally early improvement in women's rights'[10]; in the 1890s there was an unusually dynamic nexus between literature, society and politics. It is not surprising, therefore, that station readers should have taken an active interest in New Woman novelists, out of local as well as metropolitan interests. Ruth Beetham, who was responsible for much of the book selection, her two teenage daughters Thyra and Weva, and no doubt their governesses, read the New Woman novels, going by names written in some of the books. (So did John Vaughan Miller, though not necessarily from the same point of view). Thyra and Weva were both enthusiastic readers, and after her marriage to Marmaduke Bethell in 1904, Thyra went on to mix the life of a pastoralist's wife with some of the activities of a New Woman, establishing a 'new kind' of women's leadership in North Canterbury, where she was very active in voluntary work and is said to have 'dominated social life and welfare'.[11] Weva seems to have followed a different narrative model, marrying C.W.R. Nicholls-Broglie in 1913 and moving to California. In what resembles a plot by R.L. Stevenson or Conan Doyle, both very popular at Brancepeth, the Beethams believed Nicholls-Broglie was a German spy and that marrying Weva was a strategic move to insinuate himself into upper-crust New Zealand circles.[12]

On the question of the New Woman in fiction, the library offered its readers a selection of the main contenders in this heated debate. Gail Cunningham writes that Mr Roy Devereux expressed a widely held view when he announced in 1895 that life 'has taken on a strange unloveliness, and the least beautiful thing therein is the New Woman.'[13] A number of novels that supported his opinion were among those eagerly read at Brancepeth. Annie Edwards' *A Girton Girl* (1886) was one of the most heavily read books, readers perhaps agreeing with a character who asserts:

> University teaching for girls is a freak, that will die out of itself, like coal-scuttle bonnets, bishops sleeves, crinoline, or any other mode that is at once cumbersome and unbeautiful. (33)

The 'Girton Girl' was a 'recognised sub-group of the New Woman species' as Cunningham puts it, and a contentious figure.[14] Edwards' heroine, Marjorie Bartrand, employs a tutor to help her get into Cambridge. Geoffrey, the tutor, expects her to be 'an atrociously clever-looking young person . . . with a leaning to stoutness' (45), but finds a 'child' in a red and white frock. After many romantic complications and excursions into the issue of female education, including the usual warning against 'yellow back novels' (56), Marjorie abandons her Girton ambitions to become Geoffrey's wife:

> 'I desire that you will guide me.' Marjorie Bartrand had proved herself a very woman after all (485).

It is perhaps relevant to the popularity of Edwards' novel with Brancepeth readers, and in particular her attack on bluestockings, that both Thyra and Weva Beetham were educated at home. The author with the highest number of titles in the Brancepeth collection (41) was Walter Besant. Among his well-used books is the best selling futurist satire *The Revolt Of Man* (1883), which depicts a 'gynocratic England'[15] in which young men are forced against their wills to marry tyrannical (and lascivious) elderly women, who hold all the positions of power—including being dons at Oxford and Cambridge.

It is probably not a coincidence that a 'Committee of Taste' was formed at Brancepeth in 1895 about the same time as they were buying New Woman novels. The Committee of Taste, which was Miller's initiative, included Hugh and Ruth Beetham and the governess, Miss Liddle, but Miller's excoriating opinions suggest he was the driving force behind exclusions from the Brancepeth Library. After reading Sarah Grand's novel *The Beth Book* (1897), John Vaughan Miller destroyed it, and wrote a leading article for the *Wairarapa Daily Times* in which he condemned the novel and its author:

> 'The Beth Book' (which bears the most originally stupid title ever given to a book) turns the 'X-rays' on to original depravity; but the only original thing about the book is the horrible nastiness and blasphemy of the woman who wrote it and still calls herself a woman. As for the women who *read* it! 'Filth' (exclaims Maartens) 'a woman's soul may pass pure, if such be her terrible fate, through *fact*, but not through *fiction*.'[16]

Describing itself as a 'Study from the Life of Elizabeth Caldwell McClure, a Woman of Genius',[17] the 300-page novel exhaustively (and exhaustingly) follows every detail of Beth's life: genteel poverty in Ireland, her father's premature death, and marriage at sixteen to Dan McClure to escape the chilly charity of her uncle. Beth is poorly educated and naive, and takes some time to realise that her husband, a doctor, is unfaithful to her, and secretly employed at a Lock hospital where prostitutes are forcibly and hideously treated. She also discovers he is a sadist and a vivisectionist, and leaves him to become a novelist and outspoken political activist.

John Vaughan Miller's strenuous objections to *The Beth Book* focus both on the 'original depravity' of the subject matter and the reflexive effect it has on the author, who must herself be nasty and blasphemous, and capable of transferring these qualities to her female readers. This is a familiar argument in favour of censorship, perhaps particularly reflecting Miller's paternalism towards the young female readers at Brancepeth. His views would have been familiar to contemporary readers of Victorian literature, as they were often expressed in journal and newspaper articles and also by fictional characters. For example, the hero of Joseph Hocking's *All Men Are Liars* (1898; one of the most heavily read novels in the Brancepeth library), is an aspiring writer who is appalled by the 'realistic' school of novels, whose authors, 'while holding a high place in the world of letters', write of the 'sewers and cesspools of life' (88); he means the same school of writers and works that enraged and appalled Miller.

The Beth Book was not the only novel to inspire Miller's disgust. In a diary entry for 20 April 1902, he reviles a novel by Lucas Malet, which was the pen name of Charles Kingsley's daughter, Mary St Leger Harrison.

> The 'History of Sir Richard Calmady' by Lucas Malet is not only a fearfully wearisome story; it is as blasphemous and lascivious a book as ever was written—some parts are worthy of the very worst French sensualists—The way in which Lady Calverley in 618 pages inspects her moral secretions is as tiresome as it is odious—she looks at them thro' a telescope, a microscope, a magnifying glass, a monocle, a camera obscura, a horse collar, the Rōntgen Rays, a stereoscope, the electric light, and a candle with the extinguisher on. The whole motive of the book is vile and revolting in the extreme. No girl could ever be a modest girl after reading it—the book is intentionally morbid, filthy and wicked. It is sure therefore to have a large sale. It is the story of Titania and Bottom turned into monstrous lechery.

He subsequently wrote a letter to the paper, 'Fashionable Novels', in which he reiterated these views, almost word for word, for the edification of the Wairarapa public.[18] *The History of Sir Richard Calmady* (1901), one of the most famous and controversial novels of the turn of the century, included sexually explicit material and featured a New Woman 'feminist socialist activist' as its heroine. It is now considered groundbreaking for its 'psychological development and complex discourse',[19] a fact that Miller's extended denigrating comparison showed him to be disapprovingly aware of. A few days later Miller noted 'with gratitude' that *The History of Sir Richard Calmady* had been suppressed by Hugh Beetham (although it is still held in the collection) and that a novel by E.L. Voynich, *Jack Raymond* (1901), 'has been destroyed', both being written by 'vile women'.[20]

Although women novelists came in for particular contempt, the fire of Miller's pen was also directed towards some of the English realists. George Moore, one of the first English writers to imitate the French naturalist school, especially Zola, was a target. Miller declared that Moore, the author of *A Mummer's Wife* (1885) and *Mike Fletcher* (1889):

> . . . must be a dweller in one of the Cities of the Plain . . . this writer, and kindred spirits, have aimed at being original in 'realism'; they have only proved that brutal animalism is congenital. (*Wairarapa Daily Times*, 6 April 1898)

These views align Miller with the 'purity school'; he is invoking Grant Allen, who, in the preface to *The British Barbarians,* separates his own 'Hill-top' novel from the flood of 'stories of evil tendencies' that inhabit the metaphorical 'Plain'. There was some irony in Miller's reaction to Lucas Malet's novel, given that he knew her to be the daughter of a writer and thinker he greatly admired—he declared in April 1899 that 'Kingsley's *Life and Letters*' was the best book he had read for years.[21] But Miller's views on the New Woman debate, and on gender politics generally, conformed to mainstream Victorian attitudes about the perniciousness of discussing sex and especially venereal diseases, and the infectious damage such novels were believed to inflict on young women. More broadly, Miller's dislike of self-conscious and overt feminism and its disturbance of conventional gender roles, is evident in a satirical letter he wrote to the *Wairarapa Daily Times* in 1898:

A MODEST REQUEST

To The Editor
Sir,—I shall be obliged by your placing me on your staff as a leader writer. I am settled in the neighbourhood, and have leisure time in the evenings while my husband does the housework and attends to the boots. You will perceive from this specimen leader I enclose that I can turn out a finished article and that I am no literary hack. You will observe that I step off rather showily at starting, but soon settle down in a lively trot of twelve slips an hour.—I am, etc.,

JOCOSA MORDAX
December 12th, 1898.

Even though he reviled them, the New Woman novels may have sunk in: it was perhaps their exposure of venereal disease (rampant, as Gail Cunningham points out, in the Army) and the risks of the marriage market for young brides, as well as his affection for her, that prompted Miller to remark on Thyra Beetham's innocence as she left home to be married in 1904. He thanked God her marriage was to 'such a good fellow' as Marmaduke Bethell.

An author generally approved of (though not by every member of the Committee of Taste) was Marie Corelli, perhaps the bestselling of all Victorian novelists and avidly read by Queen Victoria and Gladstone. Brancepeth held 19 of her novels, though only 15 survive—the others pilfered, perhaps, or collectively read to extinction. In February 1901, Michael Ryan, the roadman and a Library Committee member, told Miller he had had to buy Corelli's *The Master Christian* (1900) for himself as the library copy was not yet available for borrowing, even though it had been received in November. The library copy was almost certainly circulating among the Beetham family and possibly their friends, but Ryan's impatience suggests that Corelli's romances had an eager following at Brancepeth. Their mix of eroticism, religiosity, spiritualism and science, as well as their often daring subject matter, attracted a large readership. At the turn of the century when modern technology was visibly advancing New Zealand into a new century—the telephone, motorcars, bicycles—Corelli's *Wormwood* (1890) set in Paris among absinthe users, exemplifies a dangerous (but attractive) modernity, even though its portrait of the fascinating world of French decadence and addiction is surrounded by the narrator's ponderous moralising. Like other celebrated and bestselling Victorian novels that are listed in the 1895 catalogue, such as Mrs Henry Wood's *East Lynne*, *Wormwood* is no longer in the collection, and it is tempting to read its absence as a sign of someone's desire to keep it.

In 1902, Miller wrote a letter to the paper about Corelli's *Temporal Power* (1902), a novel that depicts a king going in disguise among his people to find out their needs and finding out a great deal more about life on the streets. According to Miller, the book insulted the King, the Queen, the Prince of Wales, Lord Salisbury and Mr Chamberlain. Miller inveighed against Corelli for daring to 'say things which, if she were a man, would infallibly lead to her being kicked or horse-whipped.' He railed against her 'power of facile expression', and detested her political views, which he regarded as being only a 'bid for notoriety', produced by

> . . . the vitriolic ink hissing on her red-hot pen; it must surely burn holes in the paper (*Wairarapa Daily Times*, 19 December 1902).

His letter was challenged the next week by the pseudonymous 'Justitia', who takes a more approving view of 'one—and that one a woman—riding a-tilt against almost the whole of the literary world' (*Wairarapa Daily Times*, 23 December 1902). 'Justitia' finds Corelli's novels, if 'criticized fairly', are written for a good purpose, showing 'how much power for good lies in the hands of those who rule'. One might assume that Justitia's use of a feminine pseudonym denoted a woman reader who was both well read and ironic—Justitia being the name of Pontius Pilate's wife, a visionary with a 'strong heart', in Marie Corelli's bestselling *Barabbas* (1893)—but Miller's rejoinder the following week firmly addressed the author of the letter as 'he'. Always one to enjoy an argument, it was not impossible that he wrote 'Justitia's' letter himself. In any case, Miller shifted the argument to ask whether:

> In the whole range of literature, he knows anything more discreditable to the author (an unmarried woman), and more repulsive to the reader, than chapter twenty-six of 'The Sorrows of Satan'? (*Wairarapa Daily Times,* 15 January 1903)

One of the ironies here is of course Miller's revelation of his comprehensive knowledge of the spicier bits of Corelli's novels. Chapter 26 is the chapter in which the hero of *The Sorrows of Satan*, Geoffrey Tempest, discovers that the woman he has just married, Lady Sibyl ('to look at her . . . a very saint of purity'), through her extensive reading in contemporary literature and especially the New Woman novel, has become a 'contaminated creature, trained to perfection in the lax morals and prurient literature of my day.'[22] For Miller, Corelli's subject matter, despite her opposition to the New Woman, put her in the same camp as Sarah Grand or Lucas Malet. He considered her novels, like theirs, 'impure water from an unclean source'.[23] Despite Miller's strongly held views, the battered state of most of Corelli's novels suggest that the readership for them at Brancepeth was both devoted and substantial.

Although the New Woman novel attracted both readers and critics at Brancepeth, and shaped some public debate in the local paper on the questions raised, it did not dominate reading taste. The reference numbers in the Brancepeth books show historical layers of accumulation, like geological strata. The oldest layer of books, which includes novels by Wilkie Collins, Dickens and Charles Reade, has a hand-inked number series on the title page denoting acquisition order, starting in the 1860s and 70s. These historically interlinked authors constitute the core of the library—Thackeray, Smollet, Dickens, J. Fenimore Cooper, Wilkie Collins, Captain Mayne Reid, Charles Kingsley, George Eliot, Miss Ferrier, Mrs Humphrey Ward, Mrs Henry Wood, Edward Bulwer-Lytton, Charles Lever, Mrs Oliphant, George Macdonald, George Whyte-Melville, Sir Walter Scott, Trollope, Jane Austen, the Brontes, Thomas Hardy, Walter Besant and W.H. Ainsworth. The library as a whole expanded greatly in the 1890s, with the increased range of publications and the flow of cheap books in colonial editions, prompting the production of a printed catalogue in 1895 that adopted a more schematic Victorian cataloguing method. Older acquisition numbers were crossed out and an alphabetically numbered author system inserted.[24] In the 1890s and 1900s, the collection became much more focussed on current and popular fiction.

The most popular authors at Brancepeth in terms of their holdings were Walter Besant, who with his collaborator James Rice, had the highest number of titles at 41, followed by F. Marion Crawford (32); W.H. Ainsworth (30); Sir Walter Scott and Alexandre Dumas (25); Wilkie Collins and Amelia Barr (23); Captain Mayne Reid and M.E. Braddon (21); R.L. Stevenson, Marie Corelli and H. Rider Haggard (19); Bulwer-Lytton, Charles Kingsley and George Whyte-Melville (18); Dickens, Mrs Henry Wood, Stanley Weyman, Mrs Oliphant, Anthony Hope, S. Baring Gould, and Joseph Hocking (15). If those authors are recalibrated according to whose books show the heaviest use (based on dirt, damage, wear and tear), Mrs Henry Wood leaps to the top of the list, followed by Walter Besant, Wilkie Collins, M.E. Braddon, Alexandre Dumas, Rider Haggard, Rita, Anthony Trollope,

Stanley Weyman and Dickens, whose most favoured novel on this scale is *David Copperfield*. What the second list also shows is support for Dulcie Gillespie-Needham's claim that, by the 1890s,

> the quality of fiction read by settlers, no matter the social position, revealed a taste for the romantic, the spectacular and the sentimental.[25]

The shift in reading taste towards what was thought to be second-rate fiction occurred everywhere in the later nineteenth century, and was universally lamented—including in New Zealand, which was anyway, according to Charlotte Bronte's friend Mary Taylor, devoid of people literary enough to give an intelligent opinion on *Jane Eyre* (a very heavily used book at Brancepeth):

> They say 'it makes them cry' . . . I can hardly explain to you the queer feeling of living, as I do, in two places at once. One world containing books, England, and all the people with whom I can exchange an idea; the other is all that I actually see and hear and speak to.[26]

Mary Taylor was not the only person to think that the literary skills of settlers needed enhancement. Sir Robert Stout produced a pamphlet in 1908 advocating systematic reading, entitled 'How and What to Read', which observed that the 'reading of serious books' was not popular.[27] At Brancepeth, too, John Vaughan Miller's marginalia and comments in the library books showed off his expectation that other readers needed his literary expertise, which will be discussed in the next chapters. But from the 1880s, reading interest in fiction grew around the world, with a corresponding decline in systematic reading in serious disciplines, such as that undertaken by Evadne Frayling in Grand's *The Heavenly Twins*. The New Woman may have been bucking a trend, though as pointed out in the preface to the colonial edition of Blanche Atkinson's *They Have Their Reward* (1890), a novel popular at Brancepeth, widespread prejudice against the 'novel with a purpose' was because some of them failed also to be '*interesting*' (xi).

As J.E. Traue has shown, the number of public libraries in New Zealand by the end of the nineteenth century was cause for 'contemporary wonder', but this wonder was often accompanied by dismay that the overwhelming preference was for fiction, and the more popular it was, the more, in Traue's wry words, 'Satan had clearly had his way with the colonial reader'.[28] Gillespie-Needham concludes that by the 1890s most New Zealand libraries issued more than 80% fiction, and for some it might have been nearer 90%. A lecture reported in the *Wairarapa Daily Times* in 1906 noted that the Masterton library held 4000 volumes of fiction as against 1200 non-fiction, and that the borrowing rate for the fiction was six times that for non-fiction. The lecturer, Mr D. McGregor, accused the book-reading public of Masterton of cultivating a taste for trashy literature, a 'diet of sweetmeats', which were not 'vigour and health-producing'.[29] And as for systematic reading, William Pember Reeves's comment on his experience as a cadet on a sheep station was probably typical:

> I read every book I could lay my hands on, good, bad and indifferent, quite without system.[30]

What the Brancepeth library makes plain is that the authors (and books) that were the most borrowed in urban public libraries in Britain, Australia and New Zealand were also popular with their country cousins, and that the selection and quantity of books for the library were in line with contemporary tastes.[31] In a more general sense, Brancepeth is a testament to the empire-wide book market and reading culture of the time, which was characterised by the proliferation of colonial editions, efficient transport infrastructures which kept the circulation of books and review periodicals reasonably current, and the enormous popularity of newspapers. Kate Flint's point about readers wanting to be in the know is entirely germane to small remote communities like Brancepeth, whose inhabitants had more restricted recreational options than city dwellers, yet no doubt wanted to feel that they lived in the same world as everyone else. But even more to the point, the authors preferred by Brancepeth readers were *fun*.

It's not as if there wasn't plenty of popular fiction to choose from. George Gissing, whose *New Grub Street* (1891) describes an opposition between genuine artistry and commercial success in writing, deplored the huge increase in the rate of publication, remarking that the 'growing flood of literature swamps everything but works of primary genius'.[32] The question, perhaps, is not why was Brancepeth library so large (at over 2000 volumes, it was almost half the size of the municipal library in Masterton) but why wasn't it bigger? J.E. Traue has calculated that for a library buying cheap paperback reprints, a budget of £10 would purchase between 66 and 120 titles a year.[33] Brancepeth tended to order in 50–70 book lots, perhaps three times a year, with smaller orders at intervals. The size of the Brancepeth Library was probably determined by what the Beethams were prepared to spend on it, as the number of regular subscribers (about 15) could only cover part of the cost.

The choice of what to buy cannot have been easy. At the end of the nineteenth century, Walter Besant, founder of the Society of Authors, reckoned there were 1,200 novelists at work, and R.L. Wolff's bibliographical catalogue of nineteenth-century fiction estimates that there are some 42,000 published Victorian novels.[34] What readers liked at Brancepeth were the better-known names amongst the crowd, novels that had already reached a readership and were cheaply available. As the New Woman holdings and the associated debates show, there were limits as to how avant-garde they were prepared to be. The great majority of novels that they really liked, as shown by patterns of use, were variations on conservative sensational romances with 'vaguely religious'[35] overtones, whose great themes were property and class, both subjects dear to the hearts of colonial readers.

Mrs Henry Wood, whose novels top the heavy-use stakes at Brancepeth, was the author of what has been said to be the single most popular Victorian novel: *East Lynne* (1861), a 'sensation' novel. The term 'sensation novel' was first used to describe a group of bestselling serial novels published in the 1860s, which included Wilkie Collins's *The Woman in White*, Charles Reade's *Hard Cash* and M.E. Braddon's *Lady Audley's Secret.* The enormous success and appeal to readers of the first sensation novels spawned many imitations.[36] A sensation novel was topical and fast paced with multiple plot twists; as John Sutherland has put it, it was addressed to 'some journalistic sensation of the day'.[37] Dorothy L. Sayers has said it was the product of the English genius for 'melodrama with calculation'.[38] *East Lynne* is still an intensely readable narrative, frequently reprinted, and it is not hard to see why readers loved it.

In the novel, Lady Isabel Vane, who is herself the product of a Gretna Green marriage (an elopement) and whose father Lord Mount Severn has been a reckless spendthrift and gamester, is left penniless and friendless on his death. She marries her father's high-minded and intellectual lawyer, Archibald Carlyle, who has bought her old family home, East Lynne, as an act of kindness. She frankly admits she has not married him for love, and that her affections are entangled with Captain Francis Levison, a former suitor uniformly denounced as a cad, a rake and 'not a good man'. Of course, things get complicated: Isabel misconstrues her husband's friendship with another woman (clearly much more suited to him), runs off with Levison (repeating history as Victorian heroes and heroines are always bound to do), and is divorced by her husband. After a dramatic descent into desertion and childbirth, she is thought to have been killed in a train crash in France, but she returns in disguise, white-haired and wearing green spectacles, to East Lynne, as governess to her own abandoned children. The climax of the novel is when her son William dies in her arms without knowing who she is. (The stage version of *East Lynne* was the origin of Lady Isabel's famous line 'Dead! Dead! And never called me mother!' which does not appear in the novel.[39]) Although Lady Isabel's seducer is tried and convicted for the murder of another man, he does not suffer the consequences of his actions as much as she does, reflecting the inequities that New Woman novelists would attack. By 1895, *East Lynne* had sold 400,000 copies. Along with Marie Corelli's *Wormwood* and Grant Allen's *The Woman Who Did*, the Brancepeth copy of *East Lynne* is missing (stolen, or read to pieces?)—which we might legitimately take as confirmation of its extreme popularity on the farm. Fifteen of Mrs Wood's novels survived their Brancepeth readers (of at least 21, according to the catalogue numbering) and all show signs of heavy reading—opening pages are missing, the spines are falling off, and the books are covered with spills and stains and fingerprints.

Brancepeth readers might have found echoes of the attitudes expressed in *East Lynne* in the local scandal of the Earée divorce case, which was extensively reported in the paper (as described in the previous chapter). Certainly Mrs Earée, who seems from the court accounts to have suffered rejection by her husband, paid the higher price for her ill-considered extra marital affair. It is impossible to know whether Brancepeth readers made connections between events in their own locality and the luridly heightened dramas of sensational fiction, but the grip of such a narrative is easy to understand, and they were part of a global readership that devoured sensation novels and Mrs Wood's representations of Britain with gusto. According to an article in the *Spectator* in 1874, Mrs Wood was the 'leading manufacturer' of fiction for 'readers of the lower middle class, whether Church or chapel'. The *Spectator* believed that her appeal was that she dealt with solid British institutions 'the modest coroner's inquest, the homely justice-room, the unassuming smuggler's cave'. She served up, the *Spectator* said,

> murders and mutton, suicides and rice pudding, stolen cheques and thick bread-and-butter; and, as she never fails to say an emphatic grace over each heavy meal, she satisfies alike the appetite, the taste and the conscience of her readers.[40]

The popularity of this literary recipe at Brancepeth is not in doubt, given the condition of her books, and considering Miller's response to Lucas Malet and E.L. Voynich, it may also have been Mrs Wood's emphasis on despair and penitence for her wayward heroines that struck the right note with some readers on the farm.

Mrs Wood's novels follow a similar pattern. The dramatic structure is based on a family, complicated by infant and maternal deaths and the advent of stepmothers, and the plot is driven by intricacies of inheritance, succession, mysterious babies and secret elopements, with crime and mystery added to the mix. In *St Martin's Eve* [1866] for example, there are two sons from different marriages. A wicked stepmother tries to disinherit the son of the first marriage by depriving him of education, food and other comforts, but both children share a fateful birthday on St Martin's Eve. The tortuous plot of schemes, deaths, evil emotions and madness unreels to inevitable doom. Wood's novels are set in English counties and often in rural settings and deploy various nineteenth-century genre fashions—the ghost story, the bigamy plot, crime, gothic romance. Well aware of her readership, Mrs Wood's characters also like sensational fiction. In *Edina* [1876], set in a Cornish mining village, there is a 'small circulating library; or as it was called there, a book-lending club':

> the miners and the miners wives were, like their betters, fond of sensational fiction. The books consisted entirely of cheap volumes, priced at a shilling or two shillings each . . . (2)

Rises and falls of fortunes propel Mrs Wood's characters in many directions, including towards her readership in the colonies, who would have been familiar both with sudden changes of fortune and dispersed communities and families. In *Edina,* Rosaline emigrates to relatives 'near Wellington'. Indolent or vain women tend to have spent time in India, like Mrs St Clare who 'never took up a needle' and 'never cared to turn the pages of a book' (20). In *Bessy Rane* [1870] various characters depart for America or Australia. *The Channings* [1862], much of it based at a boys' school, is about a family that has, through being disappointed of a legacy, fallen on hard times. The novel pokes fun at the kind of feckless young male emigrant who expects to make his fortune effortlessly in the colonies. Roland Yorke, a young articled lawyer, who is the cause of much unhappy confusion in *The Channings*, leaves for the Cape with a mountain of buckets because he has been told there is a market for them. When asked by the elderly clerk in the law firm how he plans to make his fortune in South Africa, he cheerfully answers that they tell you that when you get there. Brancepeth readers were very familiar with that kind of young man, as is made clear by John Vaughan Miller's article, 'The Jackeroo'.[41]

Mrs Henry Wood is typical of many writers of Victorian popular fiction in the way she depicts the colonies as a normal dimension of English family life. Charles Dilke's much repeated phrase 'Greater Britain', the title of his book describing his travels around the British colonies in the

1860s, is an at-home phenomenon in Victorian fiction—characters go to the colonies as a matter of course, whether as disappointed lovers, feckless young men, ramblers or globe-trotters. The colonies figure frequently in fiction, and not always in reassuring ways. Famous examples include Magwitch's deportation to Australia in *Great Expectations*, Mr Rochester's secret wife Bertha's origins in the West Indies, and Sir Thomas Bertram's celebrated return from Antigua in *Mansfield Park*. The plot of Walter Besant's first and very popular novel *Ready Money Mortiboy* [1872], a book loved almost to death at Brancepeth, revolves around a hero who returns from being at the Cape and the Californian gold diggings to claim his inheritance. Leaving for elsewhere was not only a fact of British demography of the period—it is estimated that 12 million Britons, excluding the Irish, left for the colonies and the United States over the course of the nineteenth century[42]—it is a standard element in the narrative dynamics and motivations of British fiction.

What might this have meant to the Brancepeth readers in their choice of reading? One of the answers is surely that fiction offers a narrative of something that has happened to them. Many of the novels in the library expressed anxieties and sorrows familiar to people who had left their country of birth. *Dame Durden* (1885), a romance by Rita[43] and on the list of most heavily read at Brancepeth, features one of Victorian fiction's standard characters, the self-sacrificing woman (exemplified in New Woman fiction by Herminia Barton's tactful suicide). Rita's novel features a girl (Margaret) nicknamed 'Dame Durden' from a nursery rhyme, who from the age of 14 has to take care of her younger siblings after her mother's death. Several passages in the book have been marked by a reader. One is: 'I think life is a little bit unfair' he began, 'we are here whether we like it or not' (51). Another is a letter from a lover, writing to his sweetheart. 'Across all the wide distance that severs us . . . Have you any idea what I have suffered since we parted?' (268). Clearly, these melancholy passages spoke to someone reading them at Brancepeth. But Victorian popular fiction also offers a consoling narrative of connections maintained and absence unforgotten. The usual explanation of the settler taste for metropolitan romance is indulgent escapism—the imagination is off in London while the body lies in a hut surrounded by mud, and no doubt that was often the case. But the literary culture delivered repeated narratives in which migration to the ends of empire was part of every family; these variations on a theme rendered the world continuous, drawing a comforting circle around the lives of the vast and widely dispersed colonial readership. Mid-nineteenth-century fiction in particular reinforced the idea that international migration was part of family life, that the British world circled the globe, that property was governed by class entitlement, and that all classes—Mrs Henry Wood's Cornish miners among them—enjoyed reading fiction. As Elleke Boehmer has said, the kinds of books read by settlers 'contributed to the complex of attitudes that made imperialism seem part of the order of things'.[44]

Mary Braddon's 22 surviving titles (of at least 26) at Brancepeth are nearly all well-loved: battered, dirty, and annotated. This is unsurprising, as Braddon was one of the top-selling authors of her time. She was admired by Henry James, who compared her to Jane Austen; Thackeray, who specially loved *Lady Audley's Secret* [1862]; and Robert Louis Stevenson, who wrote to her in 1894 that in the South Seas she was 'greater than Scott, Shakespeare and Homer', and that 'everywhere in the Pacific when a new schooner came into port and the traders eagerly hoped to find on board some novel that they had not read, there was always one that they already had: M.E. Braddon's *Aurora Floyd*.'[45]

The Brancepeth station library copy of *Aurora Floyd* is

well used. First published as a triple-decker in 1863, it was reissued in a single-volume edition at a fifth of the original price only seven months later. Its success was at least partly because it immediately succeeded *Lady Audley's Secret*, also held at Brancepeth. *Lady Audley's Secret* was such a runaway bestseller that Braddon was known as Lady Audley for the rest of her long career and her first publisher Edward Tinsley built a house with the proceeds that he called Audley Lodge.[46] Both *Aurora Floyd* and *Lady Audley's Secret* feature beautiful heroines—one flaxen and the other raven-haired—with inconveniently reappearing first husbands. The raven-haired Aurora is a horsey girl, heiress to a large fortune. As a teenager she spent far too much time riding with a groom named Conyers, who was specially chosen by her father for his good looks. 'Naturally enough' as Miss Braddon's biographer Robert Wolff observes, 'this proves to be a mistake'.[47] Braddon's characteristic heroine, though she may be rich, is usually making some kind of upward social step which will be threatened by the revelation of a secret past; her upperclass characters are often revealed to be snobbish, selfish and arrogant. According to the *Spectator* in 1874, Braddon's popularity in Britain had a great deal to do with the way in which she wrote, as they put it, about 'the race-course, the music-hall, the behind-the-scenes, the lodging house life'.[48] These attractions seem to have appealed equally well to colonial New Zealand readers.

Braddon herself had a colourful life. Her father abandoned the family when she was a child, her sister married a Frenchman and went to live in Paris, her brother ended up Governor of Tasmania, and she herself worked on the stage and wrote for a living. Her novels reflect these mixed experiences and also the international nature of her extended family; her characters, like those of Mrs Henry Wood and Walter Besant, range over the empire. One of the attractions of Aurora Floyd as a character, something of a social anomaly in the Home Counties but entirely congenial to colonial girls like Thyra and Weva Beetham, is that she has caught an interest in racing from her unsuitable lover the handsome groom. When an aristocratic suitor asks her what she is thinking about so pensively, she replies 'Do you know how Thunderbolt went in the Leger?' At Brancepeth human and equine lives were just as closely entangled and mutually dependent, and Brancepeth readers liked to read about horses. Among their favourite books were John Trotwood Moore's *The Gift of the Grass* (1911), an autobiography of a race horse; George Whyte-Melville's *Katerfelto* [1875] a highwayman novel that stars a magnificent black stallion; the racing novels of Hawley Smart (for example, the heavily-read *The Pride of the Paddock*); and anything by the very popular Australian racing writer Nat Gould.

Like the novels of her great rival, Mrs Henry Wood, Braddon's fiction is preoccupied with the grand narrative of Victorian literature: the relation of property and class. The opening scene of many of her novels is a long view of a country house standing in ample grounds. In *Aurora Floyd*, 'the homeward tramping villager' pauses in the roadway to glance across the 'smooth width of dewy lawn and tranquil lake' at the stately red-brick mansion that is Aurora's home. The country house—or the farm, the grange, the manor house—is not just a staple location of Victorian fiction, but a major figure in the plot, representing status, wealth, class relations, history, conservatism and pastoral ideals. For colonial readers, it was perhaps more specifically a symbol of Englishness and an expression of nostalgia. The big house may also have represented what emigrants rejected about England: in the Wairarapa, the 'closer settlement' movement, which advocated the break up of big pastoral leases and the establishment of small farms, was very active, and the subject of ongoing debate in the columns of the local newspaper in the 1890s.[49]

But the image of the big country house was also aspirational. Edward Said has argued, somewhat controversially, that the novel and imperialism are 'unthinkable' without each other,[50] and certainly Victorian fiction is full of characters who have accumulated wealth somewhere in the empire. The ample country estate, focus of so much emotion and intrigue in Victorian fiction, is what many emigrants imagined themselves to be travelling towards. Mary Braddon's novels, like those of Mrs Henry Wood and Walter Besant, depict the empire as a distant but integral part of England's financial and social networks. Characters and their ambitions (and sometimes their bad habits) are habitually despatched to the colonies, and Brancepeth readers had only to look around them to see that the Beetham family had realised the emigrant's dream. Many of the station workers aspired to own their own land, and though for most of them it was an impossible ambition, sadly accentuated by the drifting poor of the 1890s depression, the station diary gives an intermittent history of those employees who did move on to develop smallholdings.[51]

Wilkie Collins, perhaps the most famous exponent of the sensation novel, was an earlier love of Brancepeth readers than M.E. Braddon. Like his mentor and friend Charles Dickens, Collins was a staple author for the nineteenth-century reader. In the 1895 printed catalogue, there are 23 Collins titles, as against 19 for Mrs Wood and 16 for Braddon. Collin's third novel, *Hide and Seek*, published in 1854 and dedicated to Dickens, is one of the most heavily-read books in the collection, battered and dirty, and missing all but three of the first 30 pages.[52] *Hide and Seek* is the story of a deaf and dumb foundling, Mary, known as Madonna, who is adopted from a circus by an artist and his wife. The only clue to who she might be is a hair bracelet left with her as a baby, but the mystery of her origins is lengthily and unrealistically unravelled when Matt Grice, a wild colonial who has been scalped by Native Americans (on the Amazon!), appears on the scene. Like all Wilkie Collins's novels, *Hide and Seek* is a racy read, with an exotic, driving plot that must have kept Brancepeth readers turning the pages even after a hard day's work outside. Readers might also have glimpsed themselves in its narrative of dispersed families, colonial wealth, the dangers of poverty and the return of the prodigal son.

These aspects of Wilkie Collins's novels are also fundamental to Dickens, and surely resonated at Brancepeth, which was full of stories of missing family members, and witness to the poverty and misery of swaggers arriving at the gate. Dickens, a global phenomenon by the 1870s, shaped daily life more than any other Victorian writer. His works had entered the lexicon so completely that references to Dickensian characters and works were commonplace everywhere. Edward Gibbon Wakefield's name for the manuscript of *A View of the Art of Colonization* was 'My Mrs Harris', a reference to Sairey Gamp's invisible friend, much talked about but never seen, in *Martin Chuzzlewit*. In the station diary, John Vaughan Miller referred to a shepherd who continually made requests for food supplies as suffering from 'Oliver Twist's complaint', and a new cook he disliked as 'a bad type of prizefighter', noting: 'the men say he is the original of Bill Sykes (hard on Sykes)'.[53] On Christmas Day 1900, after the whare cook stole the saloon's share of beer, Miller wrote ironically that:

> Like Mr Venus in 'Our Mutual Friend' the Head Shepherd and the Station Clerk 'floated their powerful minds in tea'.

Dickens himself was interested in New Zealand and even contemplated coming here to start a magazine in 1847, after a number of people he knew had emigrated, including Thomas Arnold, Mary Taylor and Alfred Domett. Macaulay's image of a future New Zealander (he meant a Māori) standing in a ruined London had made the prospect of New Zealand highly topical, and a number of articles about New Zealand appeared in Dickens's periodicals *Household Words* and *All the Year Round*. He was a mentor to Benjamin Farjeon who left Dunedin for London, and whose novel *Grif* [1870] was popular with readers at Brancepeth.

Dickens, both as a novelist and as a social reformer, was constantly referred to by other novelists, such as Joseph Hocking, in whose *All Men Are Liars*, Stephen Edgecumbe declares 'Charles Dickens, you know, removed, or caused to be removed, a lot of evils. That's what I'm going to do' (31). In New Zealand there were Pickwick Clubs, readings and performances, and a set of the novels of Dickens was a requirement of any library collection (alongside Sir Walter Scott, Robbie Burns and Lord Alfred Tennyson). There is a marked-up copy of *A Christmas Carol* in the Brancepeth station library, a relic of long vanished Christmas gatherings where Dickens's famous work was read aloud; and the Beetham family library contains bound volumes of *Household Words* for 1851/2 (the Christmas Issue) and four volumes of his later journal *All The Year Round* 1869/70, though curiously, no edition of Dickens's novels. The Brancepeth station library copy of Dickens is an edition in 15 volumes published by Chapman and Hall in 1880. Small print must have made them hard work by lamp or candlelight but they are almost all well used, with some clear favourites: *The Pickwick Papers*, *David Copperfield*, *Bleak House*, and *Martin Chuzzlewit*—the latter perhaps not coincidentally a novel of emigration, in which Dickens wrote of everything he hated about America.

By the 1890s, Dickens had perhaps been overtaken as recreational reading on the farm, and perhaps more generally by current trends in popular fiction, but his works, along with those of Sir Walter Scott, Thackeray and Mrs Oliphant form the essential backbone of Brancepeth as a Victorian library.

Sir Walter Scott's 25 novels, which show relatively few marks of use and seem not to have been heavily read, were also in a standard edition, published in Edinburgh in 1873. This suggests that 'sets' of the work of canonical authors were the first steps taken towards creating a 'library', as distinct from a random collection of books the family happened to own or buy (the family library also had a number of sets in it, but they tended to be reference works such as the *Encyclopaedia Britannica*). Thackeray's 14 titles were almost all editions published in 1882–3, as were a number of Mrs Oliphant's, which means these books were bought at about the time the Brancepeth library was formally established. Of Thackeray's titles the most popular is, unsurprisingly, *Vanity Fair.* The library held two copies, and both are torn off their spines and covered with dirt. In popularity, *Vanity Fair* was closely followed by *The History of Pendennis*, Thackeray's 'autobiographical masterpiece'[54]; *Henry Esmond*, whose dashing Jacobite hero is embroiled in military, political and romantic intrigue, and finally emigrates to Virginia; and its continuation, *The Virginians*, set during the American Revolution.

Mrs Oliphant's nine novels held at Brancepeth are mostly from editions published in the 1880s, though there are a few colonial editions from the next decade. By far the most popular with Brancepeth readers was *Miss Marjoribanks*, first published in 1866, which is described as the 'most sharply comic' of her Chronicles of Carlingford series.[55] Lucilla Marjoribanks is a 'Victorian Emma', determined to take charge of her widowed father and improve the 'tastes and ideas' of the village in which they live.[56] The novel features a declaration of love early on, and ten years later the patient suitor, who has been far away in India making himself worthy of Lucilla, is successful. Oliphant's theme of devotion rewarded—and enterprise paying off—is common across all Victorian genres and is, of course, the grand narrative of promotional literature for emigrants. George Eliot's eight titles in Brancepeth also belong to the early acquisitions and show varying but not heavy levels of use, the most popular being *The Mill on the Floss* and *Romola*. But though Miller refers to *Felix Holt* piously when taking Marie Corelli to task for 'too much truthtelling' in her novel *Temporal Power*, Eliot was not as popular with Brancepeth readers as Dickens and Thackeray.[57]

A surprising omission from Brancepeth is Mrs Gaskell: there are no works by Mrs Gaskell in the collection, neither extant nor missing. Again this is a gap that is difficult to interpret—was the 'social problem' category of novel antipathetic to aspiring settlers trying to build a loyal labour force? Did Mrs Gaskell's focus on free-thinking—and her depiction, in *North and South*, of the gap between the middle class comforts of the home counties and the inequities and hardships of the industrial north—strike too close to home on such issues as fair pay and labour conditions? It is impossible to know, but given Mrs Gaskell's standing as a major Victorian novelist and social commentator, her absence from the library is remarkable and puzzling.

Likewise, 'improvement literature', in the sense of self-help works, was not a favoured or dominant part of the Brancepeth library. This was possibly for class reasons. Samuel Smiles and his 'self-reliance' gospel had a big following among Methodists in Masterton, led by the redoubtable C.E. Daniell, whose building firm constructed most of the station buildings, including the homestead.[58] A number of Daniell's carpenters were enthusiastic short-term members of the library when the homestead was rebuilt in 1905. The library holds a copy of Smiles' famous book *Self-Help* [1866] which is clean and does not have signs of heavy reader use. Smiles' dictum that 'multifarious reading weakens the mind like smoking'

(325) runs counter to prevailing habits at Brancepeth, whose library subscribers liked smoking and reading, and often at the same time. Much more popular in the Brancepeth library than Smilesian self-improvement manuals were novels that explicitly dealt with moral and character improvement, either lightheartedly as in *Miss Marjoribanks,* or seriously as in Dinah Mulock-Craik's widely popular *John Halifax, Gentleman,*[59] which shows very heavy use.

John Halifax, Gentleman, first published in three volumes in 1856, the year the Beethams emigrated to New Zealand, belongs to the older segment of the collection (the library copy is 1883), and is the only heavily-read title of seven by Mulock-Craik held at Brancepeth. Described as the 'best-known fable of Smilesian self-improvement',[60] it is said by the narrator, Phineas Fletcher, the invalid son of a Quaker manufacturer, to have a 'Jonathan and David theme'. Phineas, who is angelically sweet-tempered but has weak health in some unspecified but immobilising way (one of a large crowd of similarly afflicted characters in Victorian literature[61]), persuades his father to rescue a 14-year-old orphan, John Halifax, from the street and give him a job. Phineas's 'only world' is books, of which the orphan boy knows nothing, but in a well-worn iteration of Victorian ideas about the potency of (certain kinds of) books and learning, John Halifax reveals that his most precious possession, carried in his pocket, is a book in a case of leather 'with an under one of black silk', which he 'would not let go out of his hands, but held it so I could see the leaves. It was a Greek and English testament' (13). John Halifax teaches himself to read from books sent to him by Phineas (*Robinson Crusoe*, *Pilgrim's Progress*, the *Arabian Nights* and the Bible) and rises to take over the firm and become the saviour of the Fletcher family. The valorisation of reading in *John Halifax, Gentleman*—the hero spends 'all the evening' reading aloud or 'to himself' (111)—is standard fare in Victorian fiction, but in Mulock-Craik's novel it is also a path to class elevation.

Victorian fiction generally makes it clear that education is a necessity, and that classical education is a distinction of the upper classes. In Mrs Henry Wood's novel *The Channings*, the middle son clings to his Latin and Greek classes despite having to leave school and go to work in a lawyer's office. Such exemplary devotion to study recalls Willie Beetham's anxieties about not working hard enough at Latin and Greek. In Wilkie Collins's *Armadale* [1866] the itinerant, dispossessed and abused Ozias Midwinter, on his own in the world since the age of twelve, carries the plays of Sophocles in Greek in his haversack and is able to read them, thus demonstrating his true class origins. John Halifax's social class rises once he has achieved not only literacy, but education, though the fact of his possession of a 'Greek English testament' suggests there are unknown circumstances which have caused him to fall through a class border—that he was, all along, a gentleman in disguise. Many other Victorian novels make the same point and there is little doubt that John Vaughan Miller's deployment of Latin and Greek (not to mention French, German, and Hebrew) in his marginalia and the station diary is an assertion of the social value of a classical education. Significantly, the Brancepeth station library holds no classical texts, but there are a number in the Beetham family library (Homer, Herodotus, Virgil, Horace), which have been read, annotated and cherished.

Readers at Brancepeth liked certain categories of fiction, such as historical and regional novels, that point to the role of nostalgia, patriotism and homesickness in forming their reading tastes. After Scott, W.H. Ainsworth was the leading historical novelist of the nineteenth century, though, as John Sutherland has noted, the comparison unduly flatters him. [62] Ainsworth began writing melodramas while working in his father's law office, and spent a few years in his twenties on various failed publishing and literary projects. He achieved some fame as a dandy—he was said to have the 'chest of Apollo and the waist of a gnat'[63]—before he published *Rookwood*, a novel about Dick Turpin, with great success in 1834. Brancepeth held 30 of his historical novels, all published by Routledge's Railway Library, on such topics as the Star Chamber, James the Second, the Great Fire, Guy Fawkes and the Manchester Rebels. The most popular of his novels at Brancepeth is *The Tower of London* [1840], based on the rise and fall of Lady Jane Grey, which Sutherland describes as a 'blatantly nationalist' novel (633)—indeed, that may have been an important part of its attraction. The American writer F. Marion Crawford, whose historical romances, set in such exotic locations as Roman Italy, India and Arabia, also formed a substantial holding of 32 titles, was not nearly as well read as Ainsworth, suggesting that patriotic British history had more forceful interest and relevance for station readers than the more exotic kind. Fourteen of R.D. Blackmore's historical/regional novels were held at Brancepeth, but only nine survive. Among the missing is the one he is most famous for, *Lorna Doone* [1869], but Blackmore's own favourite of his work, *The Maid of Sker* [1872], a tale about a Welsh fisherman who finds a young girl drifting in a boat and adopts her, appears to have been the least popular with Brancepeth readers. They preferred *Mary Anerly*, a smuggling romance, and Blackmore's romances of rural England, *Kit and Kitty* and *Cradock Nowell: A Tale of the New Forest,* which all show signs of heavy use.

Scottish writers, or writers about Scotland, were a substantial presence in Victorian fiction, and Scottish novels showed considerable wear and tear from the readership at Brancepeth. William Black's novels specialising in 'maiden' heroines and promoting 'Celtic' consciousness were heavily read, especially *A Daughter of Heth* [1871], which established his reputation and readership. *A Daughter of Heth* is the story of a vivacious, cultivated French girl, who, after the death of her parents, is transplanted from a convent to her uncle's puritanical Scottish manse. Her influence on the Minister's five sons and the romantic dilemmas that ensue are a vehicle for contrasting the plainness and chill of Scotland with the elegance and affection of the French heroine, who plays the piano beautifully but is constantly silenced for the unsuitability of her music or for playing on the Sabbath. The novel pays close attention to the details of manners and household interiors in lowland village life, which may have attracted nostalgic readers on the farm.

Readers also liked the work of George Macdonald, now best known for his children's fantasies such as *At The Back of the North Wind*. The library held 14 titles, mostly with Scottish settings, though the most heavily read is *Paul Faber* [1878], a didactic novel about a surgeon who is won over to religious faith. S.R. Crockett's 'Scottish vernacular fictions' set in Galloway, especially *The Grey Man* (1896), a Scottish historical novel 'interesting for the depiction of the legendary Scottish cannibal, Sawney Bean',[64] were also well used, but the best-loved Scottish and regional novelist was Amelia Barr. Set in Yorkshire and Scotland (particularly the Shetlands), Barr's novels were heavily favoured by Brancepeth readers. Their favourite seems to have been *Jan Vedder's Wife* [1885]. Set in a Shetland village in the 1830s, it is about the mysterious disappearance and resurrection of the hero, who has fallen into disgrace for spending his time drinking but eventually reforms and makes it up to his formidable wife. A highly prolific novelist, Barr met with her own reversals of fortune—her father was defrauded of his income and her husband Robert became a bankrupt. On the advice of Harriet Beecher Stowe, the Barrs migrated to America, where Robert and three children died in the 1867 yellow fever epidemic in

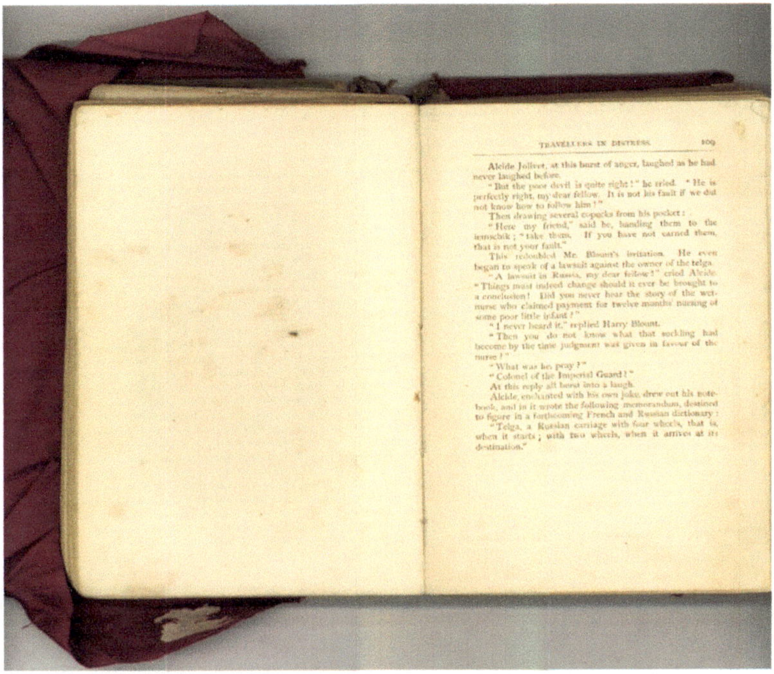

A battered copy of *Vanity Fair* showing the wear and tear of the Brancepeth Library.

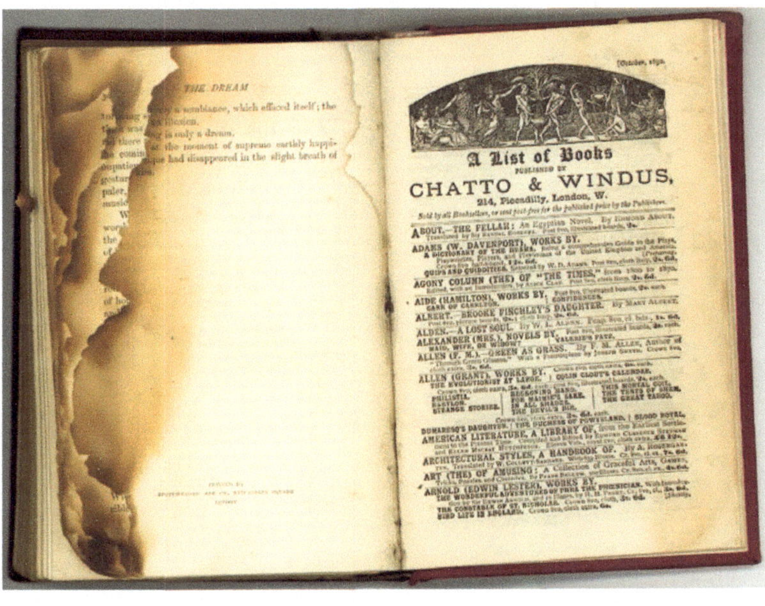

A burnt book. A number of the Brancepeth books have scorch marks, suggesting tired readers by a fire.

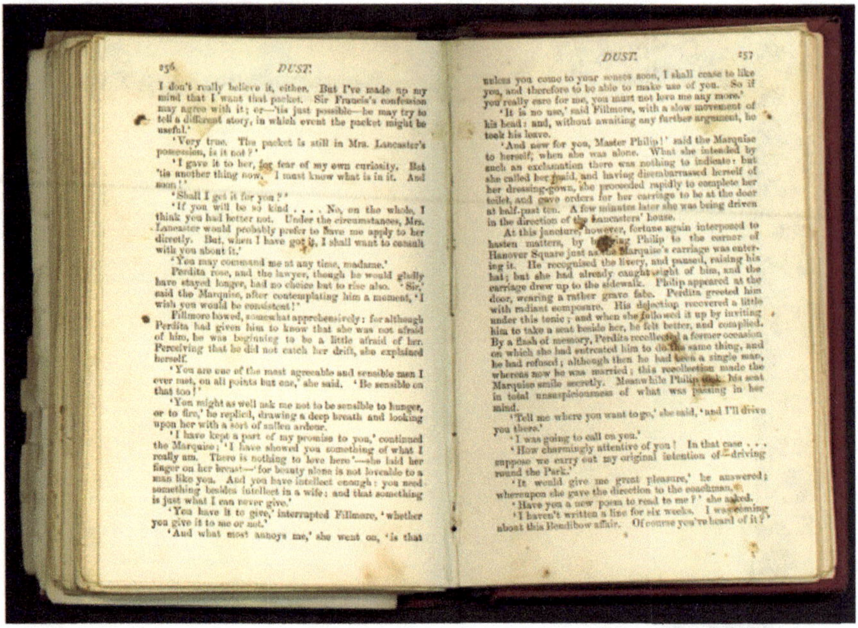

An example of the dirt that marks many Brancepeth books – here suggesting spilled food.

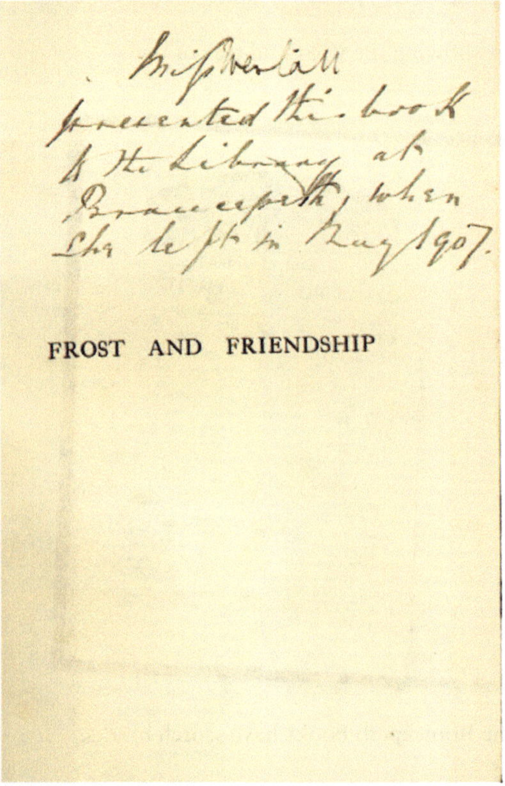

Miss Westall presented this book to the Library at Brancepeth, when she left in May 1907.

FROST AND FRIENDSHIP

Inscription in John Vaughan Miller's hand in book presented by the governess Miss Westall.

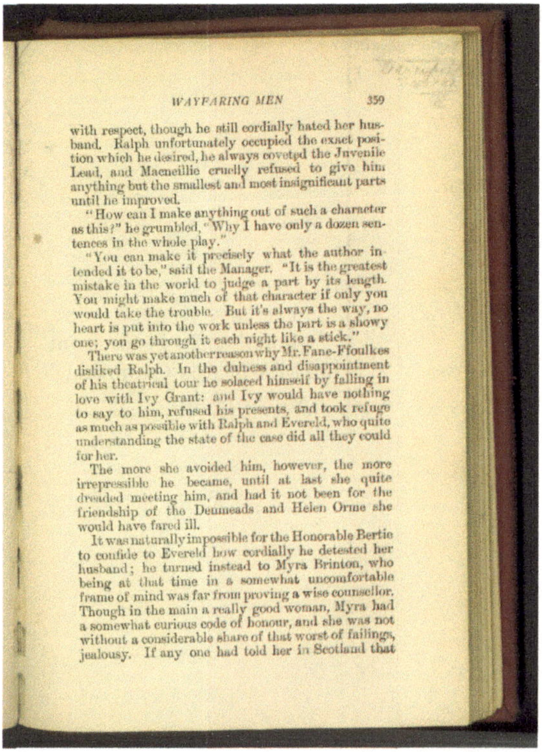

WAYFARING MEN 359

with respect, though he still cordially hated her husband. Ralph unfortunately occupied the exact position which he desired, he always coveted the Juvenile Lead, and Macneillie cruelly refused to give him anything but the smallest and most insignificant parts until he improved.

"How can I make anything out of such a character as this?" he grumbled, "Why I have only a dozen sentences in the whole play."

"You can make it precisely what the author intended it to be," said the Manager. "It is the greatest mistake in the world to judge a part by its length. You might make much of that character if only you would take the trouble. But it's always the way, no heart is put into the work unless the part is a showy one; you go through it each night like a stick."

There was yet another reason why Mr. Fane-Ffoulkes disliked Ralph. In the dulness and disappointment of his theatrical tour he solaced himself by falling in love with Ivy Grant: and Ivy would have nothing to say to him, refused his presents, and took refuge as much as possible with Ralph and Evereld, who quite understanding the state of the case did all they could for her.

The more she avoided him, however, the more irrepressible he became, until at last she quite dreaded meeting him, and had it not been for the friendship of the Denmeads and Helen Orme she would have fared ill.

It was naturally impossible for the Honorable Bertie to confide to Evereld how cordially he detested her husband; he turned instead to Myra Brinton, who being at that time in a somewhat uncomfortable frame of mind was far from proving a wise counsellor. Though in the main a really good woman, Myra had a somewhat curious code of honour, and she was not without a considerable share of that worst of failings, jealousy. If any one had told her in Scotland that

Thyra Beetham's signature and date in a copy of Edna Lyall's *Wayfaring Men*.

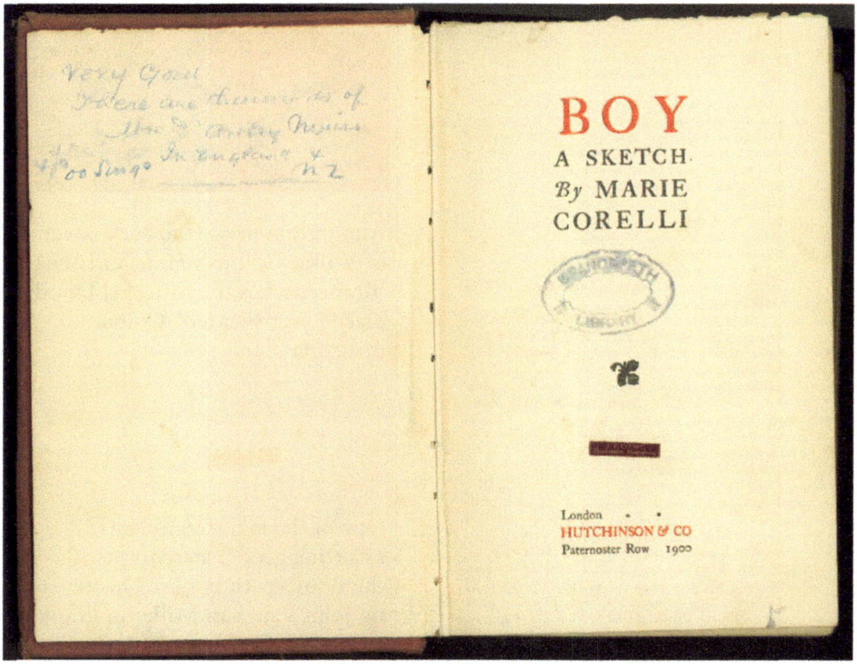

Annotation by Ruth Beetham in Marie Corelli's *Boy*: 'Very good There are thousands of Mrs D'Arcy Muirs + Poo Sings in England + NZ'.

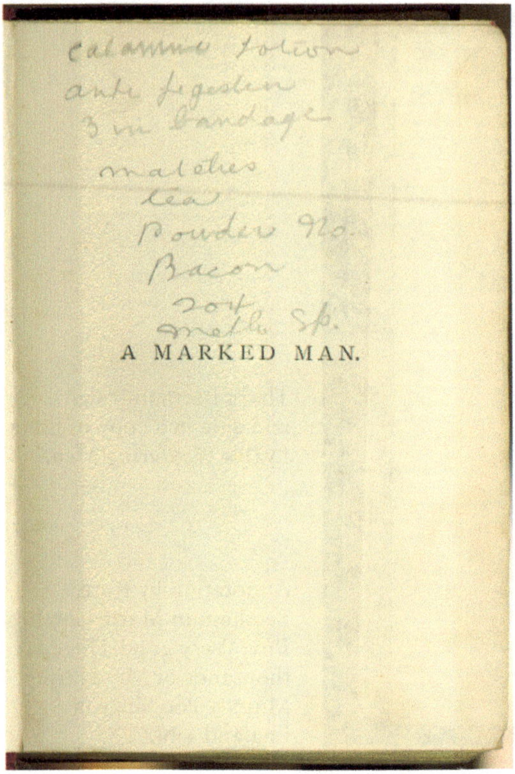

Shopping list inside front cover of Ada Cambridge's *A Marked Man.*

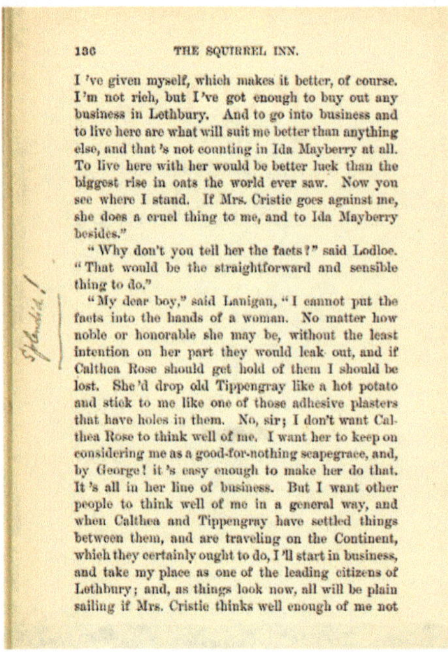

136 THE SQUIRREL INN.

I 've given myself, which makes it better, of course. I'm not rich, but I've got enough to buy out any business in Lethbury. And to go into business and to live here are what will suit me better than anything else, and that 's not counting in Ida Mayberry at all. To live here with her would be better luck than the biggest rise in oats the world ever saw. Now you see where I stand. If Mrs. Cristie goes against me, she does a cruel thing to me, and to Ida Mayberry besides."

"Why don't you tell her the facts?" said Lodloe. "That would be the straightforward and sensible thing to do."

"My dear boy," said Lanigan, "I cannot put the facts into the hands of a woman. No matter how noble or honorable she may be, without the least intention on her part they would leak out, and if Calthea Rose should get hold of them I should be lost. She 'd drop old Tippengray like a hot potato and stick to me like one of those adhesive plasters that have holes in them. No, sir; I don't want Calthea Rose to think well of me. I want her to keep on considering me as a good-for-nothing scapegrace, and, by George! it 's easy enough to make her do that. It 's all in her line of business. But I want other people to think well of me in a general way, and when Calthea and Tippengray have settled things between them, and are traveling on the Continent, which they certainly ought to do, I 'll start in business, and take my place as one of the leading citizens of Lethbury; and, as things look now, all will be plain sailing if Mrs. Cristie thinks well enough of me not

Annotation inside the back cover of Wilkie Collins's *Hide and Seek*: 'Brancepeth is the rottenest bloody place I ever sheared'. Colour inversion scan.

One of the many comments asserting gender stereotypes in the Brancepeth books. This one is by John Vaughan Miller in Frank Stockton's *The Squirrel Inn.*

Sums, inside the front cover of Mrs Oliphant's *Miss Marjoribanks*. There are numerous other examples in the library.

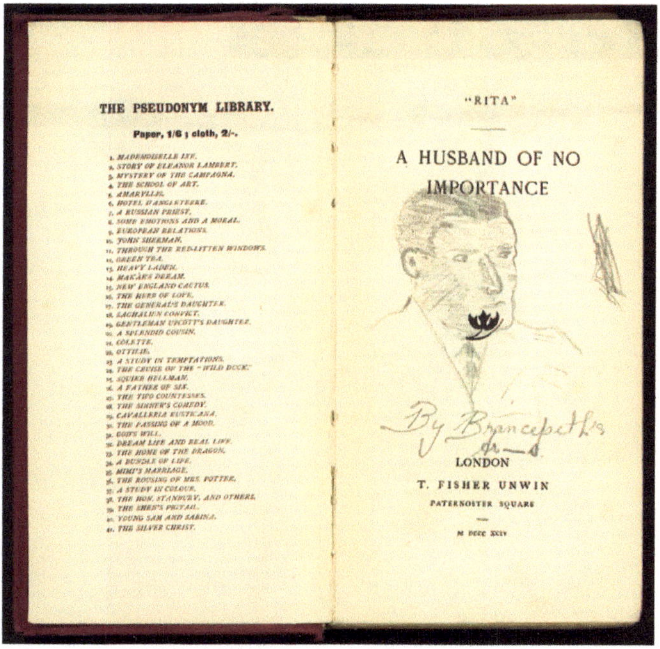

Caricature by unknown hand of Hugh Beetham in Rita's *A Husband of No Importance*.

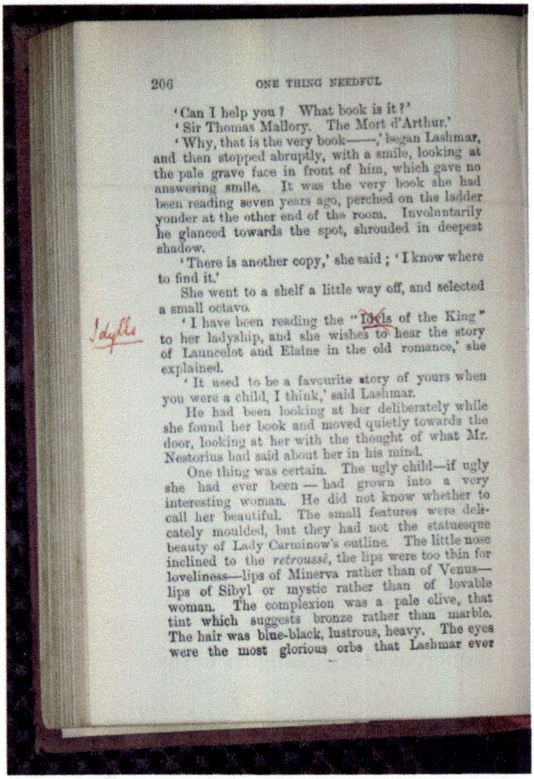

206 ONE THING NEEDFUL

'Can I help you? What book is it?'

'Sir Thomas Mallory. The Mort d'Arthur.'

'Why, that is the very book——,' began Lashmar, and then stopped abruptly, with a smile, looking at the pale grave face in front of him, which gave no answering smile. It was the very book she had been reading seven years ago, perched on the ladder yonder at the other end of the room. Involuntarily he glanced towards the spot, shrouded in deepest shadow.

'There is another copy,' she said; 'I know where to find it.'

She went to a shelf a little way off, and selected a small octavo.

'I have been reading the "Idyls of the King" to her ladyship, and she wishes to hear the story of Launcelot and Elaine in the old romance,' she explained.

'It used to be a favourite story of yours when you were a child, I think,' said Lashmar.

He had been looking at her deliberately while she found her book and moved quietly towards the door, looking at her with the thought of what Mr. Nestorius had said about her in his mind.

One thing was certain. The ugly child—if ugly she had ever been—had grown into a very interesting woman. He did not know whether to call her beautiful. The small features were delicately moulded, but they had not the statuesque beauty of Lady Carminow's outline. The little nose inclined to the *retroussé*, the lips were too thin for loveliness—lips of Minerva rather than of Venus—lips of Sibyl or mystic rather than of lovable woman. The complexion was a pale olive, that tint which suggests bronze rather than marble. The hair was blue-black, lustrous, heavy. The eyes were the most glorious orbs that Lashmar ever

Correction in John Vaughan Miller's hand in M.E. Braddon's *One Thing Needful*.

Greek gloss by John Vaughan Miller in Thomas Hardy's *Far From the Madding Crowd*.

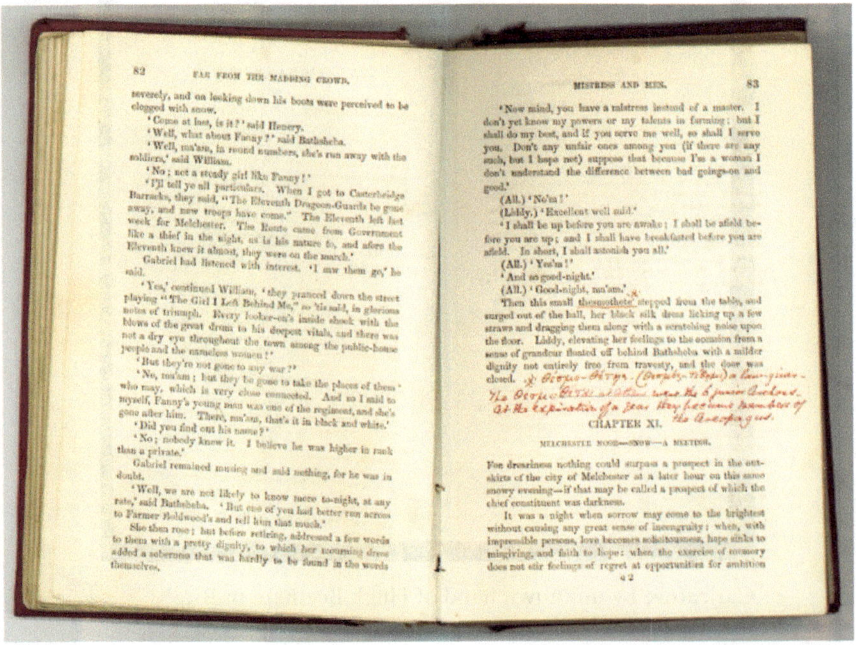

82 FAR FROM THE MADDING CROWD.

severely, and on looking down his boots were perceived to be clogged with snow.

'Come at last, is it?' said Henery.

'Well, what about Fanny?' said Bathsheba.

'Well, ma'am, in round numbers, she's run away with the soldiers,' said William.

'No; not a steady girl like Fanny!'

'I'll tell ye all particulars. When I got to Casterbridge Barracks, they said, "The Eleventh Dragoon-Guards be gone away, and new troops have come." The Eleventh left last week for Melchester. The Route came from Government like a thief in the night, as is his nature to, and afore the Eleventh knew it almost, they were on the march.'

Gabriel had listened with interest. 'I saw them go,' he said.

'Yes,' continued William, 'they pranced down the street playing "The Girl I Left Behind Me," so 'tis said, in glorious notes of triumph. Every looker-on's inside shook with the blows of the great drum to his deepest vitals, and there was not a dry eye throughout the town among the public-house people and the nameless women!'

'But they're not gone to any war?'

'No, ma'am; but they be gone to take the places of them who may, which is very close connected. And so I said to myself, Fanny's young man was one of the regiment, and she's gone after him. There, ma'am, that's it in black and white.'

'Did you find out his name?'

'No; nobody knew it. I believe he was higher in rank than a private.'

Gabriel remained musing and said nothing, for he was in doubt.

'Well, we are not likely to know more to-night, at any rate,' said Bathsheba. 'But one of you had better run across to Farmer Boldwood's and tell him that much.'

She then rose; but before retiring, addressed a few words to them with a pretty dignity, to which her mourning dress added a soberness that was hardly to be found in the words themselves.

MISTRESS AND MEN. 83

'Now mind, you have a mistress instead of a master. I don't yet know my powers or my talents in farming; but I shall do my best, and if you serve me well, so shall I serve you. Don't any unfair ones among you (if there are any such, but I hope not) suppose that because I'm a woman I don't understand the difference between bad goings-on and good.'

(All.) 'No'm!'

(Liddy.) 'Excellent well said.'

'I shall be up before you are awake; I shall be afield before you are up; and I shall have breakfasted before you are afield. In short, I shall astonish you all.'

(All.) 'Yes'm!'

'And so good-night.'

(All.) 'Good-night, ma'am.'

Then this small thesmothete stepped from the table, and surged out of the hall, her black silk dress licking up a few straws and dragging them along with a scratching noise upon the floor. Liddy, elevating her feelings to the occasion from a sense of grandeur floated off behind Bathsheba with a milder dignity not entirely free from travesty, and the door was closed.

CHAPTER XI.

MELCHESTER MOOR—SNOW—A MEETING.

For dreariness nothing could surpass a prospect in the outskirts of the city of Melchester at a later hour on this same snowy evening—if that may be called a prospect of which the chief constituent was darkness.

It was a night when sorrow may come to the brightest without causing any great sense of incongruity: when, with impressible persons, love becomes solicitousness, hope sinks to misgiving, and faith to hope: when the exercise of memory does not stir feelings of regret at opportunities for ambition

4 2

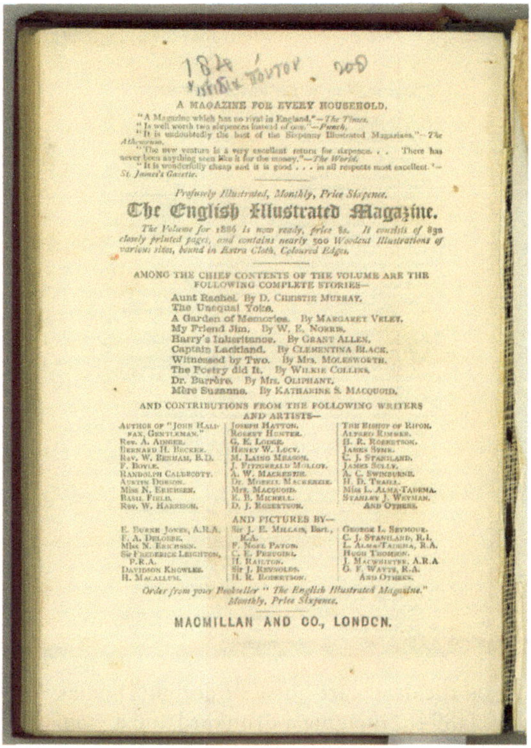

Greek phrase and page numbers noted by John Vaughan Miller at the back of Mrs Oliphant's *A House Divided From Itself*. The Greek phrase is [?]ειδεα ποντον or Homer's description 'deep-blue sea' (Odyssey 11.97) and relates to a description of the sea on p184 of the novel.

A pithy comment by an anonymous hand in A.B. Richmond's *Intemperance: The Great Source of Crime*.

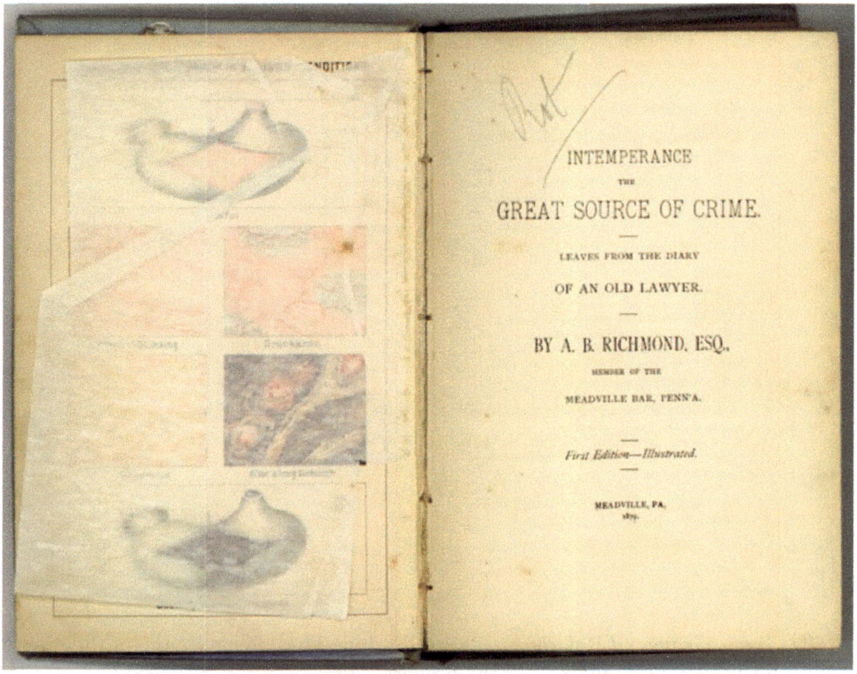

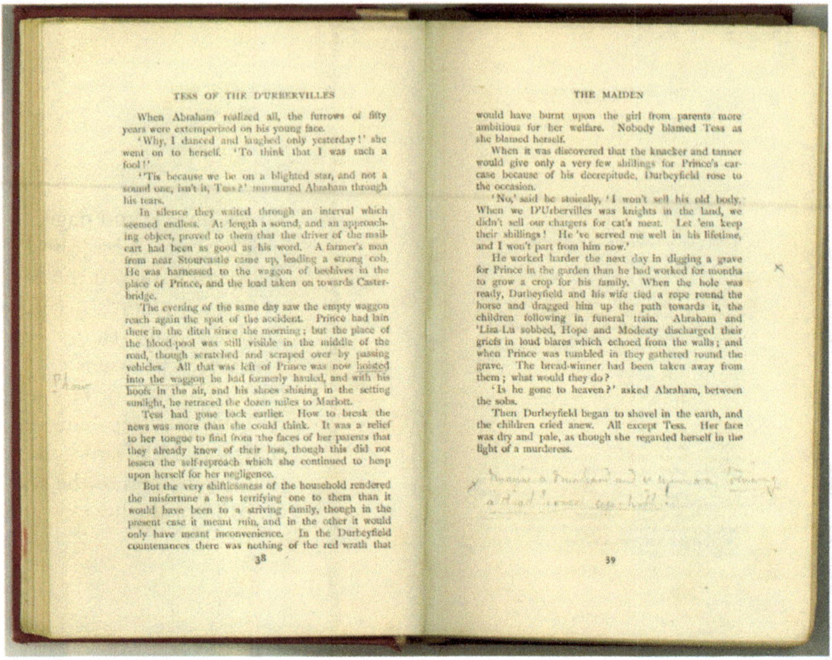

TESS OF THE D'URBERVILLES

When Abraham realized all, the furrows of fifty years were extemporized on his young face.

'Why, I danced and laughed only yesterday!' she went on to herself. 'To think that I was such a fool!'

''Tis because we be on a blighted star, and not a sound one, isn't it, Tess?' murmured Abraham through his tears.

In silence they waited through an interval which seemed endless. At length a sound, and an approaching object, proved to them that the driver of the mail-cart had been as good as his word. A farmer's man from near Stourcastle came up, leading a strong cob. He was harnessed to the waggon of beehives in the place of Prince, and the load taken on towards Casterbridge.

The evening of the same day saw the empty waggon reach again the spot of the accident. Prince had lain there in the ditch since the morning; but the place of the blood-pool was still visible in the middle of the road, though scratched and scraped over by passing vehicles. All that was left of Prince was now hoisted into the waggon he had formerly hauled, and with his hoofs in the air, and his shoes shining in the setting sunlight, he retraced the dozen miles to Marlott.

Tess had gone back earlier. How to break the news was more than she could think. It was a relief to her tongue to find from the faces of her parents that they already knew of their loss, though this did not lessen the self-reproach which she continued to heap upon herself for her negligence.

But the very shiftlessness of the household rendered the misfortune a less terrifying one to them than it would have been to a striving family, though in the present case it meant ruin, and in the other it would only have meant inconvenience. In the Durbeyfield countenances there was nothing of the red wrath that

38

THE MAIDEN

would have burnt upon the girl from parents more ambitious for her welfare. Nobody blamed Tess as she blamed herself.

When it was discovered that the knacker and tanner would give only a very few shillings for Prince's carcase because of his decrepitude, Durbeyfield rose to the occasion.

'No,' said he stoically, 'I won't sell his old body. When we D'Urbervilles was knights in the land, we didn't sell our chargers for cat's meat. Let 'em keep their shillings! He've served me well in his lifetime, and I won't part from him now.'

He worked harder the next day in digging a grave for Prince in the garden than he had worked for months to grow a crop for his family. When the hole was ready, Durbeyfield and his wife tied a rope round the horse and dragged him up the path towards it, the children following in funeral train. Abraham and 'Liza-Lu sobbed, Hope and Modesty discharged their griefs in loud blares which echoed from the walls; and when Prince was tumbled in they gathered round the grave. The bread-winner had been taken away from them; what would they do?

'Is he gone to heaven?' asked Abraham, between the sobs.

Then Durbeyfield began to shovel in the earth, and the children cried anew. All except Tess. Her face was dry and pale, as though she regarded herself in the light of a murderess.

39

John Vaughan Miller remarking on the dead cart-horse Prince, in Thomas Hardy's *Tess of the D'Urbervilles* (1894): 'Imagine a drunkard and a woman towing a dead horse uphill!'

THE GREEN GRAVES OF BALGOWRIE

more stimulating to the character than friendship. Henrietta writes an excellent letter, and enters, indeed, into all the topics of the day with Miss Margaret Pelham."

As you have seen, "all the topics of the day," as they existed for Henrietta, were mainly dissertations upon religion, mathematics, and philosophy — her only interests in life, and Maggie Pelham, a gay young maiden just entering on the pleasures of a London season, would sometimes laugh a good deal over the funnily-worded letters. But there was a touch of rareness in all that Henrietta did which made her lengthiest epistles worth the reading. She struck out new phrases and ideas constantly, and when she came down from the clouds to describe their daily life at Balgowrie to her unknown friend, she made it all so real and unconsciously touching that Maggie Pelham would cry out with moist eyes to her mother—

"Madam, do you not think we might invite Henrietta and Lucie to visit us?"

And Mrs. Pelham would shake her head regretfully, saying, "We might ask them very often, Maggie my dear, and have always the same reply. I fear Mrs. Marjorybanks is demented, poor lady, or something very like it—'tis a sad pity for the poor girls."

80

THE GREEN GRAVES OF BALGOWRIE

So time wore on, and this long lane of life that hedged in Henrietta and Lucie seemed no nearer a turning than when they had first come to Balgowrie nine long years before.

Henrietta was one-and-twenty and Lucie eighteen when an event occurred which changed the current of their lives at last.

6 81

The Green Graves of Balgowrie (1896) by Jane Findlater was one of the most popular books, as suggested by the flowers found between its pages.

Texas. Like other prolific Victorian women writers—M.E. Braddon, George Eliot, Marie Corelli and Frances Trollope, for example—Barr then supported herself, in her case by writing 'scores of potboilers'.[65] Her Scottish novels may have been popular with Brancepeth readers because her own nostalgia mirrored theirs. The shepherds at Brancepeth, as on most sheep stations, were mostly Scots, and Shetland Islanders arrived in New Zealand in significant numbers in the 1870s as a consequence of the Clearances. The drinking problems of Jan Vedder were also certainly familiar territory.

The cluster of prejudices and affiliations among the English, Welsh, Scots and Irish that played out in the relationships on Brancepeth (if Miller's diary references are a reliable guide[66]) is a feature of Victorian fiction, and is visible in the Brancepeth collection. Twenty novels by Charles Lever, the best-known Irish novelist of the nineteenth century, were held at Brancepeth; only nine survive, of which five are heavily used, with broken spines and missing pages. *Tom Burke of 'Ours'* [1844], alleged to be the best novel of the Napoleonic Wars written in England, was a hit at Brancepeth, as were Lever's 'good-humoured Irish picaresques'[67] *Charles O'Malley, Luttrell of Arran, and Jack Hinton* [1842]. The latter is about a young Guardsman who is sent to Ireland as aide-de-camp. His colourful experiences in the garrison at Dublin Castle cause him to reflect on the 'wide-sweeping prejudice' and 'certain indefinable tone of superiority' asserted towards 'our friends from across the sea' (1897 edition, 28), echoing a tone frequently adopted by Miller in the station diary. Lever was suspected by the Irish of perpetuating objectionable caricatures about them, which may have endeared him to anti-Irish readers as well as those fired by nostalgia, but his Dickensian military worlds, full of grotesques and accidents and melodrama, with illustrations by Phiz, doubtless attracted an audience reared on Thackeray, Trollope and the great man himself.

Predictably, the other pre-eminent Victorian novelist who was well read at Brancepeth was the august Edward Bulwer-Lytton: all except one of his 19 titles are still extant in the collection. The drama of Bulwer-Lytton's life seems to exemplify the raw material from which Victorian novelists drew their fictions. 'Over-educated' at home because he was thought too delicate for Eton, he had his first love affair (and wrote his first book *Ismael* about it) at sixteen. After a successful career at Cambridge where he won the poetry medal, he embarked on a 'scandalous' affair with Lady Caroline Lamb, then married Rosina Wheeler against his mother's wishes. She cut off his allowance, forcing him to write for his living, but his marriage ended in a notorious divorce. The result was a ferociously vituperative battle between Bulwer-Lytton and his wife, who published a humiliating portrait of him in her novel *Cheveley or, the Man of Honour* (1839), a novel not held at Brancepeth. Bulwer-Lytton's early bestseller that made his name, *Pelham or, Adventures of a Gentleman* [1828], was not popular at Brancepeth, nor were his two later bestsellers *The Last Days of Pompei* and *Rienzi: The Last of the Roman Tribunes*, but *The Disowned*, *Paul Clifford* (the story of a highwayman), his mystical novel *Alice* and the ghost story, *A Strange Story,* are all heavily marked by reader use. Celebrated as a novelist of ideas, Bulwer-Lytton may have been too intellectual for most of the readership at Brancepeth, but the length of his novels, some of them in four volumes, might also have had something to do with the relative unpopularity of some works. Like Dickens and Scott, Bulwer-Lytton was one of the authors considered indispensable to a library collection, with many of his titles purchased in a uniform Knebworth edition. Similarly J. Fenimore Cooper's complete works were held in an eight-volume edition published in 1883. Several of them show signs of heavy reader use, including *The Last of the Mohicans* and *The Borderers*, while *Lionel Lincoln* has the name of the bullock driver, George Parsons, and 'Brancepeth' written inside the front cover, suggesting that it was a personal copy that he left on the station. As a whole, however, Cooper's novels were not nearly as popular with readers as those of H. Rider Haggard, Robert Louis Stevenson, Stanley Weyman, Alexandre Dumas or George Whyte Melville.

It is tempting to assume that reader preferences at Brancepeth fell along gender lines, and that young and older male readers devoured Stevenson's thrilling *Kidnapped*, Whyte-Melville's *Katerfelto*, Dumas's historical adventure novel *The Page of the Duke of Savoy* and Rider Haggard's *She*, while the girls and women read the romances of Mrs Alexander and Edna Lyall. But a 1906 article by Constance Barnicoat, 'The Reading of the Colonial Girl', gives the results of a survey of 'what the girls in as many as possible of our Colonies and dependencies really do read' (939).[68] Barnicoat wrote that both British and 'Colonial and Indian' girls did indeed rate the novels of Edna Lyall at the top of their reading preferences, and liked other romance writers such as Rosa Nouchette Carey, Marie Corelli and Mrs Henry Wood. But they also liked Bulwer-Lytton, Anthony Hope, H.S. Merriman, Rider Haggard, Kipling, Conan Doyle, and Stanley Weyman. Of Weyman's 15 historical or 'costume' romances, seven were heavily used at Brancepeth, and included his novels about the Huguenots, such as *My Lady Rotha* (1894) about the St Bartholomew Massacre. Weyman's fiction was patterned on the hugely successful historical romance/adventures of Alexandre Dumas, which were also held at Brancepeth in a uniform Routledge edition and show heavy use. Anthony Hope's *The Prisoner of Zenda* (1895) and 15 other titles were all popular with Brancepeth readers, as were the works of Conan Doyle, especially *The Firm of Girdlestone* (1892) and *Strange Secrets* (1890). *The Firm of Girdlestone*, a novel of 'boom colonialism', is a satirical spoof centred on a scam to corner the South African diamond market, full of people trying to make or marry money. All the key features of the romantic/colonial adventure novel—money, scandal, intrigue and heroic daring and integrity—are grist to the mill of what Conan Doyle calls 'this small romance', which was evidently greatly enjoyed by Brancepeth readers.

Twelve of H.S. Merriman's best selling historical adventure/romance novels were held at Brancepeth and liked by readers, especially *The Slave of the Lamp* (1893) and *The Sowers* (1896). Like Stevenson and Rider Haggard, Merriman specialised in thrilling fast-paced adventure stories with a romantic element and probably appealed to the younger readers on the farm, or those looking for a night off. Captain Marryat's nautical fiction is part of the same reading taste—his most popular title at Brancepeth was *Newton Forster, or The Merchant Service* [1832], but readers also liked his land-based novels, such as *Japhet in Search of a Father* [1836], a novel about a foundling. Like escapist readers everywhere, they enjoyed Captain Mayne Reid, whose teenage adventure novels were probably also used in the schoolroom at Brancepeth.

What is clear about readers at Brancepeth is that they gravitated to the same categories of fiction loved by Victorian readers in England, America, Australia, New Zealand and the rest of the colonial world: romance (including sensational fiction) and adventure. The dominance of these genres has particular links to colonialism. Martin Green and Patrick Brantlinger have persuasively argued that adventure narratives (like *She*) were instrumental in developing the 'pervasive set of attitudes and ideas towards the rest of the world'[69] that circulated in colonial ideology and were implemented in imperial politics. As Robert Dixon has shown, the novel of imperial adventure resolved 'contradictions in the lived experience of imperialism, usually by inscribing the male reader in tales of regenerative violence on the colonial frontier'.[70]

From a quieter location on the colonial frontier, Brancepeth readers were enthusiastic consumers of these tales. There is also perhaps a sympathetic nostalgia for the frontier expressed in some of the Brancepeth popular favourites. Owen Wister's *The Virginian* (1903) was written to remember a vanished frontier world. It opens with an address to the reader:

> Had you left New York or San Francisco at ten o'clock this morning, by noon the day after tomorrow you could step out at Cheyenne. There you would stand at the heart of the world that is the subject of my picture, yet you would look around you in vain for the reality. It is a vanished world . . . [The horseman] rides in his historic yesterday . . . the last romantic figure upon our soil. (viii)

Novels about frontier life or animals, like the work of Jack London and Bret Harte, or J. Fenimore Cooper, were energetically read and circulated. It is not hard to see why men working in conditions and locations not unlike those described, might like to read about characters from a recent and more heroic past, and enjoy their affirmation of the essential qualities of the colonial male. Rolf Boldrewood, most of whose 14 titles display the damage of heavy use at Brancepeth, especially his explicitly Australian titles like *A Colonial Reformer* (1891), *Old Melbourne Memories* (1884) and *A Sydney-side Saxon* (1891), exemplified many of these characteristics—derring-do, romance, and domination of the natural and indigenous world. Steele Rudd's humorous version of the colonial working male and his manhood, *On Our Selection* (1903), possibly closer to home for Brancepeth men, was a heavily-read book, as was Henry Kingsley's *Recollections of Geoffrey Hamlyn* [1859], a family saga about early Victoria. The presence of works by Tasma, Ada Cambridge, and Mrs Praed perhaps also indicate interest in fiction about neighbouring colonies, but these do not exhibit the dirty tracks left by enthusiastic borrowers, such as those that litter the pages of James Payn, Hall Caine, Guy Boothby or Dick Donovan, early detective and mystery novels, which were perhaps passed from hand to muddy hand in the rabbiting camps.

About 140 of the 2000 books in the Brancepeth library are by American authors, which is the largest non-British category. This selection is not necessarily representative of American literature in any considered way, probably because Brancepeth was mainly buying colonial editions, and was dependent on what the publishers offered in their lists. J. Fenimore Cooper, Bret Harte and Mark Twain are significantly represented and there are four titles of Oliver Wendell Holmes, but there is no Longfellow, Louise May Alcott or Harriet Beecher Stowe. The great majority of American titles in the Brancepeth library were published in Britain—only 18 were published in the US, and a number of them were published as colonial editions. The wear and tear of the American books shows a reading preference for fiction of the outdoors, or what Frank Luther Mott calls the 'strenuous' school (Jack London, Bret Harte, J. Fenimore Cooper); [71] humorous picaresque tales or travel, especially by Mark Twain but also Kate Douglas Wiggins; and a kind of American Dream hero, from Owen Wister's *The Virginian* and A.C. Gunter's *Mr Barnes of New York* (1891) to great self-help narratives from real life like Benjamin Franklin's autobiography and Frederic T. Gammon's account of the life of President Garfield. A preference for 'masculine' fiction is clearly shown in the reading use of the American holdings. There is also a small but clear emphasis on Civil War novels, and regional or historical fiction, for example James Lane Allen's novels of Kentucky, and the novels of the American writer Winston Churchill, described by Mott as historical romances of American development that suited the patriotic climate of their times. Churchill's top-ranking bestsellers are the titles held at Brancepeth—*Richard Carvel* (1899) and *The Crisis* (1901). John Fox Jr's *The Little Shepherd of Kingdom Come* (1903), a story of an orphan's fight against the odds as he grows up into the complications of the Civil War, was also a big seller, and heavily read by Brancepeth subscribers.

The most popular American author at Brancepeth was A.C. (Arthur Clavering) Gunter, whose racy novels like *Miss Dividends*, a romance about Mormons and the American expansion in the West, have been through the mill. The hero of *Miss Dividends* (1892) appears in New York after a year in a mining camp in Southern Utah. His eye falls on a society beauty known as Miss Dividends, and he wonders, helpfully for the reader, if 'rapid Mr West should capture rich and lovely Miss East?' It's not hard to see both the relevance and the attraction of this kind of tale for the isolated working men at Brancepeth; the romantic combination of genteel money and rough manhood may have seemed particularly attractive. Gunter's most famous novel, *Mr Barnes of New York,* was rejected by Cassells and Company because Gunter would not delete 'certain unnecessary lines' from the manuscript (Frank Luther Mott believes these to have been inelegant Americanisms).[72] Gunter published it at his own expense in the summer of 1887, and the book caught on, as Mott puts it, as 'hammock reading' and on boats and trains. It became a runaway success, selling 180,000 copies in its first two years, and Gunter established a publishing house dedicated to the production of his own work. Mr Barnes is a straightforward antecedent to James Bond—a rich American travelling in Europe who is known internationally as a crack shot. He finds himself in the middle of a Corsican vendetta in which he is also able to demonstrate his prowess as a surgeon, and through various romantic complications he brings the plot to a dramatic but successful conclusion. Gunter's novels are very close to dime novels. Although they have romance plots, the action is bloody and exciting, melodramatic rather than sentimental. Mr Barnes is the popular model of a New World hero—resourceful, accomplished in frontier skills, he can patch up a leg and shoot to kill at twenty paces—but he demonstrates these skills in the more refined atmosphere of old Europe, where they stand out as manly and red-blooded. The runaway success of Gunter's novels suggests a reflexive colonial fantasy in the twist they bring to an old formula—the New World offers a reinvigorated hero who brings the mythologies of the frontier to the old world. There may have been a special connection for Brancepeth readers to novels about other colonial and Anglophone societies, demonstrating the varied, but also reassuringly similar, iterations of the British world as it liked to imagine itself.

The Brancepeth collection contained a smattering of European (mostly French) literature, including works by Tolstoy, Zola, de Maupassant, de Joncourt, Daudet, Balzac and Flaubert. But readers' main interest in reading beyond a familiar set of genres and settings was expressed in their use of the small 'miscellaneous' segment of the library. They liked travel books, for instance Sir Harry Johnstone's *David Livingstone*, Grogan and Sharpe's *From the Cape to Cairo*, and John Foster Fraser's *The Real Siberia*, which features photographs of decapitated Chinese peasants, and works by Constance Gordon Cumming, Sarah Duncan (*A Girl in the Karpathians*) and Isabella Bird. Biographies and autobiographies included *The Life of General Gordon*, Froude's *Life of Beaconsfield* and *Reminiscences of Carlyle*, the Earl of Dundonald's *The Autobiography of a Seaman*, Charlotte Yonge's *Marie Antoinette*, Fanny Kemble's *Record of a Girlhood* and the standout favourite, Benjamin Franklin's *Autobiography*, one of the top ten most-used books. But what is striking about the 'miscellaneous' list in the catalogue is precisely the miscellany. Beginning with Macaulay's essays and speeches, Carlyle's essays and *Sartor Resartus*, and Boswell's *Life of Johnson,* it quickly turns into a portrait of impressions, likes, and dislikes, current trends. There is travel writing; the rather clean copy of Smiles's *Self-Help*; collections of tales such as Hawthorne's *Tanglewood Tales*; biographies; social texts such as *Intemperance: the Great Source of Crime* and *Lives of Criminals*; *Banking Under Difficulties*, a book about life on the Australian goldfields; *The Practical Carpenter, Swiss Family Robinson,* and a lot of books about dogs, horses, poaching, hunting and fishing. These are the sort of books that might land on the unorganised shelf of any reading family, reflecting flows and shifts of interest, gifts and impulse buys.

Strikingly, there are only two New Zealand books among the heavily-used books at Brancepeth. One is F.E. Maning's *Old New Zealand, by a Pakeha Maori*, a book of perennial interest to New Zealand readers, and the other is William Churchward's historical novel set in the New Zealand wars, *Jem Peterkin's Daughter* (1892). Featuring a former whaler who has risen to 'superlative affluence' in Auckland and has a 'singularly beautiful' daughter, Jemima, with his Māori wife, the novel's clumsy prose stirs in every possible cliché of New Zealand colonial history—Pākehā Māori, warring suitors, Hauhau with 'cruel wild . . . faces' and 'crafty deep-set eyes'; a gallant independent hero, Jack Brett, who has honorable intentions, recognises the injustices being inflicted on Māori, and is saved from 'immolation' by the hei tiki he wears round his neck; and a gone-to-the-bad vicious British officer. In other words, it is a novel full of grotesque caricatures. With the exception of the beautiful heroine, who is transparently a colonial prize to be carried off to England, embodying as she does the best of interracial opportunities, Māori are 'niggers' or 'demons'. Churchward's novel exemplifies the contradictions of the colonial frontier both in its mixed stereotypes and its narrative actions, but can only resolve them by removing the hero and his bride safely to the home country. Perhaps 'new chum' readers thought Churchward would enlighten them, but the stereotypes and open racism of Churchward's novel do not mirror the more complicated situation at Brancepeth, where upper-class Māori were received as guests in the house and varying levels and kinds of interaction took place on the farm between Māori and Europeans every day. Despite Hugh Beetham's instruction to treat Māori with kindness, racism of various sorts was alive and well, as the station diary reveals when Miller expostulates against the body odour or working habits of Māori employees, or notes that the Brocken cook said he 'only swore at Maoris' (though he was dismissed because of it).[73] Perhaps the popularity of *Jem Peterkin's Daughter*, badly written and formulaic as it was, suggests a set of local recognitions.

Walter Besant's novels played to the entire mixed palette of interests of Brancepeth readers, which may be why his books constitute the largest group of any author's works (41 titles) and show consistently heavy signs of use. Trained as a mathematician, Besant was Senior Professor at the Royal College of Mauritius for six years. When he returned to Britain, he embarked on the life of a professional writer, initially with his co-author James Rice. Their first novel, *Ready Money Mortiboy*, was an enormous success, as testified to by its battered and beaten condition at Brancepeth. A prodigal son story, it deploys the usual Victorian plot mechanisms of inheritances, complex family relationships, and reversals of character and fortunes. Writing about his first book later in life, Besant described it (immodestly) as:

> The profligate with his dreadful past behind him; the low woman whom he has married; the gambler; his associate; the memory of robbery and of prison; and with the new influences around him—the girl he loves, pure and sweet, and innocent; the boy whom he picks out of the gutter; the wreck of his old

> father—form together a group which I have always thought to be commanding. Strong, attractive, interesting, much beyond anything in the ordinary run of fiction.[74]

Besant covered the literary spectrum of the nineteenth century. He wrote historical romances, the futurist novel *The Revolt of Man*, story collections, adventure and mystery novels, contemporary romances, novels of faith and doubt, and 'social-problem' novels. *All Sorts and Conditions of Men* (1882) is about the founding of a People's Palace in Stepney, and features an heiress in disguise, allegorically named Angela Messenger, who revives a downtrodden part of the East End and its labour force by setting up a workplace run on safe, improving and liberal lines (the women play lawn tennis at lunchtime). *The Children of Gibeon* (1887) deals with the exploitation of female labour in the East End. Besant was instrumental in setting up an actual People's Palace in 1887, was treasurer of the Palestine Exploration Fund and helped found the Society of Authors, which professionalised writing as an occupation. Why were Besant's novels so popular at Brancepeth? Many of them feature characters who return (like Dick Mortiboy) from the colonies or go out to them, and the combination of rip-roaring plots, social improvement and geographic range seems to have been irresistible. The displacement of some of Besant's characters may also have had a resonance with Brancepeth readers, well used to a social world full of isolated and itinerant men. Besant wrote of Dick Mortiboy, whose return to England, as a consequence of his dishevelled past, is ultimately tragic, that

> Love could not be his, nor honours, such as comes to most men, nor the quiet *vie de famille*, which is all that life really has to give worth having.[75]

But the Queen of the Brancepeth library, in all its many shapes, was romance. Janice Radway has said that though romances purport to be 'new' stories, in fact they re-tell a single tale whose final outcome their readers already know.[76] The huge popularity of romance for nineteenth-century readers, including those at Brancepeth, can perhaps be attributed to the genre's reassuring and reinforcing repetitions. Historical, adventure, mystery, sensation, society, colonial: the many tributaries of the mighty romance river flowed through all aspects of Victorian fiction and infected all its ideologies. Romance naturalised the relationship of conquered peoples to the nation that had invaded them (crudely shown in the tale of Jem Peterkin's daughter); it rescued the New Woman, brought solace to the unlucky, allowed society heroines to find their destined place, and perpetuated the idea that families and nations alike were generated by the fated discovery of a perfect match. Brancepeth readers loved romance in all its manifestations, and like the great Victorian novel-reading public, they loved it more than anything else. The clutch of writers in the Brancepeth collection who fall unequivocally into this category include Ouida, Rita, Mrs Alexander, Annie Swan, Blanche Atkinson, Lynn Linton, Rosa N. Carey, Marie Corelli, Charlotte Yonge and Edna Lyall. In a library which contained over 2000 titles by around 600 authors,[77] the bosomy and overpowering category of romance is anaemically represented by only a slim list of names. But many writers better known for other genres, like Besant and Dickens, for example, also deploy romance conventions in their novels.

Several of Mrs Alexander's very grubby nine novels have been signed by Thyra Beetham as a teenager, but are so heavily used that they must have had a wider readership than the two teenage girls who used the library. Alexander's novels revolve around a young girl torn between fortune, family and love, a romance scenario repeated everywhere. The cliché-ridden plots are peppered with 'kindly' clergymen, innocent heiresses, very 'English' Englishmen (whose nationality is demonstrated by a 'vague, instinctive sense of justice'), unscrupulous relations, and redundant characters quickly killed off by convenient machinations of empire, such as an infant 'cut off by a few hours of cholera in India', in *Her Dearest Foe* (1899, 12). Alexander's characters declaim sentences like 'Your game is over, crafty bloodhound!' (*The Heritage of Langdale,* 1894, 419), and are subject to forged wills and peremptory changes in fortune. Motherlessness is often a founding condition of the plot of a romance novel (as it is in Dickens): Annie Swan, whose *A Victory Won* (1895) was a heavily read book, described it as the 'first real desolation of life' (156). Whether the heroine is triumphant in her innocence and virtue or dies for love, as in Lucas Malet's *Colonel Enderby's Wife*, the reading satisfactions of romance reside in its variations on a theme, a theme whose ceaseless variations make it a protean beast. But it is important to remember that for a remote, overwhelmingly male and often lonely readership at Brancepeth, romance novels may have provided the only means of familial comfort at hand, offering a hope of a settled future beyond the reader's unsettled immediate circumstances.

The author nominated by Colonial and British girls at the top of their reading lists was Edna Lyall, the pen name of Ada Ellen Bayly, who wrote novels-with-a-purpose and romances, as well historical novels dealing with questions of faith and freedom. *In the Golden Days* (1891) set in the reign of Charles II, was popular at Brancepeth, as was *To Right the Wrong* (1894) a novel about John Hampden, 'statesman of the Commonwealth', set during the Civil War. The most popular of her extant books (Brancepeth held 12 titles of which only seven survive) were her romances *A Hardy Norseman* (1890) and *Wayfaring Men* (1897). Both these novels (which repeat characters from her earlier novels *Donovan* and *Knight Errant*) are about constancy, the equivalent of religious faith for lovers. *Wayfaring Men*, about an orphaned boy, Ralph, who is taken in by a dishonest guardian and has to spend some time as a young man cast out and wandering on the Scottish moors, may have struck a chord as Brancepeth readers saw the swaggers flow through the station, but it is also a precursor of J.B. Priestley's 1929 novel *The Good Companions*, describing as it does the life of a band of traveling actors. The stage is a model of decorum in comparison to the goings-on at a country-house, as one of the characters, a famous actress who has married a villain, points out

> a fortnight of country-house life, in such a place as Mearn Castle, makes one realise evil more keenly than years on the stage. (201)

New Zealand newspapers reprinted a number of interviews with Edna Lyall, whose view that novels 'can be made a great means of good' perhaps enticed parents everywhere to buy her books for their daughters—the Brancepeth novels have Thyra Beetham's name in them. Rosa N. Carey's *Wooed and Married* (1893), which was very popular at Brancepeth, hit all the keynotes of Victorian romantic fiction. The governess heroine is an orphan, given to unruly emotions that distress her saintly clergyman brother (who dies young) and which must be tamed before she can accomplish her fate of marrying the tragic hero after his first wife dies. It is effectively *Jane Eyre* embellished and decorated with more pronounced stereotypes, which would not have been a disincentive to most readers. The orphan governess heroine, Dymphna, is perpetually childlike, a 'little figure, veiled and cloaked', and her idol, the first wife of the man she loves, is called Honor and dies of fever in Florence. Brancepeth readers were not alone in their appetite for banal and clichéd romantic novels like Carey's. Her first book *Nellie's Memories*, sold over 10,000 copies, but her holdings at Brancepeth, 11 titles, were moderate. Carey, like many authors in the Brancepeth library, has one well-loved novel, which represents perhaps a certain section of the readership, or a particular reader who read and re-read it. However, Brancepeth readers seem likely to have agreed with Joanna Seaton, an omnivorous reader of light novels in Ellen Thorneycroft Fowler's very successful *Concerning Isabel Carnaby* (1899). Joanna declares to Drusilla Dallicott, a person who only reads Sir Walter Scott, Jane Austen, Plato and Aristotle, 'But don't you think that novels of all kinds—provided of course that they are good ones—help one to understand human nature?'

In the twenty-first century, the Brancepeth library seems an antiquarian relic of Victorian literature, a still-life composition of rows of rusty brown books enclosed in their glass cases. But when the books are opened, they come to life in so many ways. There are more tidal flows and pools of reader interest in the whole collection than it is possible to talk about here. I have not, for instance, discussed poetry, of which there was a small collection in the Brancepeth library: 21 titles, which included a heavily annotated edition of Milton, collected works of Pope, Burns, Scott and Lindsay Gordon, and a selection of Tennyson, who was the most popular nineteenth-century poet and who is referred to a number of times by name in the Brancepeth letters and diaries. 'Poetry' also included Shakespeare, Macaulay's *Lays of Ancient Rome* and *The Bab Ballads*. Other than Milton and Shakespeare, which may have been used as teaching texts, since the annotations tend to be explicatory, the poetry books are very lightly used. Nor have I discussed the 'History' section (42 titles), which contains a mix of canonical historical works (Carlyle, Macaulay, Gibbon), military history, ten titles from a popular historical series, 'Story of the Nation', and books about empire and New Zealand (Seeley's *Expansion of England*, Kerry-Nicholls' *The King Country*). Inevitably, like the library's original readers, I have had to find a way through the collection, running a finger or an eye along the shelves, swayed by mood and weather and time of day. I have chosen certain paths, 'separating out of the present a certain specific "past"', to borrow Donald Preziosi's description of how museums work.[78] By concentrating on fiction, the largest category of the collection and where the majority of Brancepeth readers spent their time, I have tracked the books they held most dear.

CHAPTER SIX

The Constant Reader

'The Constant Reader' was a humorous piece by W.B. Jerrold that appeared in Dickens's periodical *Household Words* in 1851. Like his more famous father Douglas,[1] Blanchard Jerrold was a close friend and literary colleague of Dickens, and earned his living as a journalist, playwright and novelist. 'The Constant Reader' paints an exaggerated and satirical portrait of a professional writer who is 'known wherever an alphabet is known' and whose 'work is unceasing and reward nil':

> My acquirements are illimitable. I can read and write at one and the same moment. Most authors can write on only one question at a time: I can tackle fifty . . . Nothing escapes me, from misdemeanour to murder; from tittle-tattle to high treason. I am, it is well-known, competent to discuss the merits of every question that ever engaged the attention of mankind.[2]

Jerrold's satiric target is the Grub Street hack who 'has not risen from his seat in fifteen months', but 'The Constant Reader' could almost have been written about John Vaughan Miller, except that he was only twelve when it was published. Miller's activity as a reader and writer was unceasing. Nothing escaped him. He wrote as an authority on everything, from the Indian Mint to Marie Corelli. He read all the new novels and, no doubt, re-read many older ones. He read poetry, essays, biography, history, collections of letters, new works on science and religion and as many periodicals and newspapers as he could get his hands on. Miller exemplified what was described in *Fraser's Magazine* in 1847 as 'book-love',[3] and there is perhaps a sense in which his love of books compensated him for the deprivation of domestic affections he endured in his long years at Brancepeth. Whatever the motivations behind his near-obsessive reading and writing, the record that he left in the station archive, his newspaper articles and in the books themselves combine to offer a rare and detailed depiction of the reader at work.

The difference between Miller and Jerrold's 'constant reader' is that Miller was not a professional journalist, although he often behaved as if he was, writing pieces for the newspaper that showed off his knowledge and education. He particularly prided himself on his literary skills, which demonstrated how well-read he was and conformed to general ideas about what a 'good' reader would have in his repertoire. Everyone who read Miller's newspaper articles would have assimilated the idea that certain values and expectations attach to reading, and that there are literary hierarchies of readers as well as authors. Miller showed off his readerly superiority by his constant use of quotations, references and allusions, and his forthright judgements about literary quality. But Brancepeth readers would also have absorbed ideas about how and what readers should read from the books themselves. Such questions not only lie behind the practices of actual readers at Brancepeth, but form part of the larger dynamic of 'book-love' that was a key element of Victorian literature and literary debate.

As already discussed, the depth and range of Victorian literary culture in colonial New Zealand (as in other settler colonies) can be measured in, for example, the expanding book market, the proliferation of colonial editions,[4] and the growth of public libraries.[5] The general 'literariness' of colonial newspapers is another indicator, as expressed in literary columns and notices, advertisements for new books, and the range and density of references and allusions employed by editors and leader writers in their articles. At the same time, the perennial question of what it means to be a good reader was a point of tension, provoked by the extraordinary growth in the numbers of published books, working authors and mass markets in the 1890s.[6] The boom in popular fiction, lamented by George Gissing,[7] and by Thackeray who called it jam tarts for the mind,[8] is reflected in anxiety about reading even in small rural towns in the Wairarapa. In a 1906 lecture on 'Books' to the YMCA Literary and Debating Society, for example, a Mr D. McGregor described the way some subscribers used the Masterton public library with palpable alarm:

> Some people . . . go and change their books every day! What sort of reading do you call that? (*Wairarapa Daily Times* 18 May 1906)

McGregor's concern about a decline in the quality of general reading taste (or in readers themselves) is also internal to Victorian literature, as a close inspection of the fictional New Woman's bookshelves reveals. In fiction, literary knowledge is a valuable attribute, demonstrating a character's judgement, authority and, usually, class. Nineteenth-century novels are full of characters who assert their status and expertise via literary knowledge. Each time Miller put pen to paper, he demonstrated his acute sense of what was at stake in being a reader, and almost every book opened by the Brancepeth subscribers would also have brought the issue to their attention.

Readers are always harder to find in history than books.[9] If we are lucky, books escape the decluttering instinct and remain on the shelves for decades, even generations; but the readers who enjoyed them leave few identifying traces, unless they are driven, like Miller, to correct, translate, emend and comment on what they find on the page. Miller's track through the Brancepeth library is wide and visible, though it is certain that the trail he left does not encompass everything he read and enjoyed. His self-presentation as a man of letters was the substance and in the end perhaps the purpose of his life, and there can have been few books in the library he did not open. His sense of a literary self was complex, profound and closely tied to the ways in which he resisted—or perhaps it is more accurate to say held himself apart from—his working situation. About half of his published articles have a literary focus or frame of reference, and their pseudonymous signatures (Nemo, Iconoclast, Jocosa Mordax, Timothy, Senex, Publicola) played to a readership that was familiar with Latin, Greek and the Bible. His references were both classical and contemporary. In his leading article 'Gracefulness of Speech' on 19 January 1898, just to give one example, he made reference to Carlyle, Hume, Cicero, Quintilian, Swift, Bacon and Dr Johnson, while his pieces about Marie Corelli, Sarah Grand and Lucas Malet reveal his more current reading. In short, Miller's writing reflected a general cultural expectation that a wide and deep literary knowledge would be part of a reader's mental furniture.

In Victorian fiction, endless possibilities, both serious and comic, gather round the figure of the aspiring literary man or woman, and their abundance demonstrates the cultural centrality of books and reading. The value and function of literary knowledge is dramatised in many of the more heavily-read books in the Brancepeth library. In Trollope's *Orley Farm*, Mary Snow is rescued from her drunken father by Felix Graham, a lawyer with prospects, and is then moulded to be his perfect wife by Mrs Thomas who runs a school for girls. Every week Mary finds time from a mountain of darning and mending to write her protector a letter (a task intended to hone her turns of phrase and modes of address), and to plough painfully through *Rasselas*, a study that Mrs Thomas intends as an initiation 'into that course of novel-reading which has become necessary for a British lady' (335). This valorisation of reading sometimes appeared in the form of an elaborate in-joke for the sophisticated reader, or a nod and a wink at the ongoing debate about 'good' and 'bad' reading. A character who despises novels and poetry in Walter Besant's *The Master Craftsman* (1896) sees a bookshelf filled with authors such Herbert Spencer and John Stuart Mill and exclaims approvingly: 'Heavens! What a serious library of solid reading'. One of the most popular Victorian novels—and certainly in the top ten at Brancepeth—was Besant's 1883 novel *The Golden Butterfly* (written with his co-author James Rice), in which Gilead Beck, a simple man who has made a fortune in California, comes to London to spend it. A number of possibilities are suggested to him: funding research, a National Theatre, supporting ragged and hungry boys. But what he wants is to host a literary dinner at which the guests will be Carlyle, Huxley, Darwin, Tennyson, Swinburne, George Eliot, Trollope, and

> 'Give me Charles Reade, Sir', said Gilead Beck. 'He is the novelist they like on our side.' (181)

The banquet scene in *The Golden Butterfly* is full of jokes for readers. Beck is a colonial buffoon, whose lack of literary sophistication is a comic measure of the distance between the metropolis and its colonies (particularly America). He mixes up the writers and their works and never realises he is at a table full of impostors. Nevertheless, his enthusiasm ironically expresses the value of literary capital in a way that Victorian fiction generally affirms when he says, about the banquet, that it seems to him as if 'for the first time, his wealth was about to bring him something worth having' (190).

Literary pretensions are always good for humour, while making a serious point. In Sarah Grand's *Babs the Impossible,* a popular novel with echoes of *Emma* and *Cranford* that was heavily read at Brancepeth, Mr Jellybond Tinney is a fake scholar—as readers would know as soon as they saw his name. His library at the 'Swiss Cottage' where he lives is

> . . . lined from floor to ceiling with learned books, handsomely bound. The books on the upper shelves were dummies, but that did not spoil the effect. Books were always lying about, some open on tables, or piled up on chairs, or even on the floor, as if in constant use . . . (129)

Mr Jellybond Tinney, who is of course a dummy himself, is caught out when he asks Montacute, brother of the heroine, what the book in his hand is:

> 'It's Virgil', said Montacute. 'In the Greek I suppose', said Mr Jellybond Tinney, blinking. (233)

The joke is further enriched because, far from being the studious academic youth Tinney takes him for, Montacute is an indolent boy who reads the classics because he must, but would rather lie in bed reading *The Woman in White.* But the joke on Tinney is also at the serious heart of Victorian literary culture. A 'real' reader would have more than a passing acquaintance with the classical canon and the serious thinkers of the past, and anyone wanting to pass themselves off as a member, or an aspiring member (Jellybond Tinney is courting Montacute's widowed mother) of the upper classes will always be caught out by deficiencies in classical learning. The opposite is also the case—a character fallen on hard times but who is really a gentleman will, at a crucial point in the narrative, produce evidence of classical knowledge as proof of gentility.

The more popular the author, the bigger the claim to

literary knowledge and insider status. Bestselling Victorian novels frequently expect readers to pick up multiple references both to the literature of the day and the great traditions of English literature. Popular authors, too, have literary reputations to make. M.E. Braddon's novels are a fine example: *Aurora Floyd* is full of references to *Othello*, *The Scarlet Letter*, Tennyson, Browning, and Dickens. Like her contemporaries Mrs Henry Wood, Marie Corelli, Walter Besant, Lucas Malet and Sarah Grand, Braddon refers to a rich literary culture, which reinforces her authorial claim to be taken seriously and includes the reader in the literary club. Picking up the references and correctly interpreting allusions or literary clues about characters allows the reader to consider themselves highly accomplished, or, conversely, helps fortify the conviction that they are not *only* readers of popular fiction. Most of the books and authors alluded to in Mary Braddon's novels are held in the Brancepeth library, which aimed to be more than simply a collection of dog-eared romances; its readers, especially Miller, were keen to display their literariness.

Literariness is more than simply a recreational taste, and more than 'book-love'. Reading is often a kind of compulsion, and self-conscious literariness is what transforms a liking for reading as a pastime into a set of skills and dispositions that allow a reader to place himself or herself in relation to literature. The literary reader exhibits a breadth of knowledge, an expertise, a familiarity that makes them 'at home' in literature, able to make fine discriminations, bring in supplementary information, write marginal glosses or critiques, create hierarchies of writers and books, and all the while, demonstrate their own refinement.[10] Most Brancepeth readers were more like Gilead Beck, reading what they knew they liked, than poor Mary Snow labouring through *Rasselas*, but that is not to say that they weren't aware of themselves as participants in a highly calibrated reading culture, where reading counted for something, and many of them drew attention to their reading presence by writing their names, dates and comments in the books.

Literariness also has a vital role to play in the negotiation of place. For a colonial reader, the connection to the print culture of London, New York, Sydney, Paris and Rome (both ancient and modern) was a vital source of agency, a way of belonging despite the fact of distance. You didn't have to live in London to know literature or, indeed, 'life'—a precept constantly iterated by fictional characters. Margaret, the heroine of Rita's *Dame Durden* describes her cloistered life thus:

> I have lived in a world of books you know. I suppose one must learn something of life in that way. (215)

Why else would John Vaughan Miller write articles on Marie Corelli for the *Wairarapa Daily Times*? As Kate Flint has said, to read is to become part of a broader community, sharing 'horizons of expectations' built up through common reading material.[11] Reading and writing about the latest novels and periodicals joined Miller to the world at large, and to a local community in which other readers acknowledged and responded to his expertise as they read his letter to the editor about 'Good Literature', or articles in which he fulminated against Lucas Malet and Sarah Grand. Reading and writing about reading, in the many forms in which Miller does it—articles, letters, diary entries and marginalia—is not merely self-expression but also dialogue, with the text, the author, and other readers. It is a way of expressing a citizenship not circumscribed by proximity. This is the 'imagined community' of print culture famously postulated by Benedict Anderson,[12] where people who do not know each other share an identity via print. It should be added that the point of many of Miller's texts is not only to claim a broad and horizontal comradeship with other imagined readers, but to demonstrate an ascendancy of learning and informed opinion over them.

Within the broader horizon of shared expectations about literary and cultural capital, Miller was a special case. He made it his business to be up with the world of letters (and current affairs) despite his long office hours and the tribulations of a rural location. But, as some of the responses to his articles, letters and poems show, he was not the only member of a literati among the readers of the *Wairarapa Daily Times*, or at Brancepeth, where there were a few kindred spirits. And though no-one seems to have matched Miller's ferocity of purpose, Brancepeth library subscribers (and indeed most of the non-subscribers on the farm)[13] would have been aware that literature in some sense defined what it meant to be British and 'civilised', even if they only went to the library to borrow detective novels by Dick Donovan or read the papers for the fifteen minutes that the rules allowed.

Who, aside from Miller, were the readers at Brancepeth? What drew their attention, and what is it possible to know about them? Are they beyond the range of historical research, as Robert Darnton has suggested the great mass of readers are?[14] Only some of the Brancepeth readers have left physical traces of their reading in the books, though many left anonymous traces of their lives, which will be discussed in the next chapter. There are some formal records of readers—the library subscriptions are recorded in the station ledgers—and the station diary notes that new lists were put up in the library every quarter, though none of these have survived. The borrowing habits of individual readers have unfortunately been lost with the Lending Book, and their individual tastes have disappeared with the Suggestion Book. Subscribers ran at about 30–40 a year; the numbers fluctuated on account of seasonal workers. There was an outer layer of non-subscribing readers, who are occasionally glimpsed in the station diary, such as when Miller comments that Clyffe Taylor, one of the shepherds, told him 'in answer to my question' that Chisholm (a rabbiter) 'avails himself of the library books that Taylor takes out—altho he is too mean to subscribe himself' (31 July 1906). There must always have been shadow readers beyond the subscribers—family, fellow workers, friends and bludgers, visitors to the homestead—although Library Rule No. 8 specifically forbids members lending books to non-members. In the search for individual readers caught in the act of reading, the small number who made their opinions known in some material way must stand in for their invisible companions.

What seems clear from the surviving records is that membership of the Brancepeth library, and especially the Library Committee, conferred prestige on a select group within the larger community on the station. The core long-term members (about 15) were closely associated with the homestead and at the more professional end of the pay scale. The committee roles (Treasurer, Secretary, Librarian) revolved around the same names, and it is likely that these people had a sense of ownership about the collection and the space in which it was housed. The library was a social gathering place, a function that Miller captures when he describes the fug of four men smoking in the room in September 1894, or when he writes that the men gathered there for a presentation to Garratt at his resignation in 1901. For a number of years, the head shepherd (Hugh Wilson) and overseer (George Garratt) shared the role of Treasurer on the Library Committee. The librarian, who received a payment for his work, was the carpenter William Richards; although afflicted with a drinking problem which caused him to have periodic binges and dismissals, Richards remained at the station for many years until his sudden death in 1907, when, Miller writes, he dropped dead on the verandah.

Names found in the books are often those of long-term employees. George Parsons, for example, whose name is written in J. Fenimore Cooper's *Lionel Lincoln* and Wilkie Collins's *The New Magdalen*, worked on the station at various times during the 1880s and 1890s, as a bullock-driver and rabbiter. He was a long-term library subscriber. In June 1894, Miller recorded in the station ledger that Parsons 'resigned from the library on his wife's orders', but by September he was being charged again as he was still 'drawing books as usual'. Hugh Wilson—the man who annoyed Miller by skiving off work with an inflamed eyelid in August 1897—was a long-term subscriber and keen reader, but Wilson, Garratt and Richards, unlike Parsons, did not leave their names in the books. Some inscriptions commemorate gifts to the library: Miss Westall, the governess, presented a copy of George Frederic Turner's *Frost and Friendship* to the library in 1907, the year she left, and Michael Ryan, the roadman who was a constant presence on the library committee presented three books in 1905.[15] J.J. (Joseph) Guest,[16] who was the schoolmaster in 1895 and who was 'invited to resign' in 1896 (Miller notes in the ledger that Guest left at his own request on 21 December to prepare for his exams by getting drunk at Taueru), presented a copy of Grant Allen's detective novel *The Scallywag* to the library in May 1896. Chas Bryant wrote his name twice in Rolf Boldrewood's *A Colonial Reformer* on the back page and cover, once in the phrase 'Chas. Bryant In the Year of Our Lord 1898', perhaps simply recording when he read it. Bryant is not recorded in the ledger, and may have been a passing visitor or even a swagger. Several other books bear the names of donors, including one presented to the school children by the School Inspector.

The most frequent signature in the Brancepeth books is a set of initials, R.C.C., which appear in at least 30 books by a range of authors, among them J.M. Barrie, Walter

Besant, Eden Philpotts, Max Pemberton, Captain Marryat, Nat Gould, George Gissing, E. Phillips Oppenheim, Charles Nordhoff and Hume Nisbet. There is no clear pattern to R.C.C.'s books, and no clue as to who owned the initials. Perhaps the books were part of a small collection which was given to the library, or left behind by someone, or bought as a job lot—Miller once recorded inspecting some 'second' books with Hugh Beetham. Like the majority of Brancepeth readers, R.C.C. remains unknown, and his initials speak of a reading history which cannot be interpreted beyond the probable fact of possession and a taste which is popular and mainstream.

A number of other names are scattered through the collection, many of them the names of men who worked on the station, who seem to have left books behind when they moved on. Edward McLean, a rabbiter who ran a poison gang, left his name and a date, 'Jany 25th, 1894', in Marie Corelli's *Barabbas*, and 'E McLean, Hineroa, Brancepeth, May 26 94', in *The Fatal Illness of Frederick The Noble*, a controversial book by the British physician Sir Morrell McKenzie about his treatment of the German crown prince for throat cancer. Both *Barabbas* (1893) and *The Fatal Illness of Frederick The Noble* (1888) were recently published, perhaps bought by McLean before he took up a life as a rabbiter. Like many others, he may have been a casualty of the 1890s depression, or an unlucky immigrant who couldn't find appropriate work. William Woof, also a rabbiter from 1887–1890, wrote 'Wm Woof' in George Sand's *Little Fadette* and G. Manville Fenn's *The Parson O'Dumford* with 'Wellington N.Z. March 4th/87', the latter suggesting he may have brought the book with him to Brancepeth.[17] James Alexander Driscoll wrote his full name and '38 Hiropi Street Wellington Sth' in a copy of Stanley Weyman's *The Red Cockade*, and R. Cade inscribed Mrs Oliphant's *Miss Marjoribanks*, a beloved book at Brancepeth, with 'R. Cade Ponto Brancepeth Masterton Wellington New

Zealand' (Ponto and Hineroa were out-stations, which gives a glimpse of the movement of books around the landscape). A marked passage in *Miss Marjoribanks* reveals someone's pleasure in the text. The marker, who may have been Cade though the novel has seen a lot of wear and tear indicating there were many readers (or multiple re-readings), has double-underlined 'take-off' in the sentence below, and written in the margin 'x good':

> Mrs Woodburn liked nothing so well as to sit by the fire and read novels and 'take-off' her neighbours (18)

J. Parker wrote his or her name three times in Benjamin Franklin's *Autobiography*; M.E. Parsons and S. Roberts left their names in copies of Trollope's novels, and H.W. Bridge in Thackeray's *Round About Papers*. But there is nothing else of these readers except the bare fact of their names and an assumption that they probably owned those books before adding them to the library shelves. What these inscriptions do show however, is that some of the men working in the rabbiting camps and out-stations, engaged in dirty hard work, isolated, cold and lonely, with no domestic comforts and nasty food, were educated readers who carried books around with them and took pleasure in reading.

The presence of men like these on Brancepeth was likely part of what encouraged the Beethams to provide a station library for the workforce in the first place. But it is also clear from inscriptions and marginalia that the Beetham family used the station library extensively. The general invisibility of women readers in the library subscriptions is countered by their presence on the Library Committee and their names in the books. Perhaps the library had a secret life during the day, when women used it, or perhaps the books took a route through the homestead before entering the collection. There is no hard evidence that women who worked in the house or who were married to men working on the station were using the library, but the wives of men with subscriptions very likely shared the books. Thyra and Weva Beetham wrote their names in a number of books, including '{Thyra Jimmy}'[18] inside the front cover of Annie Swan's *Sheila,* and 'May 29th 1898 Brancepeth Masterton T.B.' in Edna Lyall's *Wayfaring Men.* Thyra was 16 in 1898 and being taught at home, so some of these books may have been part of her tutoring, but it seems likely she sometimes jotted down her name and the actual day she was reading as a nod to memory. Her initials 'T.T.B' appear with dates scribbled in pencil on the corner of a page in *David Copperfield* 'May 5th, 1897' and Charlotte Yonge's *The Heir of Redcliffe* 'Oct 10th 1897'. Four years after Thyra read *The Heir of Redcliffe,* William Alden published a short piece in the *New York Times Saturday Review,* recalling it as the book of its year in 1853: he describes everyone reading and ' weeping over the death of Sir Guy', and parents urging their sons and daughters to read it for the good influence it 'could not fail to exercise over them'.[19] Although Thyra was reading it more than forty years after first publication, the novel still had a reputation for moral instruction that appealed to governesses and mothers. On the sketchy evidence of Ruth Beetham's reading taste, Charlotte Yonge's characteristic heroine, 'the perfect Churchwoman . . . strong in her faithful following of duty'[20] would have been an attraction. It is quite likely to have been Ruth Beetham's own copy of *The Heir of Redcliffe* that Thyra read, as some Bidwill family books are in the Brancepeth library.

According to Dulcie Gillespie-Needham, Ruth Beetham was the dominant force behind the Brancepeth collection.[21] Although her reading is only intermittently visible in the library through a sprinkling of annotations, she was a strong presence in the selection and purchase of books, and a more regular and serious reader than the annotations in her handwriting reveal. The station diary records a number of occasions when she returned from Wellington with books for the library, or when she ordered books independently and was reimbursed for them, and her taste seems likely to have dominated the Library Committee's selections. She may also be responsible for other markings in the books, such as passages marked with a pencil line and crosses. Where Ruth Beetham is visible, it is through her highly identifiable handwriting. She has corrected a misbinding in Mrs Hungerford's *Mrs Geoffrey*, alerting the reader that page 225 is 'two pages further on', and inserted a gloss inside the back cover of Henry S. Merriman's *In Kedar's Tents*: 'Kedar was the Arabian Desert—"Kedar's Tents" means houses in the wilderness of this world'. Her most extensive glosses are in Marie Corelli's *Boy*, a short novel about an indolent woman, Mrs D'Arcy-Muir, whose 'slight degree' of lower class than her husband is demonstrated in 'slovenly' behaviour and reprehensible parenting. The titular 'Boy', whose infant charms and winning ways promise a glittering future, is neglected and spoiled. Ruth Beetham's reaction to *Boy* begins on the title page:

> Very good There are thousands of Mrs D'Arcy Muirs + Poo Sings in England + NZ

Boy's father, the Honourable James D'Arcy-Muir, also known as 'Poo Sing' (which, in Corelli's sickly style, is Boy's babyish lisp of 'Poor Thing'), is a drunk and a gentleman. Ruth Beetham has marked the speech in which he asserts his gentlemanliness: 'My father was a gentleman,—and my grandfather was a gentleman—and my great-grandfather was a gentleman . . . '; and underlined, probably in approval, the narrator's scornful remark:

> Gentleman! Of course he was a gentleman! His <u>language proved it.</u> (10)

Also underlined is the description of how Mrs D'Arcy-Muir cuts her 'abundance' of hair short '<u>as soon as she married</u>'

to save herself the bother of arranging it, as is a description of her practice of wearing a 'comfortable sort of 'get-about' costume . . . morning, noon and night' (12). A page further on, Corelli's rhetorical flight about how the 'fresh rosy lips of a little child' might touch a drunkard's heart and move it to penitence and reform, has been marked, and the phrase 'As for any sacredness in the life of a child' underscored.

What does this underlining 'say', over a century later, without more explanation by the original reader? H.J. Jackson observes that marginalia has a number of functions, among them a dialogue with the author and the text, self-expression, communication intended for someone else (as a set of instructive annotations in a gift, for example, by what she calls the 'sociable' reader), and note-taking for future reference.[22] Ruth Beetham's notes in *Boy* have elements of all these purposes. She seems to be expressing agreement with a set of social observations she can link to her own environment, as well as drawing attention to specific examples that arouse a kind of class and gender indignation—slovenliness in the matter of hair and dress for instance. The bigger questions behind her comments and underlinings—what it means to be a gentleman, the care of children and parental duty towards them—are reflected more generally in the ways that ideas about culture, social standing and responsibilities were expressed at Brancepeth. When long-term employees were ill or unable to work, their families were looked after, Christmas parcels were handed out to wives of employees, and the Beethams took care of deserving cases referred to them by the local vicar. Ruth Beetham's annotations and comments are linked to the world she knew, particularly the passages about drunkenness, and about gender and behaviour—what is proper to motherhood, and the way women act towards each other. There are other marked passages in *Boy*, including this one about Mrs D'Arcy-Muir, who is described as:

> . . . one of those very common types of women who delight in making other women unhappy . . . To pick a reputation to pieces was one of her delights . . . (178)

In the margin Ruth Beetham has written: 'very good hundreds like this creature That's how all the misery arises Slobber Bellow & Bunkum'. Who is she addressing? In some senses she was talking to herself. *Boy* clearly speaks Ruth Beetham's own mind in a way she was driven to affirm, especially about the way women should behave. There is also an admonitory note in these annotations. As a mother and wife and, in a sense, lady of the manor in a small rural community, she no doubt placed great importance on questions of appropriate class behaviour and social responsibility.

Ruth Beetham's annotations are nowhere else as visible, opinionated and detailed as they are in *Boy*. Her markings tend more towards supplementary information: she provided a long note on Matthew Arnold and his father at the back of Arnold's *Essays on Criticism* for example, and in another book pasted in a picture of the Earl of Reading with a biographical note. There are also occasional glosses, such as in a volume of Charles Kingsley's sermons, and minimal notes such as the warning about the misbound pages. But she is present as a reader perhaps more often than she can be identified, in the many paragraphs marked with a pencil line. It is tempting to see her (or her husband Hugh) as the person who marked this passage from Ouida's *Guilderoy,* for example:

> 'How is it?' he thought, 'how is it we have lost the art of living in these dear old houses? Better men than we did it and were not bored by it—did not even know what being bored meant. They were cut off from the world by the impassable roads that were around them. It took weeks to get to London, and that was a portentous journey even to the nearest country town; and yet they were contented, and they were not only contented—they were often cultured scholars, true philosophers, fine soldiers when they had to draw the

> sword. They had the art of sufficing to themselves, and we have lost it. We are all of us dependent on excitement from without. (3)

There are nine marked passages in *Guilderoy*, a novel reviewed by Oscar Wilde in the *Pall Mall Gazette* in 1889. Wilde described it as:

> . . . a study of the peerage from a poetical point of view. Those who are tired of mediocre young curates who have doubts, of serious young ladies who have missions, and of the ordinary figureheads of most of the English fiction of our time, might turn with pleasure, if not with profit, to this amazing romance. It is a resplendent picture of our aristocracy. No expense has been spared in gilding. For the comparatively small sum of 1 pound, 11s. 6d. one is introduced to the best society. The central figures are exaggerated, but the background is admirable. In spite of everything, it gives one a sense of something like life.[23]

The anonymous reader who marked the text seemed to agree with the last point. The highlighted description of the old house, impassable roads and distance from London irresistibly recall Brancepeth, which was often cut off in the winter. If the annotator was Ruth or Hugh Beetham, the implicit injunction to recover the 'art of sufficing to themselves' also reflects much about the way Brancepeth was run—as a paternalist community that provided for, and regulated, itself. Most of the marked passages are sententious rhetorical pronouncements—a line about how happiness is a 'matter of our own temperament', or the rhetorical question 'what is discontent?'—and several make points about women.

Gender politics was a major trend in the marginalia, and arguably the most active area of debate in both the content and the reader response of the Brancepeth library. Some of the gender comments can be identified with John Vaughan Miller, such as the word 'Splendid!' written in the margin of an American comic novel of courtship *The Squirrel Inn*.[24]

In the passage Miller applauded, Beam Lanigan, a feckless suitor who has been away and made his fortune and now wishes to exchange his betrothed for another, says to his friend Lodloe:

> 'My dear boy,' said Lanigan, 'I cannot put the facts into the hands of a woman. No matter how noble or honourable she may be, without the least intention on her part they would leak out . . .' (136)

Marked passages about women abound in the Brancepeth collection, reflecting the views that also informed the selection of books and, no doubt, social behaviour on the station. These passages predominantly recycle conservative gender stereotypes, adages and old saws. In *Guilderoy*, for example, the narrator's assertion that the happiness of life consists in 'having learnt the art of gliding over' is followed by this marked sentence:

> That few women have this delicate art, or possess the self-control and self-negation which are required for its exercise, is a fact which lies at the root of a great deal of human unhappiness and disunion. (82)

Rita's *Corinna* has 13 ticks, an underline and a marginal line drawing attention to passages about the 'blindness of woman when she loves' (182). Annie Swan's *Who Shall Serve?*, a book Miller liked so much he wrote about it in the paper and sent a copy to his wife, has an underlined sentence which may or may not be by him, but which fits with the general trend in Brancepeth books for a reader's eye to be caught by generalisations about gender roles:

> She was one of those women who make the great mistake of putting motherly love before wifely . . . (12)

And in *Pen Sketches*, someone has been struck by Mortimer Collins's observation, in his essay 'Darwinism':

> Just now intellectual excitement is the fashion. Young ladies like a little sham theology and sham philosophy which they fancy they understand; so the atmosphere is full of adorations and genuflexions, of germs and protoplasms. The young ladies will get all right they are married; 'tis mere intellectual measles . . . (52)

Of course, many of the most heavily-read books in the collection also furnish a deep reservoir of male stereotypes, from the doubting curate to the action hero of H. Rider Haggard, all of which go unremarked by readers. Occasionally, though, there is a glimpse of generalisations running the other way. In Edna Lyall's *Wayfaring Men,* Ruth Beetham has bracketed the hero's description of his baby son:

> 'He has no eyes to speak of—just a couple of slits—and as for his face, it seems to be all nose, with just a little margin of pink puckers.' (394)

Next to it she has written 'Just a man's idea'.

The clear emphasis in the marginalia on women and gender is not particularly surprising. Victorian fiction is full of generalised assertions about femininity and masculinity, as many scholars have shown, and the politics of marriage and the family had pointed resonance in the age of the New Woman, female activism on suffrage, and significant changes in the education of women. Reader response at Brancepeth was perhaps sharpened by the scarcity of women in rural New Zealand and the more general effects of a highly mobile migrant population, where so many did not live in stable families, or experienced family break-ups due to the effects of the 1890s depression. The views of the readers at Brancepeth, while the product of local circumstances, are at the same time an illustration of the widespread and entrenched cultural and social attitudes to gender in Britain and its colonies, attitudes that produced the first wave of feminism and are reflected in the fiction of the 1880s and 1890s.

The conservatism of readers at Brancepeth shapes the collection in a particular way however. Reader comments and emphases tend to endorse stereotypical generalisations, which in turn shapes the view of the kinds of persons who made those revealing marks. It is impossible to ignore marked passages and marginal comments, which 'buttonhole' future readers.[25] You naturally find yourself wondering why these passages were marked, or why those ones attracted comment, as contemporary readers on the station must have done—which was perhaps the instructive point. It would have been interesting to find a rebel among the readers, someone whose radical views were reflected in their feminist annotations of Sarah Grand for instance. Instead, the uniformity of the anonymous marginal lines and comments shows broad reader agreement with a conservative majority culture. It was unlikely, anyway, that a person with radical views would be tolerated at Brancepeth for long. In 1899, an A. Williamson (not a library subscriber) was characterised by Miller in the ledger as a 'Socialist, Atheist and General Firebrand'. An undated note relates that he began 'idling in the kitchen' while the cook was deciding how to vote on prohibition, and 'has been in garden since'. The ledger implies that he was banned from the house, and the next year Williamson was gone from the record. This does not mean, however, that there was no resistance to the culture and society of the farm expressed in marginalia, as the next chapter will explore.

Hugh Horsley Beetham is a less visible presence in the collection than his wife. A number of the books from the earlier part of the collection which retain an acquisition number sequence and were part of collection building in the 1880s, have 'Brancepeth Library' written across page 1, or sometimes the title page, in his large and decisive hand. But whether it is Hugh Beetham who has extensively marked passages from 'Samson Agonistes', 'Paradise Lost' and 'Paradise Regained'; or the poems of Robert Burns is impossible to say. The extensive marked passages in Milton include many in a memoir of his life and long stretches of blank verse, particularly in 'Paradise Regained', but don't have comment attached. They may have been the expression of a forceful agreement, or admiration, an *aide-memoire* or something more prosaic—a member of the family or a library subscriber such as Joseph Guest studying for an exam, for example. Whatever the reason, Milton shows far more evidence of reader attention than any other poet.

A date in Hugh Beetham's handwriting occurs twice. He has written the date 'Sept 26/83' in G.P.R. James's *The Old Dominion* and in Wilkie Collins's *My Miscellaneous,* indicating perhaps the date they were put in the library, which was formally instituted about this time. Hugh Beetham's role as President of the Library Committee does not necessarily mean he was an avid reader, but in 1901 Miller notes book orders for 'Mr B' of Lord Avebury's 'book on English scenery' and E.F. Benson's *Scarlet and Hyssop,* a just published and well-reviewed novel. As the principal founder (and funder) of the library, it is likely that Hugh Beetham cared greatly about books and reading, but he seems not to have been one of those people who are irresistibly driven to record their responses. However, many of the books from the older layer of the collection have small careful scratchy ink-lines marking passages in them, clearly a different hand than the more sweeping pencil lines in the same books. There is no particular reason to think these were made by Hugh Beetham. The library was used by many other people, including his parents, William and Mary, his siblings (though by the 1880s none of them was living at Brancepeth and only George has written his name occasionally) and the household of his sister Annie and brother-in-law T.C. Williams. But they are a notable presence in the marginalia, and it is tempting to think that passages like this, from M.E. Braddon's *Weavers and Weft* (1877), are singled out because they have sparked a sharp and feeling memory:

> This was the last day. His three great sea chests, containing his clothes, books, and other property which he could not bring himself to part with, had gone on to London by that morning's luggage train. He had arranged to follow by the night mail, which left Hillborough Station at half-past nine, and would be in London at two o'clock the next morning. (257)

When I first became interested in the Brancepeth library books, now held in the Victoria University Library in Wellington, I quickly became aware that a particular hand had annotated many of the books, so many indeed that the extent of it was almost shocking. H.J. Jackson, in her history of marginalia, describes how eighteenth-century readers 'valued personal, critical marginalia', accepting them as 'natural accretions' to the text, but after 1820 attitudes to annotations in books shifted considerably:

> Writing notes even in one's own books, let alone someone else's, let alone in ink, came to be thought of as irresponsible, weak, or transgressive.[26]

The quantity of annotation by one individual in the Brancepeth books certainly seems to have crossed a tacit boundary. At first, all I knew was that this copious and constant annotator was most likely a man (many of his comments are mildly misogynist, as illustrated by 'Splendid!' above), definitely a pedant, and indisputably someone who was classically educated. It was not until I started to investigate the archives held on the station that I realised the handwriting in the library books matched that in the station diary for 1894–1908, and from there it became possible to trace some of the reading behaviour, opinions and a few biographical details of the man who wrote them—John Vaughan Miller.

A number of questions arise from the mass of records, annotation and other data Miller left behind. One of the most interesting and insistent questions is—who was he writing for? The station diary is full of indiscreet remarks that he must have feared someone might read, because the most sensitive were transliterated into Greek. Why did he so copiously annotate the books? Why did he mark passages? His annotations are undoubtedly responsive, but as a body of inscriptions in his employer's books, books which were part of a 'public' library, the scale and vigour of his annotations also seems transgressive, perhaps defiant, and certainly an act of self-assertion. There is a related question: what drove him to spend his Sundays and many of his evenings producing well-researched and reasonably long articles for the local paper? What were his circumstances and his personality? Without John Vaughan Miller's annotations and diary-keeping, the library collection would be interesting for telling us what readers at the end of the nineteenth century liked to read, and would reveal a little of some of its readers, but it would lack the organising, opinionated, assertive and altering presence of its most constant reader. In a very real sense, the Brancepeth library belongs to John Vaughan Miller, whose driven and in some ways tormented inscription of himself on the textual and social life of the station, offers a rare historical glimpse of the reader at work and his continuing and implicitly critical dialogue with the world in which he lived.

There are three ways to track John Vaughan Miller as a reader. First is the steady stream of articles he wrote for the *Wairarapa Daily Times* and other papers; then there are the diary entries in which he mentions books he has read, exchanged or lent to various people, especially the governesses; and finally, there is the marginalia in his hand. Tracking Miller through marginalia provides a slightly different picture of what he read than that offered in the more public persona of his articles and letters to the paper, and the books he lent to the governesses or mentions in the diary are another layer in his complex reading life and persona. The picture that results, while inevitably incomplete, is perhaps as detailed as it is possible to get from someone who is not a professional reader or writer.[27] Nor was he an autodidact keeping an autobiographical memoir, like the working-class British men described by Jonathan Rose.[28] Miller always described himself as a 'gentleman', a rank he reinforces and aggressively asserts through his various practises as a reader.

For a man whose job was punishingly full-time, Miller's journalistic output was impressive. He wrote articles and letters to the editor fairly steadily until eighteen months before he left Brancepeth in January 1908, in ill health and not greatly missed. Each of these publications was mentioned in the diary, usually three times: at the time of writing (usually on a Sunday), noted in the diary as 'Art:' followed by the title, for example, 'The Diet of Modern Worms'; noted again when it was sent to the editor, Joseph Payton, usually as 'Sent art: to Payton'; and then again when it was published. If he was particularly pleased with an article, he took extra copies of the paper and sent them to members of his family. It would not be possible to trace these articles and letters without the diary notes, because Miller used a range of pseudonyms, most frequently Nemo, Iconoclast and M, and only once did he use his initials as a signature.[29] In his first three years at the farm there is just a scattering of letters to the editor and five articles, but in 1897 he picked up speed and published ten letters and articles. The next year, 1898, was his most prolific with 30 articles and letters, followed by 23 in 1899, 11 in 1900, 11 in 1901 (the year his youngest son Tony died), and then a gradual tailing off—eight in 1902, five in 1903, two in 1904, five in 1905 and three in 1906. He wrote articles on gambling, religion, education, land monopoly, Cecil

Rhodes, economics, Gladstone, servants, physiology, diet, close settlement, banking, sugar duties, European politics and the South African war, including publishing a letter from his son Hubert who was a member of the 7th Contingent. Some of the subjects he chose were topical, and he perhaps wrote his articles after reading news or opinion pieces in the British papers. Some seem to relate to particular expertise—pieces on banking, trusts and tariffs, sugar bounties and the closing of the Indian Mint—which may have derived from his employment at the Admiralty. Others reflected his own experience, such as a letter, 'Guerrilla Philanthropy', signed 'Iconoclast', which responds to a 'controversy' about the work of Mr Hall, a city missionary. In the letter, Miller writes about his own experience of the four 'Scripture Readers' in his father's parish, 'who were in fact City Missionaries [and] were his right hand in dealing with sickness, want, sorrow and suffering'.[30]

Miller may himself have been to theological college, which would explain his ease with and command of Greek. He had strong views on religion, was anti-High Church and what he referred to as 'Ritual', and thought there was a 'poverty' of good clerics. He claimed the clergy no longer knew how to preach and 'made improvident marriages' (surely a reference to the Earée divorce), and he wrote critical pieces about the local vicars. He boycotted services at Brancepeth if he thought the vicar did a deficient job, and believed the church as a whole (in Britain as well as in New Zealand) was pandering to the

> . . . tastes of giddy, pleasure-loving and emotional townfolk: so that religion, which ought to combat strenuously and correct the frivolity which is the inevitable characteristic of town life, rather seeks to conciliate it . . . ('The Gentle Shepherds of the Church').[31]

Along with his religious articles went a concern about 'progress' and the general political direction of the colony (he deplored 'sham reforms' and 'dangerous abuses'). In 1899, he wrote a leader called 'Facing the Light' which could stand as a sort of credo for what he believed in. It contains a reference to John Hampden, the great statesman of the Commonwealth, who fought to preserve 'just liberties'. One of the novels in the Brancepeth collection read and annotated by John Vaughan Miller was Edna Lyall's *To Right A Wrong* (1894), a historical novel about John Hampden, which is likely to have prompted this article, making a clear link between Miller's reading in the Brancepeth library and his published pieces. Miller's editorial makes the argument that a 'true Liberal' should rule in New Zealand:

> We want our rulers to be men of a true type of manliness, fearless, frank . . . who have that kind of dignity that neither takes liberties nor allows them; men who have been well-described as having that proud dignity coupled with self-respect which makes a man acknowledge the short-comings of his position in the world while yet conscious of his own intrinsic worth . . . the man with an educated conscience. (17 November 1899)

The article goes on to say that boys should be taught the 'grand duty of looking things in the face', and women should 'awake to the fact that (as Grant Allen expressed it) "the modern system of higher education for women is helplessly wrecking the maternal powers of the best class in our community"'.

As a thumbnail self-portrait, 'Facing the Light' reiterates conservative themes common to many of John Vaughan Miller's articles, letters and annotations, and also reflected in his reading. He was a fervent Royalist who mourned when the Queen died in 1901, and wrote an energetic riposte to the *Wairarapa Star* when it published a satirical article about the female members of the Royal Family. In addition to his lampoon of the New Woman under the pseudonym 'Jocosa Mordax', he wrote an article on the 'Woman Question', making fun of the portraits of the delegates to the National Women's Council published in the *NZ Graphic*, and their resolutions ('Those Wicked Men', 27 April 1899). A week later, writing as 'Iconoclast', he published an article ('Mothers and Daughters') on the New South Wales Federal Enabling Bill, which opens with a pointedly resonant metaphor on family harmony, which Miller argued, depended on how daughters are brought up by their mothers. (2 May 1899)

Miller supported Walter Buchanan, the Liberal Member of Parliament for Wairarapa, and went so far as to put words from Lord Macaulay into Buchanan's mouth when reporting (anonymously) on an 'excellent' speech he made at Brancepeth in 1896. Buchanan's 'humble protest' against 'all attempts by combined action to interfere with free individual action in settling private affairs' was said by Miller to have concluded 'almost' in the words of Macaulay. Miller went on to quote Macaulay at length on the role of the State, which should not 'intermeddle', but should rather rely on the 'prudence and energy of the people' and leave 'capital to find its most lucrative course'. Generally Miller's political and social views allied him with his employers and with his own class status as a 'gentleman', but the contradictions of his situation are directly or indirectly evident in everything he wrote. When he found himself driven to write as an employee pointing out the inequities of labour conditions, he published his article, 'The Hire of the Labourers', in a newspaper his employers were unlikely to read.

Miller's newspaper pieces reveal his beliefs and attitudes, but also make clear how thoroughly the library collection was entwined with his writing life, as a source for quotation and argument and as inspiration for what he wrote. His arguments are buttressed by a wide range of references, some of which come from the usual authorities beloved by Victorian leader writers—Bacon, Carlyle, Hume, Cicero, Charles Lamb, Macaulay, Tennyson—but even if you imagine him scouring a dictionary of quotations for appropriate lines, his capacity for allusion is impressive, as his article 'Originals and Copies' makes clear:

> When a man has been for many years a student, and read, and re-read, all the best things said by the best men in the best possible way, his mind becomes saturated with the thoughts of these men, and the recorded expression of those thoughts is inseparable from his own ideas. He cannot, even if he would, shake himself free from them, or divest himself of their influence. This is especially the case if his memory is retentive of what he reads, and if he has books at hand to enable him to verify his quotations. (6 April 1898)

'Originals and Copies' is about the inferior skills of contemporary novelists such as Sarah Grand and George Moore, 'aboriginals of the literary world', compared to the 'Heroes of Literature' (a reference to Carlyle's famous phrase from *On Heroes, Hero-Worship, and the Heroic in History)*. It is an intemperate piece, but also a kind of self-portrait of Miller as a reader and writer. He had a reverence for literature that might seem overblown and pietistic to readers raised in modernism, but which embodies standard Victorian sentiments (held even by the writers he reviled) about the sanctity and importance of the 'accumulated wisdom of the past' and its 'imperishable words'. 'Originals and Copies' is really a continuation of Miller's various attacks on the 'realist' school of novels, which includes New Woman novelists. According to Miller, there is no living 'Laureate' of prose or poetry; modern criticism is just 'snap-shots at everyday realism with a hand camera'; and the 'bulk of modern literature is but plagiarism, that is "kidnapping".' In the article, before he takes aim at Sarah Grand and George Moore (who, in his view, are 'original' only in the sense of being depraved) he delivers a display of learning designed to dazzle his reader, tracing literary inheritances from Bacon to Solomon, Giordano Bruno, Pascal, Tennyson, St Augustine, Jeremy Taylor and Milton. He quotes French and Arabic proverbs, Augustine (in Latin), Terence, Seneca, Shakespeare and Herrick, with side trips to Ben Jonson, Goethe, Sir John Harrington, Sterne, Walter Scott's *Rob Roy* and Byron's *Childe Harold*. It is intended not just to demolish 'realism' and put Grand and Moore in their place, but to showcase his own virtuosity and put the reader, who might happen to enjoy realist novels, in their place as well. There may be, as Miller says, nothing a man can say which has not already been said far better, but taking his own advice not to throw down his pen in disappointment, Miller set out to demonstrate what a master reader and writer he was, able to 'confer great pleasure and benefit on many by his tasteful and reverent re-setting' of the gems of the old masters, an adept exponent of what we now call intertextuality.

No matter what the topic, Miller's writing always displayed some of the characteristics of 'Originals and Copies'. Well-versed in the learned style of scholarly discourse familiar from Victorian periodicals, Miller produced a kind of mimicry of what Carlyle called the 'Heroes of Literature', as he noted himself in 'Originals and Copies'. Reading is a competitive art, and in his articles, Miller's learning is athletically deployed. He builds crescendos of allusions, throws in Latin epigrams and French phrases, demonstrates his knowledge of the past and the present, and makes a point of being able to transfer his reading into judgements and observations about the state of the world. When he writes about readers in 'Originals and Copies', he is also implicitly describing himself and perhaps the other users of the Brancepeth library:

> Not many people are great readers; a still smaller number are wise readers; many have little or no access to books of

> a standard kind; many forget what they have read, or their reading is of no practical use to them in forming their own characters, or the characters, opinions, and actions of those who are under their influence.

Miller was always busy proving that he was a great and a wise reader, and judging by the regularity of his publications in the *Wairarapa Daily Times*, the editor agreed with him. As well as articles and letters, Miller contributed poems and translations to the paper. 'Slummerlied' is a satirical poem about the Rev Earée's proposal to bring people from the London slums to New Zealand:

> A parson wrote an ode,—
> (Indifferent prose
> Chopped up in Whitman's mode,
> *Mais, pas grande chose*),
> He signed it Wyndham Earée
> And worked some sums
> To prove how many a fairy
> Might fly the slums . . .
> (28 Februry 1902)

According to Miller, in 24 comic-opera stanzas, the parson's plan was to provide himself with a 'girl /To black his boots . . . a maid to fry his chops'. This was perhaps a dig at Earée's marital circumstances (and a sidelong insinuation about his previous life on the stage), which would hit the papers the following year. Miller had a sharp satirical sense: on another occasion he wrote a rejoinder to a solemn and pompous poem by Edward Holmes, 'The Agnostic to the Unknown God', reprinted in the *Wairarapa Daily Times* from the *Spectator*. Miller's riposte, 'The Unknown God to the Agnostic' (13 July 1901) is a poem of faith, but also wittily plays with the phrases and metaphors of Holmes's poem. Another ironic piece, 'The Ministry of the Interior' (25 January 1899), about human physiology, is a gently humorous, detailed description of a man, said to be 'a well-known man in the Wairarapa', five feet seven inches tall and weighing 10 ¾ stones: 'Now do any of you know who this creature is?' It is tempting to think that Miller is describing himself, as an elaborate kind of joke, in this man whose surface area contains 'nearly 28 miles of pores (A decidedly porous man)'. He also wrote satirical letters to the paper, one entitled 'What the Ministry May Do' about the Pension Bill, signed 'Balaam's Ass' which finishes

> P.S. The 'Scotchmen' in this part of the world badly want something to drink.
>
> 4th December, 1897.
> Augean Stables, Elisville.

Recording this letter in the station diary, Miller joked 'Wrote a letter from Balaam's Ass to *Wairarapa Daily Times* which will probably be DWT but is a beautiful letter'.[32] Many of his published jokes, such as this P.S., are in-jokes for a small-town newspaper where many readers knew the real identity of 'Balaam's Ass', Iconoclast, M., and Nemo. Miller also loved puns (such as the one in 'Scotchmen'), and loved to whip up a rhetorical storm in the service of something humorous. It is also possible that occasionally he wrote and replied to his own letters under different pseudonyms. Two letters signed respectively 'X' and 'Z' are both noted in the diary. It would seem to fit with Miller's sense of satire if he did, in fact, carry on a rhetorical puppet show in the letters column.

Confirming some of his reading while at Brancepeth, Miller referred explicitly in his articles to Sarah Grand's *The Beth Book,* George Moore's *The Mummer's Wife,* Lucas Malet's *The History of Sir Richard Calmady,* H. Rider Haggard's *Doctor Therne,* Marie Corelli's *Temporal Power* and Annie Swan's *Who Shall Serve?* He also referred frequently to Mark Twain and George Eliot, and mentioned Zola and the British novelist Israel Zangwill, 'the Dickens of the Ghetto'. Grand, Moore and Malet drew his most vehement critical responses, and are part of a general theme he returned to again and again: the decay of civility and what he thought of as the degradation of women, whom he believed should not abandon their 'natural' roles as mothers and wives to become New Women. Miller also had strong views on what constituted good writing. When he wrote a letter to the paper on 'Good Literature' in May 1899 asking why no one has written a 'really good novel of New Zealand life and manners', he blamed Kipling for the 'short, abrupt, jerky scenes from life' that inundated local magazines. As a counter-example of literary models that should be followed by local writers, he listed a few of the books from the Brancepeth library: two stories by W.W. Jacobs, 'Many Cargoes' and 'Sea Urchins'; James Lane Allen's *The Choir Invisible;* and Jane Findlater's *The Green Graves of Balgowrie*, a popular novel at Brancepeth which has violets pressed between the pages. *The Green Graves of Balgowrie* is a Scottish novel written by the daughter of a parson, about a country girl who goes to London and is made miserable by the society life she is expected to lead. The novel's critique of sham and pretension fits perfectly with Miller's view that one of the 'worst features of utter worldliness is its utter selfishness. Let us keep our aim in life pure and unsullied by the smoke of low desires' ('The Play's The Thing', 23 July 1903).

Miller was also full of praise for Gissing, whom he frequently invoked to carry a point, as in his letter condemning 'fashionable novels':

> What George Gissing says is true, 'The decay of religious belief is undermining morality . . .'[33]

A leader he wrote about events in Russia (perpetrated by 'the royal butchers and their ruffianly myrmidons') opens by marking Gissing's death and praising *The Private Papers of Henry Ryecroft* (1903). The most popular of Gissing's works, *The Private Papers of Henry Ryecroft* is a series of linked essays in which Gissing's intellectual history and beliefs are given fictional shape. Miller bent Gissing to his purpose and quoted him at length as a commentary on the 'savage tyrant' at work in Russia: 'If historic times had a voice, it would sound as one long note of anguish.'[34]

Miller was presented with a 'handsome' copy of Tennyson by Joseph Payton, editor of the *Wairarapa Daily Times*, as a token of gratitude for leaders supplied while Payton was ill. Miller had already been given another copy of Tennyson by Ruth Beetham in 1896 in appreciation of his work on the Library Committee. Like the rest of his generation, Miller loved Tennyson. In 1897, he wrote a comic excoriation of a poem published in a previous issue of the paper:

> May I lay my cold hand on that of the young poet who signs a name which sounds like 'Any More' (possibly Maori for Hannah More), and, having laid hold of that furtively sacrilegious member, may I give it an iron grip, and say, 'drop that Sir, or Madam, I implore, drop it. That pearl belonged to an old and revered friend of mine, named Tennyson before you spoilt its beauty and smashed up its setting'. ('Tennyson Spoiled', 30 December 1897)

He was speaking of Tennyson's famous long poem 'In Memoriam'. There are frequent references to Tennyson and Milton in Miller's published pieces; he seems to have liked reading poetry, as he recorded lending the 'Percy Reliques', a collection of old English ballads,[35] and the poems of C.S. Calverley to one of the governesses. C.S. Calverley, described by Hilda Spear as 'one of those men who become legends in their own lifetime',[36] was a mid-Victorian wit and parodist, acknowledged as a master of light verse. He wrote burlesques of Browning, Tennyson and Wordsworth, charades and pastiches of Old English, and also wrote poems in Latin and published translations of Virgil and Theocrites. Reading Calverley, it is easy to see why Miller liked him—they have a similar sense of humour, love of puns and riddles, and fondness for ballad metre. Looking backwards from Calverley to his reader is perhaps revealing about Miller, whose castigating critique, conservative political opinions, social and religious gloom and occasional flashes of personal despair were always tempered by a satirical sense of humour and a deep love of literature. When he appropriated Annie Swan's title *Who Shall Serve?* for a long comic piece about the 'delicacy' of servants, he digressed into *Vanity Fair* with comic affection:

> Delicacy means all this and a great deal more, if we are to believe the immortal volume which little boys calls 'Dixon's Johnsonry'; the volume which Becky Sharp, after putting her pale face out of the cab window, actually flung back into the garden of the Academy for Young Ladies of Chiswick Mall which was kept by the Semiramis of Hammersmith, Miss Pinkerton. (19 December 1900)

Miller, like Calverley, accepted most things as grist to his literary mill.

A list of books he lent the governess does, however, show a slightly different kind of reading persona than his track through the collection. Along with Percy and Calverley, he lent her books of sermons (*Light and Leaven* by Hensley Henson, the subtitle of which is 'historical and social sermons to general congregations'[37]) and devotional essays by Frederick Locker-Lampson. He also exchanged books with Miss Liddle, an earlier governess and member of the Library Committee; some of the station workers, especially Trigge, one of the rabbiters; Ruth Beetham, and T.C. Williams. Miller particularly liked *Social Evolution* by the British sociologist Benjamin Kidd, and noted:

> I affixed a definition of some of the hardest terms used, before putting the book in circulation—it is a first rate book.[38]

He wrote to both Miss Liddle and T.C. Williams about it, showing his role as an advocate and proselytiser. In the book,

Kidd argues that religion, which he described as an 'ultra-rational sanction' (112), was necessary to evolution, because, in a passage marked by Miller, the 'interests of the individual and those of the social organism to which he belongs are not identical' (84). Passages marked by Miller suggest a correspondence with his religious beliefs and his more general view that 'the advance of civilisation is not always progressive', a sentence he marked in H.S. Merriman's *The Last Hope,* and an opinion he reiterated in a variety of contexts. It may also have corresponded with his progressively more despairing view of his own life, which is visible in the station diary.

The books he mentions in the station diary that constitute part of his social exchange tend not to be novels. *Being and Doing* which he borrowed from Ruth Beetham and then replaced after an unexplained loss, is 'a Selection of Helpful Thoughts From Various Authors Arranged for Daily Reading', arranged by Miss Constance Wishaw. He also records ordering a prayer book, a Greek lexicon and the Falstaff edition of Shakespeare from Baillie, the bookseller used by the station. Another order Miller made in 1903, Apirana Ngata's recently published *Maori Grammar,*[39] is interesting for what it says about his intellectual engagement, both with his job and with his country of adoption, even though there is no visible use of te reo Māori in his diary entries or articles, other than an interest in recording names correctly. He corresponded with English family members about books, and asked them to send him books, such as *London Lyrics.* There is an occasional note in the station diary about books that have struck him, for example Charles Kingsley's *Life and Letters* which he ordered for his wife, and the following note about the secret medieval courts of Westphalia, described in Scott's novel *Anne of Geierstein*:

> 22 April 1899 Vehm Gerichte see pp222 et seq of Anne of Geierstein and 'Hadyn' in loco'.

If the station diary was the only way in which Miller's reading could be tracked, it would give a false impression of him as a serious, even pious reader, who amused himself after work by reading poetry, sermons or devotional texts around the fire and lending them to the governesses. But the books in the collection tell a different story. Miller left his traces on these books in several ways. A grammatical mistake, a typo, a misbind, or any other physical error in a book was like a red rag to a bull—he was driven to correct it. H.J. Jackson observes that annotators often plead that they are driven by irresistible impulse—the annotator, in some sense, is speaking to the book—and makes the point that the impulse frequently springs from noticing a mistake.[40] Miller was incapable of noticing a grammatical error and letting it be; he was compelled to address the book and improve it. He used whatever he was holding in his hand, a red pen, a blue pencil, a black pen or a soft-lead pencil, to cross out, correct, or annotate the text. There are at least a hundred books in the collection that show his annotations, ranging from *Tess of the D'Urbervilles* to novels by popular writers like Hawley Smart, Edna Lyall and Hall Caine. The sheer range of books he annotated reveals him to have been an eclectic and catholic reader, with as much enjoyment of popular fiction (or at least as much time spent reading it) as serious literary writers. He read Froude, Hardy, Gissing, Charlotte Bronte, Disraeli and Trollope, but also Adeline Sergeant, Lucas Malet, Sarah Grand, Marie Corelli, Robert Louis Stevenson, H. Rider Haggard, Mary Cholmondeley, E.P. Roe, H.S. Merriman, S. Baring Gould, Blanche Atkinson, M.E. Braddon, Mrs Henry Wood, Mrs Alexander, Grant Allen, Rita, Joseph Hocking, Israel Zangwill, Iota, and Ellen Thorneycroft Fowler, whose novel *Concerning Isabel Carnaby* contains an impressive 20 corrections, marked passages, glosses and comments by Miller, perhaps because the novel is really a dramatic dialogue about what morally responsible fiction should look like. Miller does not seem to have read some of the lighter end of the library—the horse-racing novels of Nat Gould, detective novels by Dick Donovan, or the mysteries and thrillers by the American A.C. Gunter—or at least, he left no visible trace of his reading in those otherwise very popular categories. What he read with overt attention, revealing a very different side to 'Nemo' and his other personae in the newspaper columns, leans strongly towards romance, sensation, historical novels, and the big popular novelists of his time. It seems he kept up with literary fashion and bestsellers, as many of the books he annotated were recently republished in colonial editions and still advertised in the paper.

A particular habit of Miller's was to gloss Greek and Latin words and phrases, often adding the Greek text in the margin. For example, in Hawley Smart's *Two Kisses* (a high-society romance and racing novel), Miller inserted an X in the text next to the word 'Oneiros' and glossed it at the bottom of the page. In *Far From the Madding Crowd* he underlined the word 'thesmothete' in the text, and gave the etymology in Greek at the bottom of the chapter, with the translation 'a law-giver' and a gloss explaining that 'the θεσμοθεται at Athens were the six junior Archons. At the expiration of a year they became the Areopagus' (83). This is an example of what Jackson calls a 'scholium', a note that introduces information from outside the text, which is, in her words, a 'form of interpretative labour'; when such notes mount up they can stand alone, such as the glossaries compiled by professional scholars.[41] There are dozens of scholia in Miller's hand in the Brancepeth library—he annotated almost every Greek name in Charles Kingsley's *Phaethon*, including the title. Latin phrases in the text are always translated and often glossed, and if an English word is used that seems to need its etymology explained from the Greek, as in the word 'etiolated' in Pearson's *National Life and Character*, Miller appends a note. He glosses unusual vocabulary such as the word 'sciolism' in Froude's *Short Studies*, and translates the epigram from Horace in Gissing's *The Private Papers of Henry Ryecroft*. Examples are legion.

Given that the general attitude towards annotating books, especially in ink, was no longer approving at the end of the nineteenth century, why did Miller do it? His annotations are so frequent and consistent that they are almost predictable, and surely conform to Jackson's point that every mark of annotation entails a 'degree of self-assertion, if not of aggression. The reader leaves a mark and thereby alters the object' (90). But Miller's scholia have a point beyond simply altering the object for personal use (which is more plainly the case with the marginalia by other readers). His glosses and annotations express a scholarship that is a good in itself: valuable knowledge added to the text, a personal labour of interpretation that says something forceful about the annotator and the author. It is impossible to read the Brancepeth library books a century later and not be aware of Miller's insistent, didactic presence. He has a pedantic fastidiousness that forces the less scholarly or less accurate reader to pay closer attention—in three separate texts he corrected the common misquotation of Milton's famous lines from 'Lycidas', 'To fresh fields and pastures new', crossing out 'fields' and putting 'woods'. It is at once a reproof to the book and its author, and a flag to other readers not as observant or lettered as himself. Those other readers, whether Miller's contemporaries or those of us encountering his legacy years later, find themselves 'silent witnesses', in Jackson's phrase, to the interactions between text and reader.[42]

Whom was Miller addressing? While Jackson's study of marginalia is based on privately owned books, often those owned by famous people, where there is some value in preserving the marked-up copy, Brancepeth is a rather different proposition. In terms of a community of readers, a privately-owned subscription library sits somewhere between the anonymity a reader might expect in a big municipal library (although that depends on the size of the town), and writing notes that he or she might expect will be read by people they know. The list of library subscribers was never so long that Miller wouldn't have known all of them, and in any case, his working life brought him into contact with everyone on the station, including the visitors who were often brought to the office. The other employees would have been very aware of him, as he managed their finances and many of their work conditions. It seems clear that Miller's annotations were thus, at some level, addressed to the other readers at Brancepeth, and inevitably to the Beethams. Victorian novels make much of a gentleman's classical education, and it seems likely that Miller's insistent, even hectoring, Latin and Greek glosses were designed to point out the obvious—that, like many characters in Victorian fiction, he too was in reduced circumstances, but unequivocally still a gentleman. There were other likely factors; Miller was opinionated, hated sloppiness, was highly educated and loved learning. He probably relished the scholarly work of producing glosses and corrections, and evidently took pleasure in writing as a physical and intellectual activity. His Greek words are lovingly penned. At the same time, his transliterations in the station diary suggest that he enjoyed having a secret and was not above giving his employers, and people he scorned, a good poke, in this case by insinuating that he was the most cultivated and scholarly person using the library.

It was not only in classical texts that Miller displayed his learning. *Concerning Isabel Carnaby* (1894), a novel to which Miller paid great attention, has glosses in his handwriting to *Paradise Lost*, the Bible and Shelley. He picked up echoes as well as direct quotations. When Isabel Carnaby declares, 'I have learnt in suffering what I teach in ordinary conversation', Miller added a gloss to the foot of the page: '"They learn in suffering what they teach in song", Shelley' (94). *Concerning Isabel Carnaby* is one of the most annotated books in the collection, which suggests that Miller was particularly struck by it. A bestseller (it sold a million copies), it was Ellen Thorneycroft Fowler's first novel. It is a courtship novel, about the relationship between Isabel Carnaby, recently returned from India, and her tutor, Paul Seaton, the son of a Methodist minister who has been taught that 'the only two things of importance in this life are salvation and education'. The novel is very discursive—most of the action is talk—and plays wittily with conceptions of class and belief, contrasting London society with a domesticity based on Methodist principles. Miller has made a note of this passage, which perhaps reflects his sense of himself:

> 'People are too anxious to make a stir in the world', continued her father; 'the doctrine of today is that it is disgraceful to be unknown.' (224)

Many of the novel's maxims chime with views Miller expressed elsewhere, including the distinction between good and bad novels.[43] Isabel writes a *roman à clef* 'society' novel called *Shams and Shadows* under a pseudonym. To save her the shame of this book, Paul proclaims himself to be the author, but subsequently writes a 'great book full of teaching'. Some of Fowler's jokes found their way into Miller's own annotations elsewhere. Paul Seaton's minister father, for example, tells him a story about someone giving a speech:

> She endeavoured to make use of a Latin quotation, and actually—yes, actually my dear Paul—she made a false quantity; and she the wife of a headmaster!' (319)

In the library copy of Charles Reade's *Christie Johnstone*, next to a Latin translation Miller has written 'False quantity'.

Knowing the opinionated author of the station diary makes it impossible not to read Miller's annotations as a mix of scholarly helpfulness and, sometimes, truculent self-display. His note 'Gen. xxv. 30.31' on the title page of Mary Cholmondeley's *Red Pottage,* for example, is both helpful and directive—the reader has to get out the Bible and see what he means.[44] He was quick to pick up mistakes of a practical kind, demonstrating his credentials as a man of the land and a gardener. When Thackeray describes a garden in *Pelham* as 'flaming with crocuses and sunflowers', Miller underlined 'crocuses' and 'sunflowers', leaving the reader to get the point that they don't flower in the same season. He was derisive about Hardy's description of the death of Prince, the cart-horse, in *Tess of the D'Urbervilles.* As Prince is hoisted into the wagon Miller wrote in the margin 'how?', and when he is dragged to his grave, Miller expostulated scornfully, 'Imagine a drunkard and a woman <u>towing a dead horse up-hill</u>!' These wry acknowledgements of a shared agrarian knowledge make common cause with other Brancepeth subscribers, like S. Baring Gould's reference in *Urith: A Tale of Dartmoor* to a wether as 'her'. Miller commented: 'difficult job to shear a she-wether'.

Bad writing offended him deeply. He underlined, in purple pencil without comment, this sentence from George Macdonald's *Malcolm,* describing a flock of larks:

> . . .—like air-pitcher-plants that over-flowed in song—like electric jars emptying themselves of the sweet thunder of bliss in the flashing of wings and the trembling of melodious throats . . . (63)

It is possible that the underlining is for the opposite reason, but seems unlikely in the light of other critical annotations. He was unequivocal about E.P. Roe's *Opening a Chestnut Burr,* underlining mistakes ('except' for 'accept') and repetitions, writing exclamation marks in the margin and noting sarcastically 'What exquisite English' twice—next to 'When from seeming', which is underlined, and 'death that is remediless may lurk just back of eyes that smile upon us' (124–5). Miller was just as observant of plot errors. On p367 of Mrs Eiloart's *The Dean's Wife* he has underlined 'She had never called him by his Christian name before' and written next to it 'Yes, she did on pp:291 and 315'. Social faux pas are also commented on. When a character is described as a 'thoroughbred gentleman' in Bracebridge Hemyng's story 'Captain Dayrell's Luck', Miller tells the reader to 'see page 82', where he has underlined a passage concerning accusations about money, clearly an example of ungentlemanly behaviour.

There is another category of annotation by Miller that seems to have less to do with his implicit local audience (and perhaps an imagined future readership) and his standing and relationships on the farm, and more to do with an impulse to remember passages that have struck him, or perhaps just to take note of things that mirror his life and beliefs. Many of the books have a list of page numbers in Miller's handwriting jotted inside the back cover. It is not always clear what he meant to mark. The notations are simply a pencilled dot in the margin, and often there is no mark at all. But reading the page it is frequently possible to guess what struck him. An example is the following passage from Lucas Malet's *The Carissima*, describing the heroine Miss Perry, whose claim to being the 'One Woman' is overthrown by her boots:

> . . . wide, easy, trodden over, their square toes turned badly heavenward . . . here was a detail which radically displeased, therefore Miss Perry was not the One Woman. (148)

Always attentive to his own person and very particular about his laundry and his clothes, Miller was alert to the physicality of others. He occasionally commented on the dress and appearance of women at the station, and on one occasion went so far as to note a visitor's weight. The passage above is marked with a dot, which makes it easy to identify, but Miller's attitudes and preoccupations are so widely consistent that their echoes are loud and clear. A great many marked passages concern women. In Charles Kingsley's lecture on 'Thrift', there are six marked passages about women and thrift, which really means moral virtue, Miller would have agreed with Kingsley that women should be trained 'to distinguish the good novel from the bad'.[45] Miller's endorsement of these sentiments and stereotypes is one of the most consistent features of his intellectual life, and accounts for the largest part of his annotation. This should be read in the context of his weekly exchange of letters with his wife, his frequent correspondence with his daughters, and his pleasure in the company of women he approved of. He wasn't a misogynist in the sense that he was aloof from or disliked women, but many of his attitudes and fixed ideas were founded in a philosophical and social misogyny.

Of course Miller would not have recognised his attitudes as misogynist, but seen them as a normal dimension of his wider political and social views. He marked passages which spoke to his religious belief, such as this line from Joseph Hocking's *Scarlet Woman*: '. . . many more lived in perpetual darkness when they might have felt the smiling sunshine of God' (312). Other highlighted passages concern politics, like this rhetorical question in Julian Hawthorne's *Love or a Name*:

> Where's the use of a lot of idle, shiftless ignoramuses that calls themselves politicians, and all the politics they know is to get tight on other men's whisky, and carry torches in a parade? (187)

Vehement opposition to socialism drove many of his overtly political notations, like the underlined passages in Matilda

Betham-Edwards's *The Sylvestres*, a novel about a failed experimental community, and these opinions are strongly argued in many of his newspaper articles. His social conservatism was accompanied by conservative politics and religious belief, but in practise these views were tempered by kindness and his strong sense of fairness.

Biographical information about Miller is thin. It is not quite clear why or how he wound up at Brancepeth, and there is no information about what happened in the years between his departure and his death. Although the station diary records that he sent letters to his wife at Motueka every week, amounting to hundreds over the fourteen years he worked at Brancepeth, none have survived. Other material mentioned in the diary—the gifts of books, the photographs taken of him by a professional photographer in Nelson; other photographs taken by Weva Beetham, some showing him at his desk in the office—all seem to have vanished, or perhaps been mislabelled. His surviving descendants have little knowledge of him. But it is possible to flesh out a kind of biography by looking, as this chapter has attempted to do, at the tracks he left of his reading life, which show something of his personality and perhaps hint at his feelings as well as his thoughts. Miller's love of learning, his pride and touchiness, his pedantry and fastidiousness, his attitudes about literature, religion, class, politics and gender, are all evident in his writing and his annotations. Miller's textual presence also throws some light on his workplace and social world. What he thought about his own career, from senior Admiralty clerk, to colonial landowner, to hard-pressed station clerk at Brancepeth, is implicit in the shifting attitudes towards his employers expressed in his articles and the station diary, and also seems to lie behind some of his marginalia. He has, for instance, put a dot in the margin of Israel Zangwill's *The Premier and the Painter*, next to a remark by one of the characters, Mrs Dawe, who runs a cook shop:

> 'It's no use, my dear 'Lizer,' said Mrs Dawe, rejecting the proffered journal. 'You know I can't read and write; not as I regrets it to be sure, for, as my late 'usband said, "a man as can't read or write is more likely to make his mark than a man as can".' (86)

Miller's sarcasm about his workmates and sense of unbelonging may have made Mrs Dawe's husband's observation ring uncomfortably true.

Among his many notations of page numbers are three in Trollope's *The Three Clerks*. One is a comment about the 'impotency of educated men to withstand the allurements of wealth' (347). The salutary story of Alaric Tudor—led into speculation by an upper-class rogue, tried and sent to gaol for embezzling trust funds, and finally an unsuccessful emigrant to Australia—would have appealed to Miller's hatred of gambling, which he expressed several times in his newspaper articles. But it may also have resonated as a echo of his own career, perhaps the impulse that led him to leave his safe and sure job in England (just as Alaric Tudor does) for the promise of colonial wealth. His article 'The Hire of the Labourers' argues, justly, that the only reason some people in New Zealand are wealthier than others is because they had the good fortune to arrive earlier. As Trollope's narrator declares:

> Expediency is the dangerous wind by which so many of us have wrecked our little boats. (347)

There is perhaps a kind of debate with himself carried on in his unannotated page markings: they operate as a way of expressing his feelings, which oscillate between impulses. On the one hand, in Mrs Oliphant's *A House Divided Against Itself*, he marked the sentence: 'It might even have been supposed from his conversation that he scorned rich people for being rich, which of course was an exaggeration' (208). And on the other, he singled out a paragraph from Fanny

Kemble's *Record of a Girlhood*: 'I humbly hope that I keep the sacred ground of my religion clear from whatever does not belong to the spirit of its practice' (166). He aspired to be an 'excellent man . . . glad to pick a posy of pleasure anywhere by the wayside', like the doctor in *Colonel Enderby's Wife*, a passage he has marked with a larger than usual dot. Yet he was also buffeted by irritations and contradictory emotions, plagued by his circumstances, and subject to nostalgia and regret, all of which spoke to him from his reading. Reading, we can speculate, was for Miller a way of claiming his diverse and contradictory selfhood, imposing it on other readers, and reminding himself what he valued and loved. Despite the thinness of his biographical detail, reading what John Vaughan Miller read and what he wrote about it in the margins is a rich way to know him, refracted through the fictions that sustained him. As H.J. Jackson has said, reader markings and annotations are like a letter in a bottle, picked up by chance a hundred years later.

There are two marked passages in a novel by Lucas Malet, or Mary St Leger Harrison, Charles Kingsley's daughter, and—at least before he read and hated *The History of Sir Richard Calmady*—a writer whose work seemed to appeal to Miller, if the level of annotation is a guide. *Mrs Lorimer: A Sketch in Black and White* is about a young woman, widowed early. Despite the appearance of various suitors and the promise of London life away from submission to the 'small moral and social code' of Claybrooke (the village where she has been brought up by her uncle and aunt), she chooses to remain faithful to her dead spouse and spend what turns out to be a short life on nursing the sick. The novel's social and moral pieties seem to concur with Miller's views about women and their lives, the pursuit of ambition, 'society', and wealth. But the passages he has marked are perhaps more personal in tone. They focus on Mrs Lorimer's uncle and aunt, the Rector,

Mr Mainwaring, and his wife. Miller has marked a passage when, at the end of a disagreement, they exchange a kiss:

> . . . the kiss of man and wife, in the dusty afternoon of life, when the transport and illusion of youth are dead, after long years of disappointment, struggle and hope grown tired in the stress and strain of daily living—the kiss of those two, pausing for a moment and turning to each other in faithful love, while the road stretches out before them, pale and misty, into the silence of the great unknown land . . . may well fill heaven itself . . . with a solemn gladness. (116)

Miller's separation from his wife and family, seemingly caused by his own failures and no doubt accompanied by a great deal of guilt, shame and self-recrimination, was not a condition he welcomed. Every communication from his wife and every letter he sent to her are noted in the station diary; he looked out for gifts for her, marked her birthday and their wedding anniversary, and sent her money punctiliously. Further along in the novel, he marked another paragraph that struck him, this one about the Rector musing on an unsuccessful day's hunting. It is impossible to not to imagine that John Vaughan Miller was thinking of his own life's trajectory when he carefully noted the page number inside the back cover and pencilled a little dot in the margin next to this passage:

> It struck Mr Mainwaring that his own life, looking back on it, was very like the history of that day. A cheery start in the morning sunshine; a capital horse under him; hope for the coming hours; plenty of friends; a splendid burst for a few minutes over the grass, when the pace was hot and his blood tingled with healthy excitement. Then pottering about the dreary woodlands, in the chill mist, drawing and drawing for the fox that could never be found; and, at last, the long lonely ride home in the cold and the growing darkness. The day dying, the sport all over, only the weariness and want of success left. Dirty, tired, bespattered, old—that was what it all came to in the end. Alas! For the pity of it! (222)

CHAPTER SEVEN

The Lives of Books

Robert Escarpit has said that when you hold a book in your hand, all you hold is the paper: the *book* is elsewhere.[1] Books live, in that sense, in imagination and intellect. Something of that 'elsewhere' is also how books, if they are lucky, become 'literature'—they are defined by historical period, authorship, subject and genre, become the focus of opinion and critique, and are reinvented by scholarship. But what of the book as paper object? Surely the book itself, a stack of sheets of paper glued or sewn together between hard boards or stiff paper, an object that survives into old age despite the degradation of many hands, is just as eloquent about the mysteries of the mind, heart and body as the romance printed on its pages? A book has an organic history as an object in time, a surprisingly durable object that preserves the marks of its readers as it grows old and deteriorates and becomes itself a form of memory. Fonts and typefaces go in and out of fashion; paper stock, bindings, ink and writing implements change. But books look and smell of time, and carry the physical traces of places and bodies.

As Roger Chartier and Guglielmo Cavallo have noted, reading 'involves the body, is inscribed within a space, and implies a relationship to oneself or to others'.[2] The history of reading, based as it is on elusive evidence of actual readers,[3] has tended to rely on external data to build a picture of readers and their response to reading—bestseller lists, reader surveys, library lending statistics, autobiographies. But as H.J. Jackson has argued, 'such sources can be guaranteed not to correspond to any actual reader whatever: Statistical Man is a robot'.[4] While the evidence of actual readers at Brancepeth—other than the assiduously annotating John Vaughan Miller—gives only glimpses of the reader's engagement with the text, the books themselves illuminate something of the daily lives of readers and the world in which their reading took place. Part of the attraction of a library like Brancepeth is that although most individual readers remain tantalisingly indistinct, the location of the book, in their hands and in their lives, is often written on its pages and after it is read and re-shelved, traces of the moment of reading remain. Books testify that readers were there, even though what Jackson calls the 'running mental discourse that accompanies reading'[5] has moved somewhere else. They may not provide us with a coherent narrative of reader response or labour conditions or social dynamics, but the books in the Brancepeth library tell us some things about where they have been, what other uses they were put to, and what else readers might have been doing while they were turning the pages.

The Brancepeth library books were covered with a red material Miller refers to as 'linenette', which has not aged well. Faded to a dingy brownish non-colour, it has torn and buckled, and bled a brilliant red stain onto the end pages. Still, the uniformity of the covers signals that the books are part of a library collection. Even today, the scattered library books that were missed when the collection was moved to the university stand out among the miscellaneous piles of Weva Beetham's photography manuals and forgotten paperbacks that have accumulated in the station office. The red covers also lent a protective identification to the books. Anyone removing a book from the farm or illegitimately reading one would have been conspicuous, given that the library rules stipulate that 'no book shall be lent by a member to a non-member'. On 14 July 1896, Miller wrote a circular letter to all camps and out-stations reminding them of this particular rule, but policing who read what in the rabbiting camps was obviously impossible, and it is clear from marginalia and from some of Miller's diary entries that books were used communally, perhaps read aloud, but certainly shared between friends. The primary function of covering the books, of course, was to protect them from dust and dirt and the many physical hardships of station life. For books that were not read much and stayed in the library reading room, the covers offered some protection from wear and tear. Though the spines have faded, many of these volumes have remained clean, and are still a bright red, at least where they were not exposed to the light. But those that traveled from reader to reader in the bullock dray and were read in the evening after a hard day's work outside lived a more arduous life, and it shows.

The heavily-used books in the Brancepeth library—approximately a sixth of the collection, or about 300 books—cluster in particular genres and authors, and show substantial damage: they are torn off their bindings, extremely dirty, and missing pages. Some of these very damaged books belong to the earlier phase of the library's history (the 1870s and 1880s), when the collection was small and there was much less choice about what to read. Given the greater pressure on fewer titles, it is perhaps not surprising that a number of these books lack title pages and are missing their opening pages: Trollope's titles, for example, especially *Orley Farm* and *The Prime Minister,* Fielding's *Tom Jones,* and some of George Eliot, Thackeray, George Whyte-Melville, Walter Besant and Mrs Henry Wood. But with the enormous increase in cheap editions and reprints of bestsellers like *East Lynne* or

Lady Audley's Secret, the number of books coming into the collection increased, and the status of books as durable and treasured objects changed drastically.

Colonial editions were a large and diverse category, as Graeme Johanson has pointed out,[6] and the quality of the books varied from publisher to publisher. William Milner advertised his Cottage Library of quality fiction, for instance, as cheap, complete and durable, but the belief that colonial readers were more likely to buy books than borrow them drove the British publishers to produce sets for the home reader at even lower prices (such as Macmillan's Colonial Library or Bell's Indian and Colonial).[7] What this meant is that colonial editions were more disposable. Before the 1920s, Johanson writes, the colonial edition was bound in 'colonial cloth' or paper instead of the 'more substantial cloth binding used for home editions'.[8] Although Macmillan's marketing claimed that the paper and type used in colonial editions were 'exactly the same' as the expensive English editions, a letter from Macmillan to the New York printer specified a lighter weight paper for a cheap edition of Henry James's *The Real Thing* than for the English edition,[9] and colonial institutes and libraries complained of the flimsiness of colonial editions. Binding was also subject to cost-cutting, and as a consequence books fell apart, tore, and were easier to damage[10]—in April 1906 Miller noted that he had acquired for the library a fresh copy of Conan Doyle's *White Company* because 'ours has been read to death'. Conversely, cheapness also made books easier to replace.

Unlike a municipal library, Brancepeth was not subject to regular culling and replacement of damaged books. The only other time Miller recorded asking to replace a book—it was *Vanity Fair*—he was refused permission. But he did record that a gift of old books was made to John Page, the butcher who had been a library subscriber at Brancepeth since 1894, when he departed the station in 1901:

> 19 April have reported to President that a new Hon: Treasurer must be chosen and that the Annl Gen Mtg ought to be held. Also told him of Page's hint that he would like to have all the old books no longer fit for circulation (wch Saxby picked out) presented to him on leaving the station. Mr Beetham thinks this is a very good plan for getting rid of rubbish.

Hugh Beetham's comment about 'rubbish' perhaps suggests that Saxby weeded out the 'old books no longer fit for circulation' by content as well as wear.

It is hard to believe though that there were any books less fit for circulation than some that have remained in the collection. On first encounter, their filthiness is eye-watering. Mrs Henry Wood's *St Martin's Eve* (1883) is torn off its spine, filthy and broken, falling open in chunks. Many popular novels are in a similar state, including *Vanity Fair, Kidnapped, Dawn, The Scarlet Pimpernel, David Copperfield, Hide and Seek,* Steele Rudd's *On Our Selection* and A.C. Gunter's *The King's Stockbroker.* But dirty and broken books are historical gold. The damaged books bear witness to a life of intensive use. It seems likely the most popular books went from hand to hand around the farm, recommended by one reader to the next, and many allow you to guess what the Brancepeth readers ate for dinner, or the time of day and the season of reading.

Two books have the names of out-stations written in them giving a sense of the distances they traveled. 'Ponto' which was near the homestead, is written in Mrs Oliphant's *Miss Marjoribanks,* and 'Hineroa', an out-station about 25 km to the west, in Sir Morell McKenzie's *The Fatal Illness of Frederick the Noble.* Many of the books have plainly spent some time outdoors. They have grass stains and streaks of mud; there are insects and leaf debris trapped in the gutters. A dead spider on the title page of Robert Buchanan's *The Martyrdom of Madeline* (1884) and a dead beetle in W.H. Ainsworth's *James the Second* (1854) appear to have been there some time. Moth wings, ants, desiccated spiders and silverfish litter the gutters of many books. Some books have been put face-down on the ground, and others have intensely dirty pages, like Jules Verne's *Michael Strogoff*. Pages have been badly cut on first reading or are torn and abraded; many have softened at the edges, with tide-marks of dirt reaching into the margin. Mrs Alexander's *The Wooing O'T* (1899) is one of many books to sport a ring made by a cup or glass placed on its cover, and countless books have long liquid stains running over the page, perhaps tea, cocoa or coffee, though Miller's complaints about how much tea was consumed on the station make it the most likely culprit. There were also illicit stills on the station from time to time, and despite the ban on alcohol, many potent beverages were smuggled in, which may account for the frequency of liquid accidents involving books. More dramatically, B.M. Croker's *Peggy of the Bartons* looks as if it has been dropped in the bath. Miller's alertness to body odours among the working men tends to suggest that baths were infrequent, and any bathing-related accidents to books were most likely to have happened in the homestead.

It is clear from stains and spills that books were often read over dinner. Splatters of viscous matter that have dried on the page are commonplace (stew?), and fine drifts of crumbs gather in the gutters. There are innumerable greasy fingerprints, made when someone has turned the page without wiping their hand, soaked into Mary Braddon's *Vixen* or Grant Allen's *The Scallywag*. Large numbers of books have runnels and spots of wax on the cover or on the page, like *In the Shires* (1872) a 'Sporting Novel' by Sir Randal H. Roberts. Brancepeth readers typically read after work, by candlelight and by the fire, while eating and drinking. Stoking the fire, they left large sooty thumbprints on the corners of the page; to mark their place, they turned down corners or left the book open and face down, loosening the binding and separating the gatherings. Judging by the surprising frequency of scorch marks, some readers evidently fell asleep by the fire, lost their concentration (or were interrupted) and let the book slide into the fire, or held it too close to the candle. Joseph Hocking's *The Trampled Cross* (1907), like many others, has burned edges, as does *Arctic Explorations in Search of Sir John Franklin* (1882) by Elisha Kent Kane. There are several burned pages in Marie Corelli's *Free Opinions Freely Expressed,* ironically—or who knows, deliberately?—in a chapter entitled 'The Vulgarity of Wealth', which is a sentiment unlikely to have been shared by most people at Brancepeth in the 1890s. Because the books as a whole haven't burned, it is likely they simply slipped off someone's lap into the embers, although the burn in Corelli's essay may have been an ember from a careless pipe, which someone has tried to douse, perhaps, with a splash of water.

Some books show signs of a feminine presence. Pressed flowers occur occasionally—like the violets and pansies in Jane Findlater's *The Green Graves of Balgowrie*—and the names of the Beetham daughters are written in a number of books, for example, 'Weva B R Beetham' in Rolf Boldrewood's *Plain Living.* A.J. Dawson's *Middle Greyness* has knitting instructions jotted inside the front cover. But the predominance across the collection of large thumbprints coated with soot, oil and grease suggests that the majority of readerly traces belong to men who have finished a day's hard and tiring work and have picked up a book over dinner. The burned and scorched books are likely to be the result of fatigue and inattention—the fluctuating patterns of concentration that characterise any reading session, but in this case accentuated by a life of hard physical work. Many books that open with dirty, abraded pages become cleaner and stiffer half way through, like G.A. Sala's *Gaslight and Daylight with some London scenes they shine upon* (1872), indicating where readers tended to leave off reading, having lost interest or found they didn't enjoy their choice after all. Time, in all its momentary specificity, is recorded in the Brancepeth library.

Not everyone picked up a book in order to read it. The most common jottings in the Brancepeth library (after marginalia by John Vaughan Miller) are numbers, and most of them are sums, simple additions or multiplications. The small amounts suggest personal finances. For example in Ouida's *The Massarenes,* which has a number of sums on the half title page, someone has added together 2.6.0 and 6.13.6, and written the total of 8.19.6. One of the features of the station ledgers is the large number of small transactions. Brancepeth workers bought goods on tick from the store and had them deducted from their pay, and there was always a day of final reckoning when Miller worked out what they were owed, or, in more imprudent cases, what they owed the station. The frequency of arithmetical jottings in the library books suggest that many employees had no other means at hand to keep track of their expenses. They also indicate a degree of anxiety about money. An addition on a torn half page in Walter Besant's *The Orange Girl* is followed by 'Pay bearer the sum of 22.10.4 or Help'. In Stanley Weyman's *Laid up in Lavender* someone has written a daunting list of what are probably debts:

Hamel	1.15.0
Frank	4.15.0
Tobacco	8.0
Adam	10.0
Albert	1
Taylor	1.6.0
Libray	5
	10.19

'Hamel', properly Pat Hamill, was a hawker who visited Brancepeth selling clothes, household goods and trinkets, whose regular visits were recorded by Miller in the station diary. Luckily, despite misspelling 'Library,' this anonymous debtor has miscalculated the total and owes less than they might think.

Other lists of numbers might be expenses or pay sheets. Inside the front cover of Captain Mayne Reid's *The Boy Tar* is a list of 14 amounts of shillings and pence, which vary from 1/0d to 17/6d, and are perhaps a record of money owed for hours worked. Most of the calculations and lists of figures are on the inside or back covers, but sometimes they pop up along the bottom or at the top of a page, as in Lois Hume's *An Unlucky Proposal* where a double row of crossed-out numbers on p9 looks like a score card. Some numbers are lists of measurements, once for what might perhaps be curtains ('22 1/2 green 45 connecting') in Whyte-Melville's *Katerfelto*, a novel about a highwayman's horse and one of the most heavily used books at Brancepeth.

As well as sums, there are doodles and sketches, games of noughts and crosses, a number sequence in which someone doubled numbers. There are dates (1916, inside the back cover of *King Solomon's Mines*) and phrases which seem to be reminders, like 'braised chops' inside the front cover of George Du Maurier's famous novel *Trilby*. There are several shopping lists, including one in Bret Harte's *Devil's Ford* that is entirely for varying amounts of tobacco. Tobacco was an indispensable commodity for most of the men on the station. It was the item most often bought from the station store, and was frequently smoked while reading, as the scorch holes and shreds of tobacco in a number of books testify. Other shopping lists account for goods from the store, like this one found inside the front cover of Sarah P. Carr's *The Iron Way*:

Store	
2 tins of Capstan	1/10
2 paper	8d
candles	1/-
matches	1/-

Ada Cambridge's *A Marked Man* was the repository for a more varied list: 'calamine lotion, anti-figeslin [antiphlogistine], 3 in. bandage, matches, tea, Powder No., Bacon, 204, meth sp.' The first three items tell us something of what ailed the Brancepeth workers: biting insects, sprains and muscle aches. Antiphlogistine, also known as Kaolin, was heated and applied to the body as a remedy for soreness.[11] Other items remain mysterious—'Powder No.' and '204'—although the former may be an antacid of some sort, as in the station diary Miller frequently mentions ordering and dispensing digestive remedies, such as fruit salts.

What these diverse jottings make plain is that the books provided a convenient source of writing paper in a situation where people were both poor and had few resources on hand. Collectively, these personal notes are testimony to readers, mostly men, who lived on slender means and for whom keeping track of small outgoings was an essential part of keeping afloat. They also suggest conditions with few comforts and no family life. The shoals of single men who flooded through stations like Brancepeth looking for work during the depression of the 1890s are reflected in these skimpy shopping lists and fretful arithmetic. These were men who were lucky enough to have jobs, but, as the diary repeatedly illustrates, they always had trouble making ends meet and knew they were part of a vulnerable workforce. Wages at Brancepeth were not high, and did not increase during the 1890s. It was relatively easy to get laid off if you couldn't keep up with the demands of the job or, worse, succumbed to a drinking session, since being caught drunk on the station meant instant dismissal.

In one of his articles for the *Wairarapa Daily Times,* Miller drew attention to the difficult lives endured by many working men, by way of reproof to those he named the 'decently-clad devils of society', people who have 'no mercy on any fault or weaknesses but their own':

> We think that what Charles Kingsley said is (with verbal alteration) specially applicable to men employed on station and up-country work: 'If you had ever known what it was to want, not only every luxury of the senses, but even decent bread to eat, you would think more mercifully of the man who makes up by rare excesses, and those only of the limited kinds possible to him, for long intervals of dull privation, maddening in their hateful monotony.'[12]

What Miller intended here was an indirect apologia for the infamous drinking bouts of working men (and perhaps he meant obliquely to refer to himself and the reason he ended up at Brancepeth). But he was also possibly alluding to his own job, as hateful monotony is a frequent theme in his station diary. Perhaps, too, he intended a private allusion to what it was like to be a settler in New Zealand in the 1880s after the bustle of being an Admiralty clerk in London. For Miller, as for the other Brancepeth library users, reading—and especially reading fiction—helped alleviate the 'hateful monotony', but the incidental jottings in the books also illuminate the boredom, anxiety and privations of their working conditions. It is likely that the people writing store lists and doing their arithmetic in the books were on the out-stations or in camps, where ordering from the store was not a spontaneous transaction and required careful calculation of resources. The list of debtors in *Laid up in Lavender* is suggestive not only of the all-male life of the camps, but also the cycles of lending and borrowing that occurred between them, often referred to in exasperation by Miller in his diary notes, as he was expected to untangle who owed what. The men on up-country work were also those who were paid the least.

Sometimes a comment or a witticism in the books suggests some anonymous reader's opinion of Brancepeth life. At the back of volume two of the works of Alexandre Dumas (containing *Nanon* and *The Two Dianas*), someone has written 'Wilson is in a bad temper today isnt he' in faint pencil at the top of the page, with the name 'Wilson' partly scribbled out. Hugh Wilson was the head shepherd, a man not popular with Miller, who portrays him in the station diary as bad-tempered, as well as ill-mannered and lazy. The pencil note evokes a schoolboy scribble about a teacher, and suggests that Wilson was the boss of whoever wrote it. The circumstances in which this phrase was written are intriguing to imagine. How did the book, its annotator and the person being addressed come to be in the same place as Wilson? Was Wilson addressing the other shepherds? Was he in the whare having a meal? Perhaps they were in the library, or there was a meeting at one of the camps—we cannot know, but whatever the circumstances, this chance scribble by a reader in his book opens a view of the long-vanished, transient interactions that comprised the daily life of the farm.

That Brancepeth was not always a happy place to work is indicated in Miller's fluctuating views of the station and his employers, expressed in his articles, his comments in the station diary, and his attempt at resigning from the job. Certainly Miller's personality, as revealed in his writing across all the texts he produced, was not a simple or easy one, and probably generated some of his difficulties, as did the circumstances that had led to his situation at Brancepeth. But he was not the only critical voice: other people on the farm recorded unflattering comment and critique of the station and its owners on the pages and in the margins of the library books. Notably, inside the back cover of Wilkie Collins's *Hide and Seek,* someone has scrawled in pencil 'Brancepeth is the rottenest bloody place I ever sheared', and then a name that looks like 'LBC Kaffin Brancepeth Wairarapa'. *Hide and Seek* is an early acquisition (published in 1861) so the date of this comment cannot be pinned down beyond a forty-year span, but what is interesting is that LBC Kaffin, if that is his name, felt strongly enough to leave a record of his opinion in a place where it was likely to be read by others, including the station owners. And, of course, this is part of the point of writing in the books. Shopping lists and financial records may have a strictly utilitarian and personal objective, but once annotations veer into comment or opinion, a library book is self-evidently a public place in which to record them. Most of the critical jottings are anonymous, but sometimes the intended audience is more obviously signaled.

On the title page of A.B. Richmond's *Intemperance: The Great Source of Crime* someone (not Miller) has firmly written 'Rot!', and it seems certain that the vast majority of employees at Brancepeth would have rejoiced to see it. In an even more pointed and political addition to the text, someone has produced a recognisable sketch of Hugh Beetham on the title page of Rita's *A Husband of No Importance* (1906) and added 'by Brancepeth's ar--s'. The satirical play on the title reflects on both Ruth and Hugh Beetham, and the Brancepeth 'artist' expected at least some of those who saw his work to know who he was (the cheeky abbreviation perhaps suggests a joint effort or a rude pun). Rita was a popular novelist at Brancepeth and was read with attention, as annotations and marked passages in several of her novels show—so perhaps the 'Brancepeth artist' was counting on particular readers to see the caricature. A more generic bit of reader alteration took place in Horace Vachell's *The Face of Clay,* which has had a rectangular hole cut in the title page so the half title shows through. The word 'clay' is crossed out and replaced by 'and now dust'.

Marginalia and annotations in books are always a dialogue, sometimes with the book and its author, sometimes with other readers, sometimes with oneself. Miller's annotations such as in adding scholia to the text, usually address the deficiencies of the book and its author and implicitly instruct or rebuke the other readers at Brancepeth. There are one or two examples of other readers opining or importing information to the text. These do not always address another putative reader, but sometimes seem to be driven by a desire to record something for its own sake. In the margins of p33 of *The Lost Possessions of England*, someone has made a note that a 'livre is 20 sous, or a franc/ 1 sou is about 1/2 penny /about 16 make a franc—10d'. This is a response to a passage describing how Dunkirk was sold to the French by King Charles during the Restoration for five million livres. The anonymous annotator, by noting a conversion rate, allows other Brancepeth readers to decipher the fairytale figure. If 10d meant a tin of tobacco, more or less, then Dunkirk once fetched the equivalent of 5 million tins. The helpful gloss performs a minor act of translation, but one not without political overtones on a station where wealth was so unevenly distributed.

Anonymous sketches and jottings sometimes explicitly open a dialogue with other readers, who are expected to agree with the point of view expressed or appreciate the joke. Such shafts of satiric humour, like the word 'Rot' and the sketch of Hugh Beetham appended to Rita's title, illuminate shared attitudes or anticipate solidarity. They offer a glimpse of the station world from a different perspective than the dominating runholder narrative of colonial success (as in Douglas Cresswell's biographical article of 1956 which coins the lordly phrase 'Beetham of Brancepeth'[13]) or the more ambiguous perspective of the station diary, making the homosocial working-class world of the station fleetingly visible.

As H.J. Jackson has noted, although there is no such thing as a 'typical' reader, all readers nonetheless operate under a shared system of codes of communication, which obliges them to negotiate conventions of writing, just as writers must work within conventions of reading. Jackson writes:

> Many of these tacit codes can be inferred from readers' marginalia, addressed as they are to the author or another reader. The slightest marks can tell us something. The name on the title page says, This book belongs to me and I expect it back if I lend it to you. Lines down the margin say, These are especially pertinent passages. Crosses at the beginning of a paragraph say, Take note of this . . .[14]

The tacit codes of reader marginalia at Brancepeth encompass all Jackson's examples, though some variation derives from the fact that Brancepeth, as a subscription library, sits somewhere between a public and a private collection, whereas Jackson is referring mainly to books privately owned by individuals. Although the library at Brancepeth was owned by the Beetham family, it operated as the property of a community, and its marginalia reflects a more diverse, incidental, and accidental use of the books than in the family's collection of books housed in the smoking room. When inscriptions occur in the Beethams' private collection, they are almost exclusively names, usually proclaiming ownership and often recording the circumstances of acquisition as gifts or school prizes. Many of the books in the smoking room are hardly read, and those that show signs of use tend to be reference works. Inscriptions in the station library books usually make a different point. When names occur, they commemorate a moment of reading—like Thyra Beetham's name and the date written in a number of novels, as described in the previous chapter– or they point to someone who has by choice or by accident left a book behind, or record a presentation made to the library. All these categories draw attention to the named person as a reader and book-lover, rather than an owner.

Anonymous comments and incidental use of the books' margins for drawings, lists, and sums also function as a kind of tacit code—this book does *not* belong to me and therefore I take the opportunity to deface it or use it for my own purposes. Some of these annotations are deliberately subversive and resistant ('Rot'; the sketch of Hugh Beetham). Others make their point with a kind of deliberate, insouciant willfulness—I will use this book as I like. Some are simply opportunist and reflect the paper at hand; while others note something that is perhaps intended for other readers to enjoy, or a rhyme the writer doesn't want to forget. On the whole, unlike many of Miller's annotations, the anonymous jottings do not smack of ostentatious erudition.

Various cartoons adorn the inside covers. One rather inept sketch is labelled 'Stan [or Stal] the famous halfback' which possibly refers to a person readers might know, and there are also (not very good) caricatures of male heads, drawings of ships and horses, what look like sketches of working tools, doodles that repeat titles, and frequent renditions of 'Brancepeth Library' in pencil or ink. These ornaments evoke idle time, when the blank pages of a book are fair game for a man with a pencil and nothing to do. If the use of the collection as a whole suggests a recreational need, the non-reading users expand the possibilities offered by paper and otherwise unoccupied time. A number of simple jokes or rhymes are left for other readers to enjoy, in a kind of textual camaraderie. The advertising list for Cassell's Colonial Library tipped in to the back of Joseph Hocking's *Flame of Fire*, a historical novel set at the time of the Armada, is adorned with a joke written in blotty black ink:

> Jack Brown Bull Milker Brancepeth
> Nick Lynch Worm Feeder Brancepeth

At the top of the page another name, perhaps the author of the joke, has been scrubbed out. The damaged and torn front endpaper of *King Solomon's Mines* sports a tongue twister:

> That that that was/was that that that/was not was not
> That that that was not/was that that/that was was not.

As well as these traces of people finding amusement where they can, there are also jottings that perhaps refer to Westerns (one of the most popular books in the library was Owen Wister's *The Virginian*). In Stanley Weyman's *Laid up in Lavender,* scrawled across the top of a double page is 'Tangle Trail Beau Rand outlaw story'. Elsewhere someone has written 'The ringer/ the three gun man/ the two hack bit/ and two point hit'. What do these phrases mean and why are they there? Are they just communications from the writer to himself? Is he noting a book that someone else has recommended? Is it a joke that can no longer be deciphered? It seems to me that the point is not so much to decode the meaning or the context of specific jottings by long-dead station workers (their general point is clear: the people who wrote them had read and liked Westerns), but rather, to see these fragments as an integral part of the library and, in a very general way, a memorialisation of a moment of not-reading. The reader has taken his pencil and scribbled—a fleeting thought? a reminder? a note to a friend? an idle phrase?—and in that moment, made himself visible to us, over a century later.

The debris, damage and annotations to roughly a sixth of the entire Brancepeth collection are a part of the library just as much as the selection of titles, the catalogue, the rules, red linenette covers and the specially built glass-fronted bookcases, which proclaim that the collection is not incidental, and that it is treasured. The accoutrements of the library formalise it, but the fingerprints and tears and stains personalise it, stamping the collection with temporality and making it specific to a place. The invisible readers are, however briefly, present alongside the narrative world of the text, and that momentary snapshot of the reader at his task is surrounded by the echoes of daily life on a sheep station in the 1890s.

There is very little personal memorabilia inserted into the Brancepeth books, other than pressed flowers: there are no photographs, letters, calling cards, or mementoes. There are a couple of mirror images of handwriting, from when someone has put the book they were reading face down on the still-wet ink of a letter or an invoice. A carefully cut-out reproduction of a professional pencil drawing has been tucked into the opening pages of Robert Hichens' *The Dweller on the Threshold*.[15] It shows an idealised, pensive, young woman, eyes downcast, her waving hair drawn softly back from her face and her cheek resting on her hand. In the corner is the name of the artist, and the date, 1911. The picture is a plangent reminder of the social isolation of many men in the 1890s and later,[16] and more generally the scarcity of women in nineteenth-century and early twentieth-century rural New Zealand, as manifest at Brancepeth as anywhere else. However, less romantic observations about women continued to circulate. Marie Corelli's *The Murder of Delicia* (1896) is a novel about an impeccable wife who supports her philandering titled husband's extravagant tastes by writing popular novels, until one day her eyes are opened to his nasty ways and she withdraws herself and her labour. Corelli's 'Introductory Note' is a passionate argument defending the 'clever woman' (like the eponymous Delicia, and by extension Corelli herself) who need not be 'unsexed'. The saintly Delicia exemplifies 'every sweet and sacred sentiment of womanhood'—despite her literary success and what she has endured in her marriage. Two readers have left remarks, to posterity and each other, on Delicia. Opposite the 'Introductory Note' one has written, ironically, 'Very few Delicias about in 1911'. Underneath another has added 'Fewer still in 1926'. Direct comments like these are rare, although marked passages that draw attention to stereotypical views of women are common in the Brancepeth books (many of them attributable to John Vaughan Miller). But the heavily-used romances among a mostly masculine readership, on the other hand, seem also to speak to a strongly felt absence of femininity and its consolations in the lives of working men at Brancepeth.

Although the Brancepeth library was emphatically not a self-help library full of improving literature, all libraries, by their very existence, subtly promote reader improvement. Occasionally, Brancepeth readers jotted down words without further explanation, suggesting perhaps they had come across a new piece of vocabulary and were learning it. On the title page of Mrs Henry Wood's *Anne Hereford*, someone has jotted 'hirsute', and on the back cover of a very battered copy of Henry Kingsley's *The Recollections of Geoffrey Hamlyn*, a novel that was popular at Brancepeth (perhaps because it reflected a familiar colonial narrative of migration and sheep farming but made more exciting by a melodrama of gambling, swindling, transportation and bush-ranging) there is a short list of words: 'coherent, lucid, scrupulous'. On one occasion, a reader was a tease about vocabulary. In *A Ride to Khiva* (1877) by Fred Burnaby, the author uses the word 'kibitka' without explanation when describing a wedding: the 'bride's kibitka'. Attention has been drawn to this word by inserting + into the text, and on each side of the page a teasing rhyme has been written. In the right margin, 'Pull not a face,/ But, the meaning trace+' and on the left, 'note well the line,/;+ that, happens many a time' (222).

Despite these glancing examples of devotion to grammatical self-improvement among the library's readers, Miller had a dim view of the educational accomplishments of many of the Brancepeth workers. He wrote articles on education for the *Wairarapa Daily Times*, and was particularly harsh about the demise of good letter writing and spelling: 'we scarcely know of a young man or woman in the country who can spell correctly' ('What is Education?', 14 November 1899). Two years later, he returned to his theme in 'A Liberal Education':

> . . . with many unhappy ones spelling is always a question. It is quite out of the question that any man or woman can be really sure of spelling correctly without a fair knowledge of Latin—and, we must add, Greek. (4 December 1901)

But the clincher was to follow in 1905, when Miller appeared in the correspondence column of the *Wairarapa Daily Times* under the heading 'A Specimen of Orthography'.

> Sir,—The sub-joined application, received last week, presumably from a young shepherd, for mustering work, is, no doubt, the production of a Seventh Standard youth; and yet it is difficult to believe that his education has been free, secular and compulsory. Not free—for it must have cost him a great deal to arrive at his present pitch of scholarship; not secular—for he brings the patriarch Job into his memorial; not compulsory—for surely any such education would have compelled him to turn out a more creditable communication.
>
> If a man writes in such a way, one can only wonder what sort of books he reads.
>
> After more than twenty-five years' experience of New Zealand, I have come to the conclusion that (comparatively speaking) few men, fewer women, and a still smaller proportion of children and youths, can spell ordinary English words in common use, with anything approaching to correctness.—I am, etc

> M.
> Masterton, 28th May, 1905
> [EXACT COPY]
>
> May 1905 th 18
> Dear sir—are you fuldhand and if you are not full for mursterds can you give me ay yearly Job
> [A spell on 'M's' station may enable the young shepherd to 'pass muster'. Ed. W.D.T.]

It seems unlikely that the unfortunate author of the letter read any books at all, and equally unlikely that the more illiterate workers on the farm would have spent £1 a year on a library subscription. The most popular reading matter on Brancepeth was newspapers, which were sent daily to the camps and ordered specially for the sheds when shearing was on. Quarrels about the library's provision of newspapers are the only recorded disputes in the committee records, and the library's rule that no member was to retain a newspaper or periodical for longer than 15 minutes is an indication of high demand. Sadly, newspapers, unlike periodicals and books, do not survive the present moment unless they are formally preserved. The office at Brancepeth had a book press and binder and kept bound volumes of periodicals, which were also part of the gift of the collection to the university, but no local (or foreign) newspapers have survived the passing of time, except as clippings in Ruth Beetham's scrapbook.

Writing in *The Nineteenth Century* in 1886, Edward G. Salmon described how working men read the dailies 'at their clubs, their eating-houses, and the public-house', and that the most popular magazines with British working class readers were the *Leisure Hour* and *Sunday at Home.*[17] Neither of these journals were taken at Brancepeth, but a range of illustrated periodicals, such as *The Graphic* and the *Illustrated London News* were held in the reading room, and pictures of pretty young women in the Pearson's Soap advertisements are still fastened to the walls of the groom's room. Salmon makes the point that when working men read books, 'they usually read good books' (116). He gives as examples Dickens, Shakespeare, Milton, Bunyan and the Bible. *Pilgrim's Progress* is in fact one of the least-read books in the Brancepeth collection—it is even possible that it is one of the few that have not been read at all. In contrast, both Dickens and Milton are among the heavily-used books, and in the library's edition of Milton, the memoir of his life, 'Paradise Lost', 'Paradise Regained' and 'Samson Agonistes' have numerous marked passages and show reader damage. It is of course impossible to say whether the readers of Milton and Dickens were men who worked on the farm, family members, or visitors, just as it is impossible to know who read the newspapers, and what happened to illiterate or semi-literate workers. According to Salmon, in some London work places, such as tailor shops, one worker read the paper aloud to the others (190), but Brancepeth workers were outside all day, and moving around, so it seems less likely that they enjoyed a designated reader. Still, there is some evidence of reading aloud, as in the copy of Dickens' *A Christmas Carol*, which has marked passages and the instruction 'read' in the margin, and it is not unimaginable that someone read from the papers or periodicals in the camps at night. Miller recorded men coming to hear speakers and readings in the library and being well pleased with them, but if the library offered a communal intellectual and recreational life in any regular way, it has not been recorded.

Oral tradition on the station maintains that the library was established in order to improve the literacy of the Brancepeth workers, but the annotations in the books and the range of books that were heavily used suggest that the regular readers were those employees for whom reading was an established habit. Even so, there is evidence to suggest an outer crescent of readers who enjoyed Westerns and detective novels, and whose literacy probably did not extend beyond basic schooling. It is not hard to imagine why Westerns appealed to men whose daily life was spent working outside with animals. Horses and dogs were valuable property (and often a station hand's only asset), significant companions, and, for shepherds, essential tools of their trade. Books featuring horses and dogs (like *The Virginian* and *Katerfelto*) are high on the list of heavily-used volumes, and the non-fiction part of the library collection contains a number of titles like *Our Friend the Dog, Handy Horse Book* and *The Practical Shepherd.* Idstone's *The Dog* has a marked passage about what kind of bones to feed a dog, and in *Through Stable and Saddle-Room* someone (perhaps Hugh or Ruth Beetham) has marked passages about how a stable must be kept as clean as a drawing room.

At its most elemental level, the desire to read is a form of appetite. Reading satisfies a spectrum of human needs, among them comfort, entertainment, familiarity, novelty, excitement, companionship, adventure, affection. Some of these dimensions of reading can be inferred from what readers liked best—melodramas and romances—but others are intimated by the lives of the books themselves. For each glimpse of a named reader, like Michael Ryan anxiously chasing the whereabouts of the latest Marie Corelli, there are tidemarks of fingerprints that speak of more reticent others. From this perspective, dirt is not so much proof of neglect and careless behaviour as a marvellous source of information about readers who were less verbose and ubiquitous than Miller, but just as enchanted by reading. Behind the scorch marks and the crumbs, the spilled cup of tea and guttering candle, sits someone whose hunger to finish the chapter made them oblivious to everything around them. And as the books passed through the mud and stench of working life, the occasional jaunty doodle or worried list of sums briefly illuminated the world in which their reading took place.

Conclusion

> All words have the 'taste' of a profession, a genre, a tendency, a party, a particular person, a generation, an age group, the day and hour. Each word tastes of the context and contexts in which it has lived its socially charged life.[1]

What Mikhail Bakhtin says about words can also be said of books and of collections of books. If, like me, you have been a compulsive reader and literary scholar all your life, there is deep historical magic in uncovering the evidence of past readers who have loved reading, and have often loved reading the same books as you have loved yourself. The study of literature brings the act of reading into intellectual history, but is inherently limiting, because those books preserved by time as 'great books' become the literary canon, thereby squeezing out the fertility and variety of an historical period. John Sutherland makes this point cogently when he says that generalisations about the Victorian novel are restricted to the 'dozen writers designated as "major" by the New Cambridge Bibliography of English Literature'; these are the authors found in the 'Literary Classics' sections of bookshops, and their authors are the subject of innumerable studies. But, in Sutherland's words, it is precisely their literary distinction that 'renders them necessarily unrepresentative'. He points out that estimates of book production in the Victorian period show annual totals rising from 2,000 to 8,000 new titles per year from 1837–1901; by the end of Victoria's reign, the proportion of fiction had increased from 12 to 25%.[2] Focussing on the literary canon as literary history greatly distorts the picture of what Victorian readers actually read, as if everyone was a serious literary scholar, and as if the wealth and diversity of the popular reading that surrounded them in ever-increasing quantities did not become part of their imaginations and daily lives. One of the singular features of the Brancepeth library is its concentration not only on fiction but on popular Victorian novelists, who, when they eventually became unfashionable and unpopular, were discarded by public libraries. Brancepeth's embrace of the broad range of Victorian fiction makes it an irreplaceable index of what Victorian households actually read; indeed, a number of the books held in the Brancepeth library are now the only copies in the country.

When I was first introduced to the Brancepeth library, as a collection of dirty books with faded covers in beautiful glass cases on the ground floor of the university library, I thought it would become the subject of an elegant essay about past reading habits, a little excursion into the back waters of a Victorian library. Then I opened the books, and immediately and vividly became aware that I was looking at their readers. The extent of material wear and marginalia in the Brancepeth library is astonishing, because such damage and dirt tends to be culled from current library collections, so it is rare for a twenty-first-century public library reader to encounter dramatic examples of reader use. It made me want to know more about who those readers were, and one way to find out was to look hard at what was inside the books—not only the dirt, but the content and the marginalia. Jonathan Rose has recently argued that there is no discernible pattern in marginalia, that the only pattern is no pattern.[3] The

Brancepeth library offers a forceful counter-argument, in that it constitutes a legible map of reader presence, attention, and knowledge. Not only is there a very discernible pattern in the marginalia produced by John Vaughan Miller—his marginal comments offering scholarly, emotional, psychological, historical and quantitative information about him and the world he addressed—but the Brancepeth marginalia as a whole is eloquent about who made it and the overlapping patterns of their reading and working lives.

The Brancepeth library was displaced from where it was read when it was gifted to the university in 1966. Separated from Brancepeth, the collection is presented in a very different, quite impersonal context: the implied reader at the university is someone whose interest in the books will be as fodder for literary, scholarly and academic projects. But if the Brancepeth library is considered not just as supplementary shelves of old books but as an artefact in itself, you start to wonder about its historical identity, the 'taste' of these books, the titles handwritten on their dirty spines. Who read them? What did they like? I began by visiting Brancepeth, which, as I have described in the opening chapter, though still a working farm, is also a slice of Victorian New Zealand. All the station documents remain in place, held to the walls of the office by rusty bulldog-clips, or neatly shelved as Miller and his successors must have left them. Opening the station ledgers and the diary I encountered the same hand that had inscribed so many of the books at the university, and reading Miller's entries made it clear that the library could not be considered in isolation from the social history of the station. Just as the mass of popular Victorian writers cannot be excluded from our idea of 'Victorian literature', reading was part of station life, and taking the collection back to Brancepeth was what brought the readers to life.

Many questions arose. Why did the Beethams establish

such a large subscription library and how did the collection relate to their substantial private family collection? How did the literary and artistic culture they brought with them to New Zealand shape the station world and their own lives? And what was that station world, its outlines still visible in the buildings and layout at Brancepeth? How did colonialism influence the station library? And how did the library holdings—mostly British, mostly metropolitan, mostly fiction, about half of it written by women—connect to the rural, colonial, mostly male and mostly working class readership? What was the place of reading in daily life?

'Daily life' is a simple phrase, one that suggests such a thing is easily recognisable, recovered and described. What I have called the 'social world of the reader' attempts to reconstruct some of the many interactions, relationships, behaviour, activities, emotions, hierarchies and grinding repetitions of what happened on a daily basis at Brancepeth, based on the subjective accounts of John Vaughan Miller. It is not an objective history and does not aim to be. What Miller recorded, he recorded as part of an official narrative, but it is always laced with his opinion. His gift for narrative detail makes many things—the food for example—vivid and present, while references to the things he read and wrote are interleaved with the detail of stock returns, mail deliveries and irritable accounts of the many petty tasks that occupied his long working days. Because the 'where' of reading is visible in such a rich variety of ways at Brancepeth, reading also becomes part of that daily life—which, in turn, has allowed me to make speculative connections between fiction and everything else, including colonialism, class, and gender.

This is not to say that the point of thinking about reading as part of daily life is to 'explain' how reading connects to everything else that was going on—it may, or it may not. Sometimes Miller's articles and remarks suggest a concrete, even causal connection; mostly such a link is not so clear. Rather, seeing reading as a part of daily life necessarily expands our ideas of what daily life was like. Hard-working, hard-living men spill their stew on an open copy of Marie Corelli, or jot a schoolboy note in the margin of Dumas; a sentimental type presses violets between the pages, another inserts a winsome picture of a young lady lost in thought. And, if the 'where' of reading is projected back into particular novels, then rags-to-riches narratives, and tales of debtors and orphans, brave emigrants, or missing family members, take on newly specific and local resonances.

These entanglements of reading and living are what this book is about: the intricate webs of emotions, prejudices, ideas, jokes, politics, dreams, hopes and hard physical realities that characterise the daily life of the reader on a remote sheep station and in a colony. It may have been Auden who said that the book one reads should somehow be at odds with the place in which it is read. Many of the books most heavily read at Brancepeth seem to concur with this precept, but as the particular social world of the station comes into view, the distances between page and world seem smaller.

Without John Vaughan Miller, this book would probably have remained an essay. His dominating scribal presence illuminates the many layers of daily life in the complex social world of Brancepeth, and discloses some of his own complicated story. In his scrawling hand daily life is filled with a wealth of evocative detail: a swagger dancing on the lawn, escapades in the laundry, the carpenter who moonlighted as the librarian dropping dead on the verandah, plums stolen in the night, cuts of mutton sliced 'the wrong way', the vicar's dubious past, and the parade of 'cringing bloaters', insurance 'drummers', and 'naked' lonely men who passed through the farm gates in the hope of a meal and a few days' work. Miller illuminates the diversity of relationships with Māori; collective anxieties about 'progressive' women and the advance of women's rights; the state of education; and the many variations in the workforce that might, as a simple list of names in the ledgers, seem homogenous, but under Miller's recording pen turn out to be Cornish, Irish, Scots, Welsh, Australian, Canadian, Swedish, Norwegian, and Japanese, not to mention absconded sailors. Not least Miller's cumulative writings show how an intellectual life might be pursued under less than promising circumstances, and how such a life might spring from a whole spectrum of motivations, from vanity to intellectual curiosity. Miller allows me to make the argument this book presents, that discovering the 'where' of reading opens new views not only of readers and their books, but also of the singular and lively world they inhabited. It is both ironic and moving that Miller, who did not seem to enjoy most of his working life at Brancepeth and thought it was high time someone in New Zealand wrote a 'really good novel of life and manners', produced—in his tireless diary entries, annotations, letters and articles—the next best thing.

Notes

Chapter One: The Romance of the Archive

1 Greg Dening, *History's Anthropology: The Death of William Gooch* (Lanham, MD: University Press of America, 1988) 1.
2 A Category I site is defined by the New Zealand Historic Places Act 1993 as a place of 'special or outstanding historical or cultural heritage significance or value'.
3 See James Belich, *Paradise Reforged: A History of the New Zealanders from the 1880s to the year 2000* (Auckland: Allen Lane / The Penguin Press, 2001) 128; David Yerex *They Came to Wydrop* (Masterton: Published on behalf of Hugh Beetham of Brancepeth and Tom Williams of Te Parae; Distributed by GP Publications, 1991) 96–102.
4 James Belich, *Making Peoples: A History of the New Zealanders from Polynesian Settlement to the End of the Nineteenth Century* (Auckland: Allen Lane /The Penguin Press, 1996) 400.
5 A block of 275,000 acres was bought by Donald McLean, the Crown purchaser, in 1853 after negotiation with the local iwi. The Crown paid £2500. Paul Goldsmith, *District 11A Report—Wairarapa* (Wellington, NZ: Waitangi Tribunal Rangahaua Whanui Series, July 1996), Chapter 3 'The First Crown Purchases: 1853 to January 1854.' http://www.waitangi-tribunal.govt.nz/doclibrary/public/researchwhanui/district/11A/Chapt03.pdf 22 (accessed 5 May 2010).
6 Brancepeth is the name of a village and castle in Country Durham, adjacent to Westmoreland where the Beetham family originated. It is likely the name 'Brancepeth' was already familiar to the Beethams; a similar (and possibly apocryphal) derivation is claimed for the village.
7 For example G. Hall 'Terrace' Station, Hororata, and P.R. Harding 'Mt. Vernon' Station, Waipukurau. See Dulcie Gillespie-Needham 'The Colonial and His Books' (Ph.D. thesis, Victoria University of Wellington, 1971) 134.
8 *Wairarapa Daily Times* 3 December 1895, 2.
9 Rough draft of the Annual Report of the Brancepeth Library [1892?], Brancepeth office papers.
10 Jonathan Rose, *The Intellectual Life of the British Working Classes* (New Haven and London: Yale University Press, 2001) 1.
11 See for example Jonathan Rose, *The Intellectual Life of the British Working Classes*, Simon Eliot, 'Public Libraries and Popular Authors, 1883–1912' (*The Library*, Sixth Series, VIII [1986] 322–350), and

Alberto Manguel, *A History of Reading* (New York: Viking, 1996). Tim Dolin has moved in this direction in his study of the South Australia Institute borrowing records, 'First Steps toward a History of the Mid-Victorian Novel in Colonial Australia' (*Australian Literary Studies* 22, 3 [2006] 273–293), but does not have access to individual readers. The notable exception is Kate Flint, *The Woman Reader, 1837–1914* (Oxford: Clarendon Press, 1993), but her focus is only on the woman reader.

12 J.E. Traue, 'The Public Library Explosion in Colonial New Zealand,' *Libraries & the Cultural Record* 42:2 (2007): 151–164. Traue's figures are: 1878, one library for every 1,529 people; 1898, one for every 2608; 1906, one for 2099 (152).

13 'Review.' *New Zealand Journal*, 6 July 1844, quoted in Traue (2007) 155.

14 Belich, *Making Peoples* 326 passim.

15 Lady Mary Anne Barker, *Station Amusements in New Zealand* (London: William Hunt, 1873).

16 Gillespie-Needham as above (419) and also discussed by Judy Klaus, 'Shearers Reading Shakespeare: How Unique was Brancepeth Station Library in the Late 1800s' (Master of Library and Information Studies research project, Victorian University of Wellington, 1999).

17 Tony Ballantyne, *Orientalism and Race: Aryanism in the British Empire* (Houndmills, Basingstoke, Hampshire; New York: Palgrave, 2002).

18 Dening, *History's Anthropology* 1.

19 Belich, *Making Peoples* 401.

20 Ellis Rowan, *A Flower Hunter in Queensland and New Zealand* (Sydney: Angus and Robertson, 1898) 222.

21 Belich, *Making Peoples* 393.

22 Martyn Lyons and Lucy Taksa, *Australian Readers Remember* (Melbourne: Oxford University Press, 1992) 7.

23 Belich, *Making Peoples* 393. Belich draws on Chapters 5–6 of Charlotte Macdonald, *A Woman of Good Character* (Wellington: Allen & Unwin/Historical Branch, 1990).

24 Amy Cruse, *The Victorians and Their Books* (London: George Allen & Unwin Ltd, 1935) 14.

25 See, for example Paul Erickson 'Help or Hindrance? The History of the Book and Electronic Media' in *Rethinking Media Change: The Aesthetics of Transition*, ed. David Thorburn and Henry Jenkins (Cambridge, MA: MIT Press, 2003) 95–116. See also Robert Darnton, 'First Steps Towards a History of Reading' in *The Kiss of Lamourette: Reflections in Cultural History* (New York and London: W.W.Norton, 1990) 177.

Chapter Two: Willie's Diary

1 MS Diary kept by William (Willie) Beetham, Beetham family papers. The diary has been typed and was available to me in the typescript. There may be transcription errors, but I am inclined to think the punctuation, syntax and spelling belong to Willie.
2 MS draft letter, Beetham family papers.
3 C.G. H[amilton], *Margaret Waldegrave; or, The Power of Truth* (Edinburgh 1846). Charles Gillingham Hamilton was also the author of *The Curate Of Linwood; or, The Real Strength Of The Christian Ministry* (1845) and *Amy Harrington; or, A Sister's Love* (1848).
4 It is not clear what Willie was referring to.
5 22 November 1851.
6 Beatrice Webb, *My Apprenticeship* (London: Longmans, 1926) 13. Cited in Walter E Houghton, *The Victorian Frame of Mind 1830–1870* (New Haven: Yale University Press, 1957) 188
7 In 1867, William Beetham Sr. wrote from the Hutt Valley to a friend called 'George' that 'we see all matters of that kind by the "Illustrated London News"' . . . which we receive here about 7 weeks old'. MS draft letter, Beetham family papers.
8 Thomas Dick, *On the Improvement of Society by the Diffusion of Knowledge: or, An illustration of the advantages which would result from a more general dissemination of rational and scientific information among all ranks* (NY: J & J Harper, 1883).
9 John Claudius Loudon (1783–1843). An extraordinary polymath (and garden designer), Loudon produced many famous works, including a number of well-known encyclopaedias. Willie could have been referring to *An Encyclopaedia of Gardening* 1822; *An Encyclopædia of Agriculture* 1825; *An Encyclopedia of Cottage Farm and Villa Architecture and Furniture* 1833; *The Encyclopedias of Plants* 1828/29; *An Encyclopaedia of Trees and Shrubs* 1842.
10 It is not clear what Willie is referring to, but it may be Sir William Strickland's *Journal of a tour in the United States of America 1794–1795* (London: Printed by W.Bulmer & Co, 1801).
11 Mrs Burbury, 'French Hay, or: Lost and Found, a Tale of English Village Life.' Serialised in *The Illustrated Magazine of Art* 23:4 and ff., 1854.
12 Mary Louise Pratt discusses the conventions that dominated travel writing in her famous book *Imperial Eyes* (London: Routledge, 1992), though many of these relate more to explorers and professional travelers than to passengers like Willie Beetham.
13 Edward Wakefield, 'New Zealand and Mr Froude.' *Nineteenth Century,* CXIV (August 1886) 174.
14 Jim McAloon has discussed the Canterbury rural elite and their strong

sense of class responsibility in *No Idle Rich* (Dunedin: University of Otago Press, 2002). Stevan Eldred-Grigg's *A Southern Gentry* (Wellington: Reed, 1980) is a history of South Island landed gentry.

15 Ernest Betham, ed., *A House of Letters* (London: Jarrold & Sons, n.d.) 16. Purchased by Hugh Horsley Beetham in August 1905.

16 Bernard Burke, *A Genealogical and Heraldic History of the Colonial Gentry*. 2 vols. (London, Harrison, 1891–1895) 97.

17 A.G. Bagnall, *Wairarapa* (Masterton: Hedley's Bookshop for the Masterton Trust Lands Trust, 1976) 51.

18 Written on the spine of this home-bound book is 'Press Paragraphs—Family Affairs'.

19 A short newspaper article containing this information is pasted into Ruth Beetham's press cutting book. 'The Betham Family of Towcett' came from the *Penrith Observer* and is dated 27 December 1911. Like other colonial families, the Beethams carried on family place names. William Beetham's house in Masterton was called Towcett.

20 See Egerton Castle, ed., *The Jerningham Letters* (1780–1843) 2 vols. (London: Richard Bentley & Son, 1896). The majority of letters are between Lady Frances Jerningham and her daughter Charlotte, who became Lady Bedingfield.

21 Betham, *A House of Letters* 35–6.

22 Paula R. Feldman, ed. *British Woman Poets of the Romantic Era* (Baltimore, Maryland: The Johns Hopkins University Press, 1997) 91.

23 Betham, *A House of Letters* 76. See *The Complete Poetical Works of Samuel Taylor Coleridge*, ed. Ernest Hartley Coleridge (Oxford, Clarendon Press, 1912), Vol. II, 374–75.

24 Betham, *A House of Letters* 127.

25 Elaine Bailey, 'Matilda Betham: a new biography.' *Wordsworth Circle* Summer 2007 http://findarticles.com/p/articles/mi_hb347/is_3_38/ai_n29371919/?tag=content;col1 (accessed 1 June, 2010).

26 Matilda Betham, 'The Lay of Marie', 1816, a facsimile reprint chosen and introduced by Jonathan Wordsworth (NY: Woodstock Books, 1996).

27 John Sutherland, *The Stanford Companion to Victorian Fiction* (Stanford, CA: Stanford University Press, 1989) 62.

28 W.B. Rhodes, a pastoralist, merchant and investor. By 1853 he was already being referred to as the 'millionaire of Wellington'. See entry in the online Dictionary of New Zealand Biography (DNZB) http://www.dnzb.govt.nz/dnzb/alt_essayBody.asp?essayID=1R7 (accessed 20 May 2010)

29 Brian Easton. 'William Beetham's *Portrait of Dr Isaac Featherston with the Maori Chiefs Wi Tako and Te Puni.*' *Bulletin of New Zealand Art History*, 12 (1991) 29–34. Roger Blackley, *A Nation's Portraits*

(Wellington: Art History, Victoria University of Wellington, 2005) 33.

30 An unsourced press cutting of William Beetham's obituary has been kept in Ruth Beetham's 'Press Paragraphs' scrapbook.

31 Nuku Tewhatewha was moved to George Beetham's house in Moturoa St, Thorndon when William died, and then to Brancepeth on 16 January 1906, after George had returned to live in London. In 1982 it was gifted to the Dowse Museum in Lower Hutt.

32 Blackley, *A Nation's Portraits* 33.

33 Undated MS letter, Beetham family papers.

34 Te Manihera Te Rangi-taka-i-waho (Ngāti Kahungunu) ?-1888. Te Manihera travelled with Charles Bidwill, Henry Petre, Charles Clifford and William Vavasour to Palliser Bay and South Wairarapa and managed the lease negotiations for the Māori owners. See entry in the online DNZB: http://www.dnzb.govt.nz/dnzb/alt_essayBody.asp?essayID=1T69 (accessed 1 June 2010).

35 'Pioneer Days—Settling the Wairarapa.' *Dominion* 14 September 1923, 8.

36 McAloon, *No Idle Rich*.

37 Bagnall, *Wairarapa* 357.

38 Bagnall, *Wairarapa* 359.

39 See David Yerex, *They Came to Wydrop* (Masterton: Published on behalf of Hugh Beetham of Brancepeth and Tom Williams of Te Parae; Distributed by GP Publications,1991) 66.

40 See DNZB entry for Te Korou, Te Retimana (?—1882). http://www.dnzb.govt.nz/DNZB/alt_essayBody.asp?essayID=1T46 (accessed 18 January, 2010).

41 Letter from Richmond to his father, 25 April 1856, quoted in Yerex, *They Came to Wydrop* 42.

42 Bagnall, *Wairarapa* 97.

43 Bagnall, *Wairarapa* 213.

44 There may have been more to this story than meets the eye. The *Nelson Evening Mail* reported that the plaintiffs, who included Taiawhio Te Tau, claimed that the article alleging dog-tax evasion imputed that 'they as chiefs were disreputable and dishonourable, utterly degraded and unfit to hold tribal rights', and sued 'Aporo and Tamahau Mahuhui' (Piripi Aporo and Tamahau Mahupuku), the writer and publisher, for £100 in damages. They eventually settled for £15 and a published apology. 'A Maori Libel Action.' *Nelson Evening Mail*, 26 March 1903, 3.

45 From 'Press Paragraphs—Family Affairs' the family press clipping album maintained by Ruth Beetham. Not all the clippings are dated and sourced.

46 *Wanganui Herald* 22 June 1906, 5.

47 Brancepeth station diary, 2 September 1907.
48 Thomas Richards, *The Imperial Archive* (London New York: Verso, 1993) 4.
49 D.F. McKenzie *Bibliography and the Sociology of Texts* (Cambridge: Cambridge University Press, 1999). This sentence is a summary of part of McKenzie's argument, and is drawn from Roger Chartier's discussion of McKenzie in *On the Edge of the Cliff: History, Language and Practices* (Baltimore: John Hopkins University Press, 1997) 83.
50 J.R. Seeley, *The Expansion of England* (London: Macmillan and Co, *1883)*; Charles Wentworth Dilke, *Greater Britain* (London: Macmillan & Co, 1868).
51 Marie Zielie Hermanze Frere was born in Picardy. Her obituary claimed that she had a very vivid memory of the Franco-Prussian War, and 'was the last woman to leave Paris at the time of the siege in 1870'. *Wairarapa Daily Times* 14 October 1918.
52 Belich, *Making Peoples* 445.
53 Ralph Beetham in later life was a collector of early New Zealand books, and it is possible these were bought by him. But it is also quite likely Selwyn visited at some point.
54 See entry in online DNZB for Taiawhio Te Tau: http://www.dnzb.govt.nz/dnzb/alt_essayBody.asp?essayID=3T21 (accessed 30 May 2010).

Chapter Three: The Clerk's Tale

1 Station Diary, 2 February 1908.
2 '(Sir) Alexander Mackenzie, (1842–1902) a civilian and Lieutenant Governor of Bengal from December 1895 to April 1898. Educated at Grammar School, Birmingham and Trinity College, Cambridge, Mackenzie arrived in Calcutta as an ICS member in December 1862. Before he became the Lt Governor of Bengal, Alexander Mackenzie held many high positions of administration including Home Secretary to the Government of India, 1882; Chief Commissioner of the Central Provinces, 1887; Chief Commissioner of Burma, 1890 and Member of the Supreme Council, 1895.' From *Banglapedia: National Encyclopedia of Bangladesh*. Web. http://www.banglapedia.org/httpdocs/HT/M_0008.HTM (accessed 19 June 2010).
3 Station Diary, 13 November 1897. Mrs Richmond Beetham was Lucilla Swainson, daughter of William Swainson the naturalist and artist, who lived in the Hutt. The Swainsons were early friends of William Beetham and his family. E(dwin) N(ewcome) Swainson was Assistant Secretary to the Lords Commissioners of the Admiralty Board, famous for his severity, and survived a bomb attack in his office in 1885. For a full account of Swainson, see Iain Hamilton, 'The Difficulties of an Admiralty Reformer in the later Nineteenth Century: The Case of

E.N. Swainson.' *International Journal of Naval History* 7:1, April 2008. Web. http://ijnhonline.org/volume7_number1_apr08/PDF%20 apr08/article_hamilton_apr08.pdf (accessed 21 January 2010).

4 Station Diary, 13 January 1906.

5 Nelson *Colonist* 25 January 1893, 3.

6 Nelson *Colonist* 5 April 1893, 3.

7 There was another employee called Miller, Charles R. Miller, who was in charge of Westmere, on the west side of the station. His movements are regularly noted in the station diary and there is a tone of animosity about them but also insistent interest.

8 Herbert, Hubert, Margaret, Arthur, Basil, Mary, Maud, Anthony, Ruth. Surviving family members no longer know which one of the daughters was known as 'Queenie' but it was probably Margaret.

9 The stanza is from 'Resignation' by Henry Wadsworth Longfellow in *The Seaside and the Fireside (By the Fireside)* 1850; and the reference to John Keble's famous prayer book *The Christian Year*, probably the Tenth Sunday after Trinity when Christ is weeping over the city (Luke XIX, 41).

10 The Miller family now knows little about their great-grandfather. An email from Jan Miller said the family story was that he had lost the land at Kaiteriteri through drinking, which is supported by his bankruptcy and the prohibition order taken out against him in 1893. These were sometimes applied for by the person affected. His disparaging remarks about people who drank at Brancepeth were perhaps a reaction to a drunken past.

11 Miles Fairburn, *Nearly Out of Heart and Hope: The Puzzle of a Colonial Labourer's Diary* (Auckland: Auckland University Press, 1995) 241.

12 Station Diary, 26 May 1904

13 By 'two', Miller presumably means 'at odds.'

14 Station Diary, 1 January 1904.

15 'Guerilla Philanthropy,' *Wairarapa Daily Times* 17 August 1898.

16 Tony Ballantyne, *Orientalism and Race* (London: Palgrave Macmillan, 2007), 3–17.

17 Eric Wolf, *Europe and the People without History* (Berkeley: University of California Press, 1982), cited in Ballantyne, *Orientalism and Race* 3. I use the phrase here as an apt description of Miller's circumstances and context.

18 J.A. Froude, *Oceana or, England and her Colonies* (London: Longmans, Green & Co, 1886) 308.

19 See Dulcie Gillespie-Needham, 'The Colonial and his Books' (PhD thesis, Victoria University of Wellington, 1971).

20 Gillespie-Needham, 'The Colonial and his Books' 419.

21 'Tennyson Spoiled,' *Wairarapa Daily Times* 30 December 1897, 2.

22 Ellis Rowan, *A Flower Painter in Queensland and New Zealand* (Sydney: Angus & Robertson, 1898), 222.
23 Te Parae was the station homestead belonging to T. C. Williams and had its own work gang.
24 Benedict Anderson, *Imagined Communities: Reflections on the Origin and Spread of Nationalism*. Revised Edition. (London, New York: Verso, 1991), 35–6.

Chapter Four: The Social World of the Reader

1 Miles Fairburn, *Nearly Out of Heart and Hope* (Auckland: Auckland University Press, 1995) 1.
2 *David Copperfield* was the most popular of Dickens's novels at Brancepeth, while H. Rider Haggard's books were among the most heavily read.
3 Robert Darnton, in *The Kiss of Lamourette: Reflections in Cultural History* (London and New York: W.W. Norton and Company, 1990), has called for more attention to be paid to the 'where' of reading (167).
4 Belich, *Making Peoples: A History of the New Zealanders, from Polynesian Settlement to the End of the 19th Century (*Auckland: Penguin Press, 1996) 336.
5 Lawson worked on newspapers and as a schoolteacher in New Zealand and wrote a number of stories set here. See W.H. Pearson, *Henry Lawson Among Maoris (*Canberra: Australian National University, 1968).
6 A.H. McLintock, '1890–1919 The Liberal Era.' *An Encyclopaedia of New Zealand 1966*, online at Te Ara Encyclopaedia of New Zealand http://www.teara.govt.nz/en/1966/history-settlement-and-development/13 (accessed 5 June 2010). On closer settlement, see also Belich, *Making Peoples* 408–10.
7 Belich, *Making Peoples* 328.
8 Belich, *Making Peoples* 428–9. He notes that overseas sailors came 'in thousands and stayed in hundreds from the 1820s', and as late as 1860, probably constituted a majority of Europeans to have visited New Zealand. They continued to be important both as settlers and sojourners.
9 'Naked' seems to mean they arrived with no swag, rather than no clothes.
10 MS letter, Beetham family papers.
11 See Belich, *Making Peoples* 421–423 for a discussion of Miles Fairburn's theory of atomism, as expressed in *The Ideal Society and Its Enemies: The Foundations of Modern New Zealand Society, 1850–1900* (Auckland: Auckland University Press, 1989).

12 'The Hire of the Labourers.' Nelson *Colonist* 31 May 1901.
13 Belich, *Making Peoples* 429–436.
14 Edward Wakefield, *New Zealand After Fifty Years(*London, 1889), 153–4, quoted in Belich, *Making Peoples* 431.
15 See Belich, *Making Peoples* 401.
16 Belich, *Making Peoples* 344.
17 Phormium cookianum 'Tricolor': 'According to Mr L. Robinson, a Masterton nurseryman, this cultivar was discovered in the late 1880's (sic) on the banks of the Wainuioru River in the Wairarapa, by a Mr W. Summers, who was a gardener at Brancepeth Station. Mr Summers is said to have found the plant growing on a steep papa bank and had himself lowered on the end of a rope so that he could obtain it. In the Wairarapa district it is grown as P. colensoi "Summersii" but this name is not valid.' L.J. Metcalf, *The Cultivation of New Zealand Trees and Shrubs* (Wellington: A.H. & A.W. Reed, 1972), 209–10. Thanks to Gareth Winter, Wairarapa Archive, for this reference.
18 Station Diary, October 1895.
19 Belich, *Making Peoples* 433.
20 Nelson *Colonist* 31 May 1901.
21 Joseph Guest later became well known as an artist and lived in the Chatham Islands. There are several charming sketches of Brancepeth done by Guest in the family papers.
22 Belich, *Making Peoples* 438.
23 Frederic Wallis (1853–1928), Bishop of Wellington 1895–1911.
24 Fairburn, *The Ideal Society and Its Enemies* 191ff.
25 Fairburn, *The Ideal Society and Its Enemies* Chapter VII.
26 Paul Husbands, 'The People of Freemans Bay 1880–1914.' (M.A. Thesis, University of Auckland, 1992), Chapter 5; and Caroline Daley, 'Taradale Meets the Ideal Society and its Enemies,' *New Zealand Journal of History* 25 (1991), cited in Belich, *Making Peoples* 414.
27 Robert Dixon has charted the growth of colonial and imperial adventure novels from 1875–1914 in *Writing the Colonial Adventure: Race, Gender and Nation in Anglo-Australian Popular Fiction, 1875–1914* (Cambridge: Cambridge University Press, 1995). Republished, Cambridge: Cambridge University Press, 2009.
28 Station diary, 3 March 1895
29 Belich, *Making Peoples* 426.
30 Belich, *Making Peoples* 326.
31 Belich, *Making Peoples* 354.
32 As described in Miles Fairburn's *Nearly Out of Heart and Hope* (1995), based on the diaries of an itinerant worker, James Cox, who turned up at Brancepeth as a swagger.
33 Belich, *Making Peoples* 406.
34 Belich, *Making Peoples,* discussing Fairburn (1989) notes that some

prominent factors of bondlessness 'are likely to have been *caused* by atomism: high rates of hitting, suing and bingeing—arrests for drunkenness tended to stem from being very drunk and a little disorderly in public places rather than private tippling' (413). The station diary records many episodes of employees being arrested for drunken behaviour in Masterton and Taueru, but the farm itself functioned like a 'public' place in that drunkenness and disorderly behaviour is visible in the records but 'private tippling' is not. Station hands were dismissed both for being drunk on the station and for missing work days when bingeing.

35 *Wairarapa Daily Times,* 16 Sept 1903.

36 *Wairarapa Daily Times,* 16 Sept 1903.

Chapter Five: What They Read

1 Dates in round brackets refer to the publication dates of copies in the Brancepeth collection. If there is a large gap between original publication and the Brancepeth copy, the date of first publication is given in square brackets.

2 Gail Cunningham, *The New Woman and the Victorian Novel* (London: Macmillan Press, 1978). Cunningham divides New Woman novelists into the 'purity school' also known as 'hill-top' novels (a phrase coined by Grant Allen) and the 'neurotic school'. Sarah Grand was one of the former. As Cunningham explains, 'purity' novelists adhered to the idea of a feminine ideal, and advocated the 'purity of truth, personal integrity and freedom' which 'inevitably brought them into head-on collision with social convention', whereas the 'neurotic school' placed more emphasis on sexual freedom for women and were 'far less concerned with establishing an ideal of femininity' (50–51).

3 Herbert Spencer was well known for, among many other works, *The Principles of Ethics* (1879–93), *The Man Versus the State* (1884), *The Principles of Sociology* (1876–96); Francis Galton, a cousin of Charles Darwin was famous for many books, including *Hereditary Genius* (1869) and *The Art of Travel* (1872). Both Spencer and Galton were social Darwinists.

4 For example, the incestuous attraction between 'Madonna' and Zack Thorpe, who turns out to be her half brother, in Wilkie Collins's *Hide and Seek* (also a favourite at Brancepeth) is also instantly dismissed.

5 Cunningham, *The New Woman* 11.

6 John Sutherland, *The Stanford Companion to Victorian Fiction* (Stanford, California: Stanford University Press, 1989) 20.

7 Kate Flint, 'The Victorian Novel and Its Readers.' In *The Cambridge Companion to the Victorian Novel,* ed. Deirdre David (Cambridge: Cambridge University Press, 2001) 31.

8 Rudyard Kipling, 'The Song of the Cities,' in *The Seven Seas* (London: Methuen and Co Ltd, 1907) 15.
9 Tim Dolin, 'First Steps Toward a History of the Mid-Victorian Novel in Colonial Australia.' *Australian Literary Studies* 22:3 (2006) 273–293; 277
10 James Belich, *Paradise Reforged* (Auckland: Allen Lane/ The Penguin Press, 2001) 46
11 DNZB entry for Marmaduke Bethell and Thyra Talvase Bethell, http://www.dnzb.govt.nz/dnzb/alt_essayBody.asp?essayID=4B28 (accessed 19 June 2010).
12 See David Yerex's *They Came to Wydrop* (Masterton: Published on behalf of Hugh Beetham of Brancepeth and Tom Williams of Te Parae; Distributed by GP Publications, 1991) 143–4. In her press clipping book, Ruth Beetham pasted two short articles from the *Dominion* describing Prince Jacques de Broglie's tour of New Zealand in 1925. According to the articles, he was a member of one of the 'best-known and most distinguished families in France' and married Dame Clara Butt's pianist in Sydney in 1926. Perhaps the family connection reassured them about Weva's marriage.
13 Cunningham, *The New Woman* 1.
14 Cunningham, *The New Woman* 2.
15 Sutherland, *The Stanford Companion to Victorian Fiction* 530.
16 John Vaughan Miller,'Originals and Copies.' *Wairarapa Daily Times* 6 April 1898.
17 Penny Boumelha (1997) has pointed out that the phrase 'Woman of Genius' used by a number of New Woman novelists makes a claim to intellectual and creative equality with men, but is inherently doomed to contradiction, as the Woman of Genius must also fail as an artist if she is to represent authentic cultural values. Grand's heroines for example, however free-thinking they might be, like Angelica in *The Heavenly Twins*, ultimately always choose marriage and 'proper' womanhood.
18 John Vaughan Miller,'Fashionable Novels.' *Wairarapa Daily Times* 5 May 1902
19 Talia Schaffer, 'The History of Richard Calmady.' *The Literary Encyclopedia*. 24 January 2002. http://www.litencyc.com/php/sworks.php?rec=true&UID=595 (accessed 15 October 2009)
20 Ethel Lillian Voynich, daughter of the Irish mathematician George Boole, who married a Polish Count, Wilfrid Voynich. Her most successful novel was *The Gadfly* (1897) about an international revolutionary in Italy during the uprising of 1848, which was immensely popular in Russia. *Jack Raymond* is a coming of age novel in which people are not what they seem, including the vicar, which may have been what Miller objected to.

21 *Charles Kingsley: His Letters and Memories of His Life, Edited by his wife* (London: Macmillan & Co, 1899).
22 Marie Corelli, *The Sorrows of Satan* (Oxford: Oxford World's Classics, 1998) 242.
23 *Wairarapa Daily Times* 15 January 1903.
24 Authors were numbered more or less alphabetically and each of their titles followed in sequence of acquisition. For example Disraeli's *Sybil* was the third title acquired under 94 (Disraeli) so it is catalogued as 94/3.
25 Dulcie Gillespie-Needham, 'The Colonial and His Books.' (Ph.D. thesis, Victoria University of Wellington, 1971) 2.
26 Mary Taylor to Charlotte Bronte, Letter 16, 24 July, 1848, in *Mary Taylor, Friend of Charlotte Bronte: Letters from New Zealand & Elsewhere,* ed. Joan Stevens (Auckland: Auckland University Press/ Oxford University Press, 1972) 75, 77. Cited by Gillespie-Needham, 'The Colonial and His Books,' 250.
27 Sir Robert Stout, *How and What to Read (*Auckland: Book Exchange, 1908).
28 J.E. Traue, 'A Paradise for Readers? The Extraordinary Proliferation of Public Libraries in Colonial New Zealand.' In *Script & Print: Bulletin of the Bibliographical Society of Australia and New Zealand (*Special Issue: *Paradise: New Worlds of Books and Readers),* 29: 1–4 (2005), 335
29 'An Important Subject: The Kind of Books That Are Read.' *Wairarapa Daily Times* 18 May 1906
30 William Pember Reeves, 'Papers', MS., and typescript, Alexander Turnbull Library, n.d, cited by Gillespie-Needham, 'The Colonial and His Books', 354–7.
31 For borrowing data of the time, see Gillespie-Needham, 'The Colonial and His Books', and Traue, 'A Paradise for Readers?' See also Dolin, 'First Steps,' which shows that the list of top 40 authors and top loan titles from the South Australian Institute 1861–2 has significant correspondences with Brancepeth. Also, Simon Eliot's 1986 study of Victorian popular authors judged by their holdings in public libraries shows a close correspondence with the heavily used authors at Brancepeth. Simon Eliot, 'Public Libraries and Popular Authors, 1883–1912.' *The Library*, Sixth Series, Vol VIII (1986) 322–347.
32 George Gissing, *New Grub Street.* Ed John Goode (Oxford: Oxford University Press, 1998) 493.
33 J.E. Traue 'The Public Library Explosion in Colonial New Zealand'. *Libraries and the Cultural Record* 42:2 (2007) 161.
34 John Sutherland, *Victorian Fiction: Writers, Publishers, Readers* (Basingstoke, New York: Palgrave Macmillan, 2006) 159–160.
35 I borrow the phrase from Margaret Dalziel, who, in describing the

stereotypical Victorian romance heroine, noted 'It is equally essential that the heroine should be religious in a vague kind of way.' *Popular Fiction 100 Years Ago* (London: Cohen & West, 1957) 86.

36 The appeal of the sensation novel extends to the present day, with the recent example of Sarah Waters' bestselling Victorian pastiches *Tipping the Velvet* (1998) and *Fingersmith* (2002), which use all the familiar plot elements—abduction, bigamy, murder, asylums, secret identities and fatal discoveries—but include a new 'sensation' as narratives of lesbian desire.

37 Sutherland, *The Stanford Companion* 562–3. Such journalistic sensations included the bigamy in *Lady Audley's Secret,* which derived its 'contemporary piquancy' from a notorious divorce scandal of 1861, or the forced incarceration of sane people in mental asylums in Charles Reade's *Hard Cash,* also a plot driver in Sarah Waters' *Fingersmith* (2002). Sutherland notes that sensation novels were also known as 'newspaper novels' and were shaped by the needs of serial publication, in which every instalment had to end with the reader wanting more.

38 Dorothy L. Sayers, *Wilkie Collins: A Critical and Biographical Study.* Ed. E.R. Gregory (Toledo, OH: The Friends of the University of Toledo Libraries, 1977) 25.

39 See John Sutherland, *The Stanford Companion* 204.

40 Robert Wolff, *Sensational Victorian: The Life and Fiction of Mary Elizabeth Braddon* (New York and London: Garland Publishing, 1979) 246.

41 'The Jackeroo.' *Wairarapa Daily Times* 28 June 1899.

42 Eric Richards, *Britannia's Children* (Hambledon and London: St Martin's Press, 2004).

43 Eliza Humphreys (1850–1938).

44 Elleke Boehmer, *Colonial and Postcolonial Literature: Migrant Metaphors* (Oxford/ New York: Oxford University Press, 1995) 3.

45 Quoted in Wolff, *Sensational Victorian* 9.

46 Wolff, *Sensational Victorian* 9.

47 Wolff, *Sensational Victorian* 149.

48 *The Spectator* 17, 1874, 1303–1304. Quoted in Wolff, *Sensational Victorian* 245.

49 See James Belich, *Making Peoples* (Auckland: Penguin Books, 1996) 408–9.

50 Edward Said, *Culture and Imperialism* (New York: Knopf, 1993) xii.

51 For example George Garratt, the overseer, whose negotiations over the price of a piece of land with Hugh Beetham are referred to, and who acquired a small farm at Taueru.

52 Tim Dolin's study of the lending patterns of the South Australian Institute 1861–2 noted that *Hide and Seek* was the most borrowed Collins title after *The Woman in White.* Dolin, 'First Steps' 285.

53 Station Diary, 7 December 1906.
54 Sutherland, *The Stanford Companion* 496.
55 Sutherland, *The Stanford Companion* 438. Recently, *Miss Marjoribanks* has been nominated as one of the 100 best Scottish books of all time. Kenny Hodgart, Miss Marjoribanks—Mrs Oliphant (1866),' *The List*, 2005/2007. http://www.list.co.uk/article/2788–miss-marjoribanks-margaret-oliphant-1866/ (accessed 14 June 2010).
56 Sutherland, *The Stanford Companion* 438.
57 John Vaughan Miller, 'Temporal Power.' *Wairarapa Daily Times* 19 December 1902.
58 Tim Shoebridge, *The Good Citizen: A Life of C.E. Daniell of Masterton* (Masterton: Fraser Books, 2009) 66–67.
59 Dolin's study shows *John Halifax Gentleman* to have been 5th of the top loan titles at the SA Institute, 1861–2.
60 Sutherland, *The Stanford Companion* 336.
61 Dorothy L. Sayers gives a list of 28 characters with deformities and physical afflictions in novels by Dickens, Charles Reade, Wilkie Collins and Trollope, who she says deprived Signora Neroni in *Barchester Towers* of the 'use of her legs for no very obvious cause', and noted there are also others 'too numerous to mention.' Sayers, *Wilkie Collins* 108.
62 Sutherland, *The Stanford Companion,* 14.
63 Sutherland, *The Stanford Companion* 13.
64 Sutherland, *The Stanford Companion* 161.
65 Sutherland, *The Stanford Companion* 46.
66 In the diary Miller refers to a 'Welsh shuffler', a 'paddy in distress', the 'bad kind of Irishman', cockneys, Jews, a 'Brummagem youth', and has numerous things to say about Scotsmen, especially shepherds.
67 Sutherland, *The Stanford Companion* 372.
68 Constance Barnicoat, 'The Reading of the Colonial Girl.' *Nineteenth Century,* December 1906, 939. Barnicoat's article was a response to an article by Florence B. Low in the same magazine earlier the same year, about the reading habits of British girls.
69 Patrick Brantlinger, *Rule of Darkness: British Literature and Imperialism, 1830–1914* (Ithaca: Cornell University Press, 1988) 8.
70 Robert Dixon, *Writing the Colonial Adventure: Race, Nation and Gender in Anglo-Australian Popular Fiction, 1875–1914* (Cambridge: Cambridge University Press, 1995) 1.
71 Frank Luther Mott, *Golden Multitudes: The Story of Best Sellers in the United States* (New York, Bowker, 1966).
72 Mott, *Golden Multitudes* 176.
73 25 September 1904. The Brocken was one of the largest out-stations and always had its own cook.
74 *My First Book,* ed. Jerome K. Jerome (London: Chatto & Windus,1894) 12.

75 Besant wrote these lines about Dick Mortiboy, the hero of his very successful first novel *Ready-money Mortiboy*, in *My First Book* 14.

76 Janice Radway, *Reading the Romance* (North Carolina: The University of North Carolina Press, 1984).

77 It is hard to be exact, because the numbering system stops at 481—Zola—and begins again for non-fiction.

78 Donald Preziosi, 'The Art of Art History.' *The Art of Art History: A Critical Anthology*, ed. Donald Preziosi (Oxford: Oxford University Press, 1998) 511. I thank Rebecca Rice for bringing this to my attention.

Chapter Six: The Constant Reader

1 Douglas Jerrold was a famous wit. He started by contributing to *Blackwood's Magazine,* but made his name at *Punch*. He was also a playwright, founded a monthly magazine and edited *Lloyd's Weekly Newspaper*. John Sutherland, *The Stanford Companion to Victorian Fiction (*Stanford, California: Stanford University Press, 1989) 332–3.

2 *Household Words* 111, 13 September 13, 1851; 599. Cited in J.S. Ryan, ed. *Charles Dickens and New Zealand* (Wellington: A.H. & A.W. Reed, 1965) 77.

3 'Book-Love.' *Fraser's Magazine* 36 (1847). Cited in Kate Flint, *The Woman Reader 1837–1914,* (Oxford: Clarendon Press, 1993) 11.

4 See Graeme Johanson, *Colonial Editions in Australia, 1843–1972* (Wellington: Elibank Press, 2000).

5 J.E. Traue, 'A Paradise for Readers? The Extraordinary Proliferation of Public Libraries in Colonial New Zealand.' In *Script & Print: Bulletin of the Bibliographical Society of Australia and New Zealand (*Special Issue: *Paradise: New Worlds of Books and Readers),* 29: 1–4 (2005).

6 See John Sutherland, *Victorian Fiction: Writers, Publishers, Readers* (London: Palgrave, 2006) 159–160.

7 See George Gissing's *New Grub Street* (1891), a satirical attack on the contest between literature and journalism.

8 Cited in Sutherland, *Victorian Fiction* ix.

9 Robert Darnton has noted that the reading experience of the great mass of readers lies beyond the range of historical research, but that historians should be able to 'capture something of what reading meant for the few persons who left a record of it'. See *Kiss of Lamourette: Reflections in Cultural History* (New York and London: W.W.Norton, 1990, 177); also cited in H.J. Jackson, *Marginalia (*New Haven and London: Yale University Press, 2001) 255.

10 Pierre Bourdieu calls this a 'habitus', that is, a set of common properties and classifying systems. See *Distinction: A Social Critique of the*

Judgement of Taste, trans. Richard Nice (London: Routledge, 1996) 101–2.

11 Kate Flint, *The Woman Reader 1837–1914* (Oxford: Clarendon Press, 1993) 42.

12 Benedict Anderson, *Imagined Communities* (London: Verso, 1991).

13 Miles Fairburn's *Nearly Out of Heart and Hope* (Auckland: Auckland University Press, 1995) describes the life of James Cox, an itinerant labourer who wrote immensely detailed diaries. Cox read the fiction in the Carterton library, and visited Brancepeth looking for work. Despite the miseries of his life and its exiguous and sad circumstances, Cox kept up his participation in a literate and literary culture. He would not have been the only one of the almost 1000 swaggers who travelled to Brancepeth who did this.

14 Darnton, *Kiss of Lamourette* 177.

15 Marie Corelli *God's Good Man,* Rider H. Haggard *The World's Desire* and John Morley's *The Life of William Ewart Gladstone.*

16 Guest became a minor artist. There are some charming sketches of Brancepeth by him from 1895.

17 G. Manville Fenn wrote more than 60 books, most of them adventure stories for boys in the manner of G.A. Henty. *The Parson O'Dumford* is one of his adult novels and is subtitled 'A Story of Lincoln Folk'. Fenn grew up in Lincolnshire and perhaps the regional location is what appealed to William Woof.

18 Thyra Beetham referred to herself as 'Jimmy' in a correspondence with one of her female cousins, probably Elfie Williams ('Bill').

19 William L. Alden, 'London Literary Letter.' *New York Times* Saturday Review, 27 April 1901.

20 Amy Cruse, *The Victorians and their Books* (London: George Allen & Unwin, 1935) 42. This is an unreferenced quote from Martha Roscoe Garnett, *Samuel Butler and his Family Relations* (London: J .M. Dent & Sons Limited, 1926) in which the author described his sister May, whose prototype was to be found in Charlotte Yonge's heroines.

21 Dulcie Gillespie-Needham, 'The Colonial and His Books.' (Ph.D. thesis. Victoria University of Wellington, 1971) 419.

22 H. J. Jackson, *Marginalia.* This is a summary of her general points.

23 Oscar Wilde, 'Ouida's New Novel.' *Pall Mall Gazette,* May 17, 1899.

24 Frank R Stockton, *The Squirrel Inn* (London: Sampson, Low, Marston, 1891).

25 Leah Price, summarising H. J. Jackson, *Marginalia,* in her review 'Tres Vrai.' *London Review of Books.* 18 October 2001, 27–30.

26 Jackson, *Marginalia* 74.

27 Although in some ways Miller was a professional writer, but supported himself as a record-keeper, and did not primarily write for a living.

28 Jonathan Rose *The Intellectual Life of the British Working Classes*

(New Haven and London: Yale University Press, 2002).

29 Unusually he signed his poem 'The Unknown God to the Agnostic' (July 13, 1901) with his initials, perhaps because it expresses his own strongly-held sentiments ('I am God, the Father of Jesus, thy Lord and Giver of life').

30 *Wairarapa Daily Times* 22 August 1898.

31 *Wairarapa Daily Times* October 9 1900.

32 My guess is that DWT stands for Disappeared Without Trace.

33 *Wairarapa Daily Times*, 5 May 1902.

34 'Breaking the Chains' *Wairarapa Daily Times*. 11 March 1905.

35 Thomas Percy, *Reliques of Ancient English Poetry: Selection* (Gottingen: Printed for Victorinus Bossiegel, 1767). Often reprinted as, for example, *Reliques of Ancient English Poetry* (London: Dent, 1906).

36 Hilda D. Spear, ed., *The English Poems of Charles Stuart Calverley* (Leicester: Leicester University Press, 1974) 9.

37 Henley Henson, *Light and Leaven* (London: Methuen 1897).

38 Station Diary, 22 June 1896. The definition of terms Miller recorded no longer exists.

39 Apirana Ngata, ed. *Complete Manual of Maori Grammar and Conversation, with Vocabulary.* (Christchurch: Whitcombe and Tombs, 1901).

40 Jackson, *Marginalia* 82.

41 Jackson, *Marginalia* 45.

42 Jackson, *Marginalia* 100.

43 In Sarah Grand's collection of stories *Our Manifold Nature* (1894), Miller has marked a sentence that describes the 'round of Society' as the 'deadliest level of deadly dullness in living' (136).

44 Sometimes he gives the line and sometimes not—George Macdonald's *Malcolm* has a reference in the text to Isaiah lviii.6, and Miller has written the line in full in the margin.

45 Charles Kingsley, 'Thrift,' in *The Works of Charles Kingsley.* (London: Macmillan and Company, 1880, Vol. XV111) 77–104. Kingsley opines that young ladies should spend their leisure time collecting wild flowers and identifying them correctly, rather than 'lounging on benches on the esplanade, reading useless novels . . .' (95–6).

Chapter Seven: The Lives of Books

1 Robert Escarpit, *The Book Revolution* (London: Harrap; Paris: Unesco, 1966) 17.

2 Guglielmo Cavallo and Roger Chartier, eds., *A History of Reading in the West.* Trans. Lydia G. Cochrane (Amherst: University of Massachusetts Press, 1999).

3 As Jonathan Rose notes, it is 'relatively easy to recover the reading experiences of professional intellectuals . . . But what record do we have of "common readers" . . . ?' *The Intellectual Life of the British Working Classes* (New Haven and London: Yale University Press, 2002) 1. Readers at Brancepeth did not leave autobiographies, as have been used by historians like Richard Altick and David Vincent to reconstruct the common reader, yet as this chapter makes plain, the lives of common readers are materially inscribed all over the collection.
4 H.J. Jackson *Marginalia* (New Haven and London: Yale University Press, 2001) 253.
5 Jackson, *Marginalia* 256.
6 Graeme Johanson *Colonial Editions in Australia, 1843–1972* (Elibank Press: Wellington, 2000).
7 Johanson, *Colonial Editions in Australia* 161.
8 Johanson, *Colonial Editions in Australia* 12.
9 Johanson, *Colonial Editions in Australia* 117.
10 Johanson, *Colonial Editions in Australia* 115.
11 I owe this reference to Pamela Wood, author of *Dirt: Filth and Decay in a New World Arcadia* (Auckland: Auckland University Press, 2005), who saw this list and interpreted it for me.
12 'Philadelphia', *Wairarapa Daily Times* 9 February 1898.
13 'Beetham of Brancepeth', a biographical article in Douglas Cresswell, *Early New Zealand Families* 2nd Series (Christchurch: Whitcombe and Tombs, 1956). Cresswell's standard formula couples station owners with the names of their runs, in the style of a landed aristocracy. Cresswell's focus on the family and their estate is an example of how the Wakefieldian project of systematic colonisation was meant to work. As Jim McAloon has said, it intended to 'transplant hierarchical English rural society overseas.' McAloon, *No Idle Rich: The Wealthy in Canterbury and Otago 1840–1914* (Dunedin: University of Otago Press, 2002) 19.
14 Jackson, *Marginalia* 257.
15 Hichens made his name with a satire on ultra-aestheticism *The Green Carnation* (1894) which featured lightly disguised versions of Oscar Wilde and Lord Alfred Douglas. John Sutherland, *The Stanford Companion to Victorian Fiction* (Stanford: Stanford University Press, 1989) 295.
16 See Miles Fairburn, *Nearly out of Heart and Hope* (Auckland: Auckland University Press, 1995).
17 'What The Working Classes Read.' *The Nineteenth Century* July 1886, 108–117.

Conclusion

1 Mikhail Bakhtin, *The Dialogic Imagination*. Ed. Michael Holquist. Trans. Caryl Emerson and Michael Holquist (Austin and London: University of Texas Press, 1981) 293.
2 John Sutherland, *Victorian Fiction: Writers, Publishers, Readers* (Basingstoke: Palgrave Macmillan, 2006) 159.
3 A keynote address by Jonathan Rose, quoted in Lawrence (Lou) Duggan, 'Librarians have much to Offer in Solving the Mystery of Reading.' *APLA Bulletin*, Volume 72. http://www.apla.ca/node/86 (accessed 29 January 2010).

APPENDIX 1

Heavily Used Books in the Brancepeth Library

(an impressionistic classification)

W.H. Ainsworth	*The Tower of London*
Mrs Alexander	*The Heritage of Langdale; The Wooing O'T*
Grant Allen	*The British Barbarians*
Blanche Atkinson	*The Web of Life*
Amelia Barr	*Jan Vedder's Wife; A Daughter of Fife*
Frank Barrett	*Breaking the Shackles*
Walter Besant	*All in a Garden Fair; Amorel of Lyonesse; Dorothy Forster; All Sorts and Conditions of Men; The City of Refuge*
with James Rice	*The Golden Butterfly; A Matter of Fact; My Little Girl*
William Black	*A Daughter of Heth; Macleod of Dare*
Rolf Boldrewood	*A Sydney-side Saxon; A Colonial Reformer; Plain Living*
Guy Boothby	*Doctor Nikola*
M.E. Braddon	*Rough Justice; Lady Audley's Secret; Mohawks; Vixen; Aurora Floyd; Weavers and Weft*
Charlotte Bronte	*Jane Eyre*
Robert Buchanan	*The Master of the Mine*
E. Bulwer-Lytton	*Alice; A Strange Story*
Hall Caine	*The Deemster; The Shadow of a Crime; The Bondman*
Rosa N. Carey	*Barbara Heathcote's Trial*
Sarah P. Carr	*The Iron Way*
W.B. Churchward	*Jem Peterkin's Daughter*
Wilkie Collins	*Hide and Seek; The Black Robe; A Rogue's Life; The Law and the Lady; Say No*
Marie Corelli	*Barabbas; The Murder of Delicia; The Master Christian*
Arthur H. Davis [Steele Rudd]	*On Our Selection*
Richard Dehan	*The Dop Doctor*
Charles Dickens	*David Copperfield; Bleak House; Martin Chuzzlewit*

Dick Donovan	*Who Poisoned Hetty Duncan?; The Man from Manchester; Caught at Last!; In the Grip of the Law; Tracked and Taken*
A. Conan Doyle	*The Firm of Girdlestone; The Sign of Four; The Captain of the Polestar and other Tales*
Alexandre Dumas	*The Russian Gipsy; The Beau Tancrede; The Page of the Duke of Savoy*
Annie Edwards	*A Girton Girl*
B.L. Farjeon	*Grif; Aaron the Jew*
Henry Fielding	*Tom Jones*
Mrs Alexander Fraser	*The Match of the Season*
John Foster Fraser	*The Real Siberia*
John Fox Jr.	*The Little Shepherd of Kingdom Come*
Benjamin Franklin	*Autobiography*
James Grant	*The Cameronians; Derval Hampton*
S. Baring Gould	*Red Spider*
A.C. Gunter	*The King's Stockbroker; Mr Barnes of New York; Mr Potter of Texas; Miss Dividends; Jack Curzon*
Frederic Gammon	*The Canal Boy Who Became President*
Nat Gould	*On and Off the Turf in Australia; Life's Web*
Sarah Grand	*The Heavenly Twins*
Maxwell Gray	*In the Heart of the Storm*
H. Rider Haggard	*Jess; Dawn; The World's Desire; Colonel Quaritch V.C.; Eric Brighteyes; The Witch's Head*
Bret Harte	*Flip and Other Stories; Californian Stories*
Julian Hawthorne	*Love—Or a Name; Dust*
Mary Cecil Hay	*Dorothy's Venture*
W. Stephens Hayward	*John Hazel's Vengeance*
S.B. Hemyng	*The Stockbroker's Wife*
Joseph Hocking	*All Men Are Liars*
Antony Hope	*The Prisoner of Zenda*
Lois Hume	*The Bloom of the Peach*
Mrs Hungerford	*Mrs Geoffrey; Molly Bawn*
Mrs Alfred W. Hunt	*The Leaden Casket*
W.W. Jacobs	*Many Cargoes*
Mrs Robert Jocelyn	*The Criton Hunt Mystery*
Sir H.H. Johnstone	*David Livingstone*
Mrs Edward Kennard	*A Homburg Beauty; Matron or Maid*
Arthut Keyser	*An Exile's Romance*
Charles Kingsley	*Two Years Ago*
Henry Kingsley	*The Recollections of Geoffrey Hamlyn*

Charles Lever	*Jack Hinton; Tom Burke of 'Ours'; Luttrell of Arran*
Edna Lyall	*A Hardy Norseman; Knight Errant; To Right the Wrong*
Captain Marryat	*Japhet; Newton Forster, or The Merchant Service; Olla Podrida; Monsieur Violet*
Florence Marryat	*My Own Child*
Justin McCarthy	*My Enemy's Daughter; Making His Pile; Miss Misanthrope*
H.S. Merriman	*The Slave of the Lamp*
John Trotwood Moore	*The Gift of the Grass*
D. Christie Murray	*Val Strange; The Way of the World; A Life's Atonement*
Hume Nisbet	*The Queen's Desire*
N.P. O'Donoghue	*Unfairly Won*
George Ohnet	*The Ironmaster*
Mrs Oliphant	*Miss Marjoribanks*
E. Phillips Oppenheim	*The Traitors; The World's Great Snare; The Governors*
Baroness Orczy	*The Scarlet Pimpernel*
John Oxenham	*Under the Iron Flail*
Ouida	*The Massarenes; Guilderoy*
Gilbert Parker	*Mrs Falchion*
James Payn	*The Luck of the Darvells; Lost Sir Massingberd; A Confidential Agent*
Eleanor C. Price	*Mrs Lancaster's Rival*
Charles Reade	*A Woman-Hater; Good Stories of Man and Other Animals*
Captain Mayne Reid	*Gaspar the Gaucho; The Wood-Rangers; The White Chief; The Guerilla Chief and Other Tales*
Rita	*Corinna; Fragolette; Dame Durden; Kitty the Rag; Peg the Rake; Gretchen*
Lord Roberts	*Forty-One Years in India*
Morley Roberts	*The Promotion of the Admiral and other sea comedies*
E.P. Roe	*He Fell in Love with his Wife; A Young Girl's Wooing*
E. Rogers	*Madeline's Mystery*
Dora Russell	*Annabel's Rival*
W.C. Russell	*My Danish Sweetheart; The Romance of Jenny Harlow; Is He The Man?; The Two Captains*
R.H. Savage	*My Official Wife; An Exile from London*
Adeline Sergeant	*A Deadly Foe*

Hawley Smart	*Two Kisses; Saddle and Sabre; Beatrice and Benedick; Long Odds; Courtship; The Pride of the Paddock*
Albert Smith	*The Adventures of Mr Ledbury and His Friend Jack Johnson*
R.L. Stevenson	*Kidnapped; St Ives*
Annie Swan	*Sheila; Elizabeth Glen M.B.; A Stormy Voyager; A Victory Won*
M. Taylor	*A Noble Queen*
W.M. Thackeray	*The History of Pendennis; The Virginians; Vanity Fair*
Antony Trollope	*Kept in the Dark; The Prime Minister; Orley Farm; The Way We Live Now*
Louis Tracy	*Waifs of Circumstance*
Mark Twain	*The Gilded Age; The Prince and the Pauper; A Tramp Abroad*
George F. Underhill	*A Nasty Cropper*
Captain N. Urner	*Dynamite Aboard!*
Louis J. Vance	*The Black Bag*
Jules Verne	*Tigers and Traitors; Michael Strogoff*
L.B. Walford	*Troublesome Daughters*
Artemus Ward	*Artemus Ward Complete*
Mrs Humphrey Ward	*Robert Elsmere*
Florence Warden	*A Sensational Case*
H.G. Wells	*The War of the Worlds*
Stanley Weyman	*Under the Red Robe; My Lady Rotha; The Story of Francis Cludde; The Man in Black; The Red Cockade; From the Memoirs of a Minister of France*
Steward E. White	*The Silent Places*
G.J. Whyte-Melville	*Katerfelto; The Brooks of Bridlemere; Sarchedon; Contraband*
Owen Wister	*The Virginian*
Mrs Henry Wood	*St Martin's Eve; Edina; The Red Court Farm; Elster's Folly; The Unholy Wish & Other stories; The Shadow of Ashlydat; Lord Oakburn's Daughters; Anne Hereford; Johnny Ludlow; Mildred Arkell; Trevlyn Hold; Bessy Rane*
Emma Jane Worboise	*The Brudenells of Brude*
Charlotte Yonge	*The Armourer's Prentice*
Emile Zola	*The Dream*
Anon	*[Tasma] The Fate of Fenella* *A Fool's Errand*

	Won By a Neck
	Pauline
[Catherine Martin]	*An Australian Girl*

History & Miscellaneous

Sir Bernard Burke	*Family Romance*
Fred Burnaby	*A Ride to Khiva*
[F.E. Maning]	*Old New Zealand*
Robert McKenzie	*America A History*
Samuel Warren	*Passages from the Diary of a Late Physician*
'A Brutal Saxon'	*John Bull's Neighbour in her True Light*
'Wanderer'	*Fair Diana*
[W. & R. Chambers]	*Tales from Chambers's Journal*
[Clarence J. Howard]	*Howard's Recitations*
[Johann David Wyss]	*The Swiss Family Robinson*
Anon	*Encyclopaedia of New Zealand* 1897

Poetry

Robert Burns	*Poetical Works*
John Milton	*Poetical Works*

APPENDIX 2

John Vaughan Miller's Newspaper Publications

(Not all the articles he mentioned sending to the *Wairarapa Daily Times* in the station diary have been traced.)

Wairarapa Daily Times
9 February 1894 Letter
26 November 1894 Letter
10 December 1894 'Outlook'
11 September 1895 Letter 'Religious Instruction in Schools'
21 September 1895 Letter 'Apologia Neminis Pro Litera Sua'
3 January 1896 'Hector vs Salisbury'
14 October 1896 'Prohibition in South Africa'
1 December 1896 'Mr Buchanan at Taueru'
7 December 1896 'Political Freedom'
1 April 1897 Letter 'Ruskin's View'
29 June 1897 Letter 'The Makers of New Zealand' signed 'Huki Waaka'
7 July 1897 Letter 'All Saints' signed 'E Pluribus Unum'
13 July 1897 Letter 'All Saints' signed 'Nemo'
4 December 1897 Letter 'What the Ministry May Do' signed 'Balaam's Ass'
28 December 1897 Letter 'Tennyson Spoiled' signed 'Not "Any More"'
7 January 1898 'Has India a Grievance?'
12 January 1898 'Closing of the Native Mints in India'
13 January 1898 'Toleration in Matters of Opinion'
19 January 1898 'Gracefulness in Speech'
9 February 1898 'Philadelphia'
16 February 1898 Letter 'The Sign of the X' signed 'Senex'
6 April 1898 'Originals and Copies'
16 April 1898 'Independence'
11 July 1898 'Banking'
18 July 1898 'The Closing of the Indian Mints'
27 July 1898 'The Limitations of Science'
29 July1898 'Close Settlement'
10 August 1898 'Bismarck'
12 August 1898 'Banks'
17 August 1898 Letter 'Guerilla Philanthropy'
5 September 1898 'The Ethics of Debate'
21 September 1898 'Tyrannicides'
23 September 1898 'Fashions in Names'

27 September 1898 'British Enterprise in China'
4 October 1898 ' A Hop-Famine in England'
5 October 1898 'The Muscovite Lion-Tamer'
8 October 1898 'Anarchy'
10 November 1898 'France'
24 November 1898 Letter 'A Genuine Cat's Tale' signed 'Timothy'
26 November 1898 'France and Russia'
15 December 1898 Letter 'A Modest Request' signed 'Jocosa Mordax'
29 December 1898 'The Opinion in the Old Country'
4 January 1899 'What Frenchmen Say of Themselves'
18 January 1898 'The Church of England'
25 January 1899 'The Ministry of the Interior'
20 April 1899 'The Decay of the Latin Races'
27 April 1899 'Those Wicked Men'
2 May 1899 'Mothers and Daughters'
19 May 1899 'Priests and People'
23 May 1899 Letter 'Good Literature'
7 June 1899 'Cock and Bull Stories about the Royal Family'
28 June 1899 'The Jackeroo'
1 July 1899 'The Unrest in the Transvaal'
27 July 1899 'Humanity'
15 August 1899 'Sugar Bounties and Countervailing Duties'
17 August 1899 'Countervailing Sugar Duties'
30 August 1899 'Women's Rights'
26 September 1899 'The Transvaal'
13 October 1899 'Un Roi Sans Couronne S'Amuse'
14 November 1899 'What is Education?'
17 November 1899 'Facing the Light'
15 December 1899 'An Open Letter to Mr W.C. Buchanan'
27 February 1900 'Untimely Criticism'
2 March 1900 'The British Army'
31 March 1900 'Monopoly of Land'
17 May 1900 'War Hymn' by Mrs Bromley (sent in by Miller)
6 June 1900 'The Raad and its President'
9 October 1900 'The Gentle Shepherds of the Church'
17 October 1900 'The Subjugation of the Boers'
14 November 1900 'Quo Vadis'
19 December 1900 'Who Shall Serve?'
6 March 1901 'A Station Labour Problem'
14 May 1901 Letter 'Six of one and Half a Dozen of the Other'
16 May 1901 'Trusts and Tariffs'
29 May 1901 'British Commerce'
13 July 1901 Poem 'The Unknown God to the Agnostic'
30 September 1901 'Our Boys at the Front' Letter from Hubert Miller

about the 7th Contingent in South Africa
25 November 1901 'The Diet of Modern Worms'
4 December 1901 'A Liberal Education'
1 February 1902 Letter 'Bullets and Billets' signed 'Publicola'
28 February 1902 Poem 'Slummerlied'
2 May 1902 'Workmen *versus* Workmen'
5 May 1902 Letter 'Fashionable Novels'
8 June 1902 'Sugar Bounties and Countervailing Duties'
19 December 1902 Letter 'Temporal Power'
15 January 1903 Letter 'Marie Corelli'
19 May 1903 'The Victorian Strike'
23 July 1903 'The Play's The Thing'
14 January 1904 'A Falling Barometer'
25 November 1904 'The True End of Government'
11 March 1905 'Breaking the Chains'
30 May 1905 Letter 'A Specimen of Orthography' signed 'M'
25 October 1905 Letter 'Melodrama in Excelsis' signed 'X'
30 October 1905 Letter signed 'Y'
21 May 1906 Letter 'Levelling Means Stagnation' signed 'M'
16 June 1906 'Hic Jacet'
18 June 1906 'A Master Builder' In Memoriam R.J.S. [Seddon]

Wairarapa Star
9 February 1894 Letter 'The Pastoral Industry'

Colonist
31 May 1901 'The Hire of the Labourers'

References

Primary Sources

1. Beetham family

Beetham family MS papers-letters, poems, diaries, press cuttings book, scrapbooks. Private collection.

Beetham family photographs and photograph albums. Private collection.

Beetham family sketches. Private collection.

MS letters in possession of Beetham family.

Sketches of Brancepeth 1896–7 by Joseph Guest in Beetham family papers. Private collection.

2. Brancepeth Library

Brancepeth Library catalogue 1895, Brancepeth Station Library Archives, held in the J C Beaglehole Room, Victoria University of Wellington Library.

Brancepeth Station Library, held in the J C Beaglehole Room, Victoria University of Wellington Library

Brancepeth Station Library archives, held in the J C Beaglehole Room, Victoria University of Wellington Library

Brancepeth Station Diaries 1890–1908. Private collection.

Brancepeth Station Ledgers 1890–1908. Private collection.

3. Wairarapa Archive files

4. Newspapers

Colonist

Dominion

Evening Post

Wairarapa Daily Times

Wairarapa Star

Secondary Sources

Altick, Richard, D., *The English Common Reader: A Social History of the Mass Reading Public, 1800–1900,* Second Edition. Columbus: Ohio State University Press, 1998.

Anderson, Benedict, *Imagined Communities: Reflections on the Origin and Spread of Nationalism.* Revised Edition. London, New York: Verso, 1991.

Bagnall, A.G., *Wairarapa: An Historical Excursion.* Masterton, New Zealand: Hedley's Bookshop for the Masterton Trust Lands Trust, 1976.

Bailey, Elaine, 'Matilda Betham: a new biography.' *Wordsworth Circle,* Summer 2007 http://findarticles.com/p/articles/mi_hb347/is_3_38/ai_n29371919/?tag=content;col1 Accessed 1 June, 2010.

Bakhtin, Mikhail, *The Dialogic Imagination: Four Essays.* Edited by Michael Holquist; Translated by Caryl Emerson and Michael Holquist. Austin and London: University of Texas Press, 1981.

Ballantyne, Tony, *Orientalism and Race: Aryanism in the British Empire.* Houndmills, Basingstoke and New York: Palgrave, 2002.

Belich, James, *Making Peoples: A History of the New Zealanders, from Polynesian Settlement to the End of the 19th Century.* Auckland: Allen Lane / The Penguin Press, 1996.

Belich, James, *Paradise Reforged: A History of the New Zealanders from the 1880s to the Year 2000.* Auckland: Allan Lane / The Penguin Press, 2001.

Betham, Ernest, ed. *A House of Letters.* London: Jarrold and Sons, n.d.

Blackley, Roger, *A Nation's Portraits.* Art History Lecture Series 03. Wellington: Art History, Victoria University of Wellington, 2005.

Boehmer, Elleke, *Colonial and Postcolonial Literature: Migrant Metaphors.* Oxford and New York: Oxford University Press, 1995

Bloom, Harold, ed., *The Victorian Novel.* New York: Chelsea House, 2004.

Bodenheimer, Rosemarie, *The Politics of Story in Victorian Social Fiction.* Ithaca and London: Cornell University Press, 1988.

Boumelha, Penny, *Thomas Hardy and Women: Sexual Ideology and Narrative Form.* Brighton: Harvester Press, 1982.

Boumelha, Penny, 'The Woman of Genius and the Woman of Grub Street: Figures of the Female Writer in British *Fin-de-Siècle* Fiction'. *English*

Literature in Transition, 1880–1920 40, 2 (April 1997): 164–180.

Bourdieu, Pierre, *Distinction: A Social Critique of the Judgement of Taste.* Translated by Richard Nice. London: Routledge and Kegan Paul, 1986 (1984).

Brantlinger, Patrick, *Rule of Darkness: British Literature and Imperialism, 1830–1914.* Ithaca: Cornell University Press, 1988.

Bulwer-Lytton, Edward, *The Disowned.* London: Chapman and Hall, 1852.

Burke, Bernard, *A Genealogical and Heraldic History of the Colonial Gentry.* 2 vols. London, Harrison, 1891–1895.

Calverley, Charles Stuart, *The Complete Works of C.S. Calverley.* London: G. Bell and Sons, 1901.

Calverley, Charles Stuart, *The English Poems of Charles Stuart Calverley.* Edited by Hilda D. Spear. Leicester: Leicester University Press, 1974.

Calverley, Charles Stuart, *Verses and Fly Leaves.* London: G. Bell and Sons, 1894.

Castle, Egerton (ed), *The Jerningham Letters* (1780–1843). 2 vols. London: Richard Bentley & Son, 1896.

Cavallo, Guglielmo and Roger Chartier, eds., *A History of Reading in the West.* Translated by Lydia G. Cochrane. Amherst: University of Massachusetts Press, 1999.

Chartier, Roger, *On the Edge of the Cliff: History, Language and Practices* Baltimore: John Hopkins University Press, 1997.

Coleridge, Samuel Taylor, *The Complete Poetical Works of Samuel Taylor Coleridge.* Ed. Ernest Hartley Coleridge. 2 vol. Oxford: Clarendon Press, 1912.

Cresswell, Douglas, *Early New Zealand Families. Second Series.* Christchurch: Whitcombe and Tombs, 1956.

Cruse, Amy, *The Victorians and Their Books.* London: George Allen and Unwin Ltd, 1935.

Cunningham, Gail, *The New Woman and the Victorian Novel.* London: Macmillan Press, 1978.

Dalziel, Margaret, *Popular Fiction 100 Years Ago: An Unexplored Tract of Literary History.* London: Cohen and West, 1957.

Darnton, Robert, *The Kiss of Lamourette: Reflections in Cultural History.* London and New York: W.W. Norton and Company, 1990.

Darnton, Robert, 'Review: The Symbolic Element in History.' *The Journal of Modern History*, 58, 1 (March 1986): 218–234. http://www.jstor.org/stable/1881570 Accessed: 27 Jan 2010.

Dening, Greg, *History's Anthropology: The Death of William Gooch*. Lanham, MD: Unversity Press of America, 1988.

Denning, Michael, *Mechanic Accents, Dime Novels and Working Class Culture in America*. London: Verso, 1998.

Dilke, Charles Wentworth, *Greater Britain: A Record of Travel in English-speaking Countries During 1866 and 1867*. London: Macmillan, 1868.

Dixon, Robert, *Writing the Colonial Adventure: Race, Gender and Nation in Anglo-Australian Popular Fiction, 1875–1914*. Cambridge and New York: Cambridge University Press, 1995.

Dolin, Tim, 'First Steps toward a History of the Mid-Victorian Novel in Colonial Australia'. *Australian Literary Studies* 22, 3 (2006): 273–293.

Duggan, Lawrence J. (Lou), 'Librarians have much to Offer in Solving the Mystery of Reading'. *APLA Bulletin* 72, 1 (Fall 2008) http://www.apla.ca/node/146 Accessed 29 January 2010.

Eagleton, Terry, Fredric Jameson and Edward W. Said, *Nationalism, Colonialism and Literature*. Minneapolis: University of Minnesota Press, 1990.

Easton, Brian, 'William Beetham's *Portrait of Dr Isaac Featherston with the Maori Chiefs Wi Tako and Te Puni*'. *Bulletin of New Zealand Art History* 12 (1991): 29–34.

Eldred-Grigg, Stevan, *A Southern Gentry: New Zealanders Who Inherited the Earth*. Wellington: A.H. and A.W. Reed, 1980.

Eliot, Simon, 'Public Libraries and Popular Authors, 1883–1912'. *The Library*, Sixth Series, VIII (1986): 322–350.

Erickson, Paul, ' Help or Hindrance? The History of the Book and Electronic Media' in *Rethinking Media Change: The Aesthetics of Transition*. Ed. David Thorburn and Henry Jenkins. Cambridge, MA: MIT Press, 2003, 95–116

Escarpit, Robert, *The Book Revolution*. London: Harrap; Paris: Unesco, 1966.

Fairburn, Miles, *The Ideal Society and Its Enemies: The Foundations of Modern New Zealand Society, 1850–1900*. Auckland: Auckland University Press, 1989.

Fairburn, Miles, *Nearly Out of Heart and Hope: The Puzzle of a Colonial Labourer's Diary*. Auckland: Auckland University Press, 1995.

Feldman, Paula R., ed., *British Women Poets of the Romantic Era: An Anthology*. Baltimore, Maryland: The Johns Hopkins University Press, 1997.

Fernando, Lloyd, *'New Women' in the Late Victorian Novel*. University Park and London: The Pennsylvania State University Press, 1977.

Flint, Kate, *The Woman Reader, 1837–1914*. Oxford: Clarendon Press, 1993.

Flint, Kate, ed., *The Victorian Novelist: Social Problems and Social Change*. London: Croom Helm, 1987.

The Friends of the Turnbull Library, *Edward Gibbon Wakefield and the Colonial Dream: A Reconsideration*, Wellington: GP Publications, 1997.

Froude, J.A., *Oceana, or, England and her Colonies*. London: Longmans, Green and Co., 1886.

Gillespie-Needham, Dulcie, *The Colonial and His Books: A Study of Reading in Nineteenth Century New Zealand*. PhD thesis, Victoria University of Wellington, 1971.

Gilmour, Robin, *The Novel in the Victorian Age: A Modern Introduction*. London: Edward Arnold, 1986.

Gissing, George, *The Crown of Life*. Edited by Michael Ballard. Hassocks, Sussex: Harvester Press, 1978.

Gissing, George, *New Grub Street*. Edited by John Goode. Oxford: Oxford University Press, 1998.

Gissing, George, *The Private Papers of Henry Ryecroft*. London: Constable, 1903.

Goldsmith, Paul, 'The First Crown Purchases: 1853 to January 1854.' Chapter 3 of *District 11A Report—Wairarapa*. Wellington, NZ: Waitangi Tribunal Rangahaua Whanui Series, July 1996. http://www.waitangi-tribunal.govt.nz/doclibrary/public/researchwhanui/district/11A/Chapt03.pdf 22 Accessed 5 May 2010.

Grogan, Ewart S., and Arthur H. Sharp, *From the Cape to Cairo: The First Traverse of Africa from South to North*. London: Hurst and Blackett, 1900.

Guy, Josephine M., *The Victorian Social-Problem Novel: The Market, the Individual and Communal Life*. Houndsmills, Basingstoke: Macmillan Press, 1996.

Houghton, Walter E., *The Victorian Frame of Mind, 1830–1870*. New Haven and London: Yale University Press, 1957 (1985).

Hunter, Shelagh, *Victorian Idyllic Fiction: Pastoral Strategies*. London, Macmillan: 1984.

Jackson, H. J., *Marginalia: Readers Writing in Books*. New Haven and London: Yale University Press, 2001.

James, Louis, *The Victorian Novel*, Malden, MA: Blackwell Publishing, 2006.

Jerome, Jerome K, ed., *My First Book*. London: Chatto & Windus, 1894

Johanson, Graeme, *A Study of Colonial Editions in Australia, 1843–1972*. Wellington: Elibank Press, 2000.

Kane, Penny, *Victorian Families in Fact and Fiction*. New York: St Martin's Press, 1995.

Keen, Suzanne, *Victorian Renovations of the Novel. Naarrative Annexes and the Boundaries of Representation*. Cambridge: Cambridge University Press, 1998 (pbk 2005).

Kingsley, Charles, *Alton Locke, Tailor and Poet: An Autobiography*. London: Macmillan, 1887.

Kingsley, Charles, *Charles Kingsley: His Letters and Memories of his Life. Ed. by his Wife*. London: Macmillan and Co., 1883.

Kingsley, Charles, *Hypatia*. New York and London: Garland Publishing, 1975.

Kingsley, Charles, *Literary and General Lectures and Essays*. Second Edition. London: Macmillan, 1890.

Kingsley, Charles, *Yeast: A Problem*. London: Macmillan, 1888.

Kipling, Rudyard, 'The Song of the Cities' in *The Seven Seas*. London: Methuen and Co Ltd, 1907.

Klaus, Judy, 'Shearers Reading Shakespeare: How Unique was Brancepeth Station Library in the Late 1800s?' (Master of Library and Information Studies research project, Victorian University of Wellington, 1999).

Lester, Alan, *Imperial Networks: Creating Identities in Nineteenth-century South Africa and Britain*. London and New York: Routledge, 2001.

Lever, Charles, *The Novels of Charles Lever*. Edited by his daughter [Julia Kate Neville]. London: Downey and Co., 1897–1899.

Lyons, Martyn and Lucy Taksa, *Australian Readers Remember: An Oral History of Reading, 1890–1930*. Melbourne: Oxford University Press, 1992.

McAloon, Jim, *No Idle Rich: The Wealthy in Canterbury and Otago 1840–1914*. Dunedin, University of Otago Press, 2002.

Macdonald, Charlotte, *A Woman of Good Character: Single Women as Immigrant Settlers in Nineteenth-century New Zealand*. Wellington: Allen and Unwin/Historical Branch, 1990.

McKenzie D.F., *Bibliography and the Sociology of Texts*. Cambridge: Cambridge University Press, 1999.

Manguel, Alberto, *A History of Reading*. New York: Viking, 1996.

Metcalf L.J, *The Cultivation of New Zealand Trees and Shrubs*. Wellington: A.H. & A.W. Reed, 1972.

Meyer, Susan, *Imperialism at Home: Race and Victorian Women's Fiction*. Ithaca, New York: Cornell University Press, 1996.

Morris, Virginia B., *Double Jeopardy: Women Who Kill in Victorian Fiction*. Lexington, Kentucky: University Press of Kentucky, 1990.

Mott, Frank Luther, *Golden Multitudes: The Story of Best Sellers in the United States*. New York: The Macmillan Company, 1947.

Nadel, Ira Bruce, ed., *Victorian Fiction: A Collection of Essays from the Period*. New York and London: Garland Publishing, 1986.

Ngata, A.T., ed., *Complete Manual of Māori Grammar and Conversation with Vocabulary*. Christchurch: Whitcombe and Tombs, 1901.

O'Gorman, Francis, ed., *The Victorian Novel*. Oxford and Malden, MA: Blackwell Publishing, 2002.

Pearson, W.H., *Henry Lawson among Maoris*. Canberra: Australian National University Press, 1968.

Percy, Thomas, *Reliques of Ancient English Poetry*. London: J.M. Dent and Sons, 1906.

Pratt, Mary Louise, *Imperial Eyes: Travel Writing and Transculturation*. Routledge: London and New York, 1992.

Preziosi, Donald, 'The Art of Art History', in *The Art of Art History: A Critical Anthology*. Ed. Donald Preziosi. Oxford: Oxford University Press, 1998.

Price, Leah, 'Tres Vrai', review of H.J. Jackson, *Marginalia* (2001), *London Review of Books* (18 October, 2001) 27–30.

Radway, Janice, *Reading the Romance*. North Carolina: The University of North Carolina Press, 1984.

Richards, Eric, *Britannia's Children: Emigration from England, Scotland, Wales and Ireland since 1600*. London and New York: Hambledon and London, 2004.

Richards, Thomas, *The Imperial Archive: Knowledge and the Fantasy of Empire*. London, New York: Verso, 1993.

Richardson, LeeAnne M., *New Woman and Colonial Adventure Fiction in Victorian Britain: Gender, Genre, and Empire*. Gainesville: University Press of Florida, 2006.

Rose, Jonathan, *The Intellectual Life of the British Working Classes*. New Haven and London, Yale University Press, 2002.

Rowan, Mrs [Ellis], *A Flower-hunter in Queensland and New Zealand*. Sydney: Angus and Robertson, 1898.

Ryan, J. S., *Charles Dickens and New Zealand: A Colonial Image; Selected from the Periodical Publications of Charles Dickens*. Wellington: A.H. and A.W. Reed for the Dunedin Public Library, 1965.

Said, Edward W., *Culture and Imperialism*. New York: Knopf, 1993.

Sayers, Dorothy L., *Wilkie Collins: A Critical and Biographical Study*. Edited from the manuscript, Humanities Research Center, Austin, Texas, by E.R. Gregory. [Toledo, Ohio]: The Friends of the University of Toledo Libraries, 1977.

Schaffer, Talia, 'The History of Richard Calmady.' *The Literary Encyclopedia*. 24 January 2002. http://www.litencyc.com/php/sworks.php?rec=true&UID=595 Accessed 15 October 2009.

Seeley, J.R., *The Expansion of England: Two Courses of Lectures*. London: Macmillan and Co., 1883.

Shattock, Joanne, *The Cambridge Bibliography of English Literature, Volume Four 1800–1900*, 3rd edition. Cambridge: Cambridge University Press, 1999.

Shoebridge, Tim, *The Good Citizen: A Life of C.E. Daniell of Masterton*. Masterton, New Zealand: Fraser Books, 2009.

Stafford, Jane and Mark Williams, *Maoriland: New Zealand Literature 1872–1914*. Wellington: Victoria University Press, 2006.

Sturm, Terry, ed., *The Oxford History of New Zealand Literature in English*, 2nd ed. Auckland: Oxford University Press, 1998.

Sutherland, John, *The Stanford Companion to Victorian Fiction*. Stanford: Stanford University Press,1989. [First published as *The Longman*

Companion to Victorian Literature. Harlow, Essex: Longman, 1988.]

Sutherland, John, *Victorian Fiction: Writers, Publishers, Readers*. Basingstoke and New York: Palgrave Macmillan, 2006.

Taylor, Mary, *Mary Taylor, Friend of Charlotte Bronte; Letters from New Zealand and Elsewhere*. Ed. Joan Stevens. Auckland: Auckland University Press; Wellington: Oxford University Press, 1972.

Tennyson, Lord Alfred, *Enoch Arden and In Memoriam*. London: Macmillan, 1891.

Traue, J.E. 'A Paradise for Readers?: The Extraordinary Proliferation of Public Libraries in Colonial New Zealand'. *Script and Print: Bulletin of the Bibliographical Society of Australia and New Zealand* (Special Issue: *Paradise: New Worlds of Books and Readers)* 29: 1–4 (2005), 323–340.

Traue, J.E., 'The Public Library Explosion in Colonial New Zealand'. *Libraries and the Cultural Record* 42:2 (2007),151–164.

Trodd, Anthea, *Domestic Crime in the Victorian Novel*. New York: St Martin's Press, 1989.

Uffelman, Larry, K., *Charles Kingsley*. Boston: Twayne Publishers, 1979.

Wakefield, Edward, 'New Zealand and Mr Froude'. *Nineteenth Century*, CXIV (August 1886): 171–82.

Wheeler, Michael, *English Fiction of the Victorian period, 1830–1890*. London and New York: Longman, 1985.

Wolff, Robert Lee, *Sensational Victorian: the life and fiction of Mary Elizabeth Braddon*. New York: Garland Pub., 1979

Wood, Mrs Henry, *East Lynne/Ellen Wood*. Edited by Andrew Maunder. Peterborough, Ont.; Orchard Park, New York: Broadview Press, c2000

Wood, Jane, *Passion and Pathology in Victorian Fiction*. Oxford: Oxford University Press, 2001.

Yerex, David, *They Came to Wydrop: The Beetham and Williams Families of Brancepeth and Te Parae, Wairarapa, 1856–1990*. Masterton, New Zealand: Published on behalf of Hugh Beetham of Brancepeth and Tom Williams of Te Parae; Distributed by GP Publications, 1991.

Brancepeth Library Titles Discussed in the Text

Ainsworth, W.H., *The Tower of London*. London: Routledge, 1891.

Allen, Grant, *The Woman Who Did*. [Listed in 1895 Catalogue, missing from Brancepeth Collection.]

Allen, Grant, *The British Barbarians: A Hill-top Novel*. London: Lane; New York: Putnam, 1895.

Allen, James Lane, *The Choir Invisible*. London: Chatto and Windus, 1897.

Alexander, Mrs [Annie French Hector], *Her Dearest Foe*, London: Macmillan, 1899.

Alexander, Mrs [Annie French Hector], *The Heritage of Langdale*. London: Hutchinson, 1894.

Atkinson, Blanche, *They Have Their Reward: A Novel*. Melbourne: Petherick, 1890.

Barr, Amelia, *Jan Vedder's Wife*. London: Warne, 1892.

Besant, Walter, *The Children of Gibeon*. London: Chatto and Windus, 1886.

Besant, Walter, *All Sorts and Conditions of Men: An Impossible Story*. London: Chatto and Windus, 1889.

Besant, Walter, *The Master Craftsman*. London: Chatto and Windus, 1896.

Besant, Walter, *The Revolt Of Man*. Edinburgh: Blackwood, 1883.

Besant, Walter, and James Rice, *The Golden Butterfly: A Novel*. London: Chatto and Windus, 1892.

Besant, Walter, and James Rice, *Ready-money Mortiboy: A Matter-of-fact Story*. London: Chatto and Windus, 1883.

Betham-Edwards, Matilda, *The Sylvestres*. London: Warne, [1877?].

Black, William, *A Daughter of Heth*. London: Low, Marston, Searle and Rivington, 1892.

Boldrewood, Rolf, *A Colonial Reformer*. London: Macmillan, 1891.

Boldrewood, Rolf, *Old Melbourne Memories*. Melbourne: George Robertson, 1884.

Boldrewood, Rolf, *A Sydney-side Saxon*. London: Macmillan, 1891.

Braddon, M.E., *Asphodel*. London: Simpkin, Marshall, Hamilton, Kent, 1890.

Braddon, M.E., *Aurora Floyd: A Novel.* London: Simpkin, Marshall, Hamilton, Kent, 1864.

Braddon, M.E. *Lady Audley's Secret: A Novel.* London: Simpkin, Marshall, Hamilton, Kent, 1908.

Carey, Rosa N., *Wooed and Married.* London: Bentley, 1893.

Cholmondeley, Mary, *Red Pottage.* London: Longmans, Green, 1899.

Churchill, Winston, *Richard Carvel.* London: Macmillan Company, 1899.

Churchill, Winston, *The Crisis.* London: Macmillan, 1901.

Churchward, William, *Jem Peterkin's Daughter: An Antipodean Novel.* London: Robertson, 1892.

Collins, Wilkie, *Armadale.* London: Chatto and Windus, 1891.

Collins, Wilkie, *Hide and Seek; or, The Mystery of Mary Grice*, London: Sampson Low, 1861.

Collins, Wilkie, *My Miscellanies.* London: Chatto and Windus, [1863?].

Collins, Mortimer, *Pen Sketches by a Vanished Hand, From the Papers of the Late Mortimer Collins.* 2 volumes. Edited by Tom Taylor with notes by the editor and Mrs. Mortimer Collins. London: Bentley, 1879.

Corelli, Marie, *Barabbas: A Dream of the World's Tragedy.* London, Methuen, 1894; 2nd copy, Sydney: Edwards, Dunlop, [1893?]

Corelli, Marie, *Boy: A Sketch.* London: Hutchinson, 1900.

Corelli, Marie, *The Master Christian.* London: Methuen, 1900.

Corelli, Marie, *Temporal Power: A Study in Supremacy.* London: Methuen, 1902.

Crockett, S.R., *The Grey Man.* London: Fisher Unwin, 1896.

Dickens, Charles, *The Works of Charles Dickens.* 30 volumes. London: Chapman and Hall, 1880.

Doyle, A. Conan, *The Firm of Girdlestone.* London: Chatto & Windus, 1892.

Doyle, A. Conan, *Strange Secrets.* London: Chatto & Windus, 1890

Dumas, Alexandre, *The Page of the Duke of Savoy.*_London: Routledge, [1889?].

Edwards, Annie, *A Girton Girl.* London: Bentley, 1886.

Eiloart, Mrs, *The Dean's Wife.* London: White, 1883.

Findlater, Helen Jane, *The Green Graves of Balgowrie*. London, Methuen, 1896.

Fowler, Ellen Thorneycroft, *Concerning Isabel Carnaby*. London: Hodder and Stoughton, 1899.

Fox, John Jr, *The Little Shepherd of Kingdom Come*. Westminster: Constable, 1903.

Gissing, George, *New Grub Street: A Novel*. London: Smith Elder, 1893.

Gissing, George, *The Private Papers of Henry Ryecroft*. London: Constable, 1903.

Gould, S. Baring, *Urith A Tale of Dartmoor*. Melbourne: Petherick, 1891.

Grand, Sarah, *Babs the Impossible*. London: Hutchinson, 1902.

Grand, Sarah, *The Beth Book*. [Listed in 1895 Catalogue, missing from Brancepeth Collection.]

Grand, Sarah, *The Heavenly Twins*. London: William Heinemann, 1894.

Grand, Sarah, *Ideala: A Study from Life*. London: Heinemann, 1893.

Gunter, Archibald Clavering, *Miss Dividends: A Novel*. London: Routledge, 1892.

Gunter, Archibald Clavering, *Mr Barnes of New York. A Novel*. London: Routledge, 1891.

Haggard, H. Rider, *She*. London: Longmans, Green, 1898.

Hardy, Thomas, *Tess of the D'Urbervilles*. London: Bell, 1894

Hawthorne, Julian, *Love or a Name*. London: Chatto & Windus, 1885.

Hocking, Joseph, *All Men Are Liars*. London: Ward, Lock, 1898.

Hope, Anthony. *The Prisoner of Zenda*. London: Macmillan, 1895.

Hungerford, Mrs, *Mrs Geoffrey*. London: Smith, Elder, 1885.

Iota, *A Yellow Aster*. London: Hutchinson, 1894.

James, G.P.R., *The Old Dominion*. London: Routledge, [186–].

James, G.P.R., *One in a Thousand*. London: Routledge, [186–].

Kidd, Benjamin, *Social Evolution*. London: Macmillan, 1895.

Kingsley, Henry, *Recollections of Geoffrey Hamlyn*. London: Ward, Lock, 1894.

Lever, Charles, *Jack Hinton*. London: Warne, 1886.

Lyall, Edna, *In the Golden Days*. London: Hurst and Blackett, 1891.

Lyall, Edna, *A Hardy Norseman*. London: Hurst and Blackett, 1890.

Lyall, Edna, *To Right the Wrong*. London: Hurst and Blackett, 1894.

Lyall, Edna, *Wayfaring Men*. London: Longmans, Green, 1897.

Macdonald, George, *Malcolm*. London: Kegan Paul, Trench, [1880s?].

Macdonald, George, *Paul Faber*. London, Chatto & Windus, 1883.

Malet, Lucas, *The Carissima*. London: Methuen, 1896.

Malet, Lucas, *Colonel Enderby's Wife*. London: Kegan Paul, Trench, [1885].

Malet, Lucas, *The History of Sir Richard Calmady*. London: Methuen, 1901.

Malet, Lucas, *Mrs Lorimer A Sketch in Black and White*. London: Macmillan, 1886.

Marryat, Captain, *Japhet in Search of a Father*. London: Routledge, [1873].

Merriman, Henry S., *In Kedar's Tents*. London: Macmillan, 1897.

Moore, George, *A Mummer's Wife*. London: Vizetelly, ?1885.

Morrell, Sir McKenzie, *The Fatal Illness of Frederick The Noble*. London: Sampson Low, Marston, Searle & Rivington, 1888.

Mulock-Craik, Dinah, *John Halifax, Gentleman*. New York: Green's, 1883.

Oliphant, Mrs, *Miss Marjoribanks*. Edinburgh: Blackwood, 1869.

Ouida, *Guilderoy*, London: Chatto & Windus, [1889].

Reade, Charles, *Christie Johnstone*. London: Chatto & Windus, 1890.

Rita, *Corinna*. London: Blackett, [188–?].

Rita, *Dame Durden*. London: Maxwell, [188–?].

Roe, E.P, *Opening a Chestnut Burr*. London: Ward, Lock and Co., [18–].

Smiles, Samuel. *Self-Help: With Illustrations of Conduct and Perseverance*. London: Murray, 1882.

Smith, Albert, *The [Struggles and] Adventures of Christopher Tadpole*. London: King, 1893.

Steele, Rudd, *On Our Selection*. Sydney: The Bulletin, 1903.

Stevenson, R.L., *Kidnapped*. London: Cassell, 1891.

Stockton, Frank R., *The Squirrel Inn*. London: Sampson, Low, Marston, 1891.

Swan, Annie, *Who Shall Serve*. Edinburgh: Oliphant, Anderson and Ferrier, 1891.

Swan, Annie, *A Victory Won*. London: Hutchinson, [1895].

Thackeray, William Makepeace, *The History of Henry Esmond Esq.* London: Smith, Elder, 1884.

Thackeray, William Makepeace, *The History of Pendennis*. London: Smith, Elder, 1883.

Thackeray, William Makepeace, *Vanity Fair*. [London: Routledge, 1891].

Thackeray, William Makepeace, *The Virginians*. London: Smith, Elder, 1882.

Trollope, Anthony, *Orley Farm*. [London: Chapman and Hall, 188–?].

Trollope, Anthony, *The Three Clerks*. London: Bentley, 1891.

Twain, Mark, *The Adventures of Huckleberry Finn, (Tom Sawyer's Comrade)*. London: Chatto and Windus, 1898.

Whyte-Melville, G.J., *Katerfelto*. London: Ward, Lock [190–?].

Wister, Owen, *The Virginian: A Horseman of the Plains*. London: Macmillan, 1903.

Wood, Mrs Henry, *Bessie Rane*. [London: Bentley, 1872].

Wood, Mrs Henry, *East Lynne*. [Listed in 1895 Catalogue, missing from Brancepeth Collection.]

Wood, Mrs Henry, *Edina*. London: Bentley, 1882.

Wood, Mrs Henry, *A Life's Secret: A Story*. London: Macmillan and Co., 1901.

Wood, Mrs Henry, *St Martin's Eve*. London: Bentley, 1883.

Zangwill, Israel, *The Premier and the Painter*. London: Heinemann, 1895.

Index

I1 denotes photographs in the first insert, after page 96
I2 denotes photographs in the second insert, after page 192
[ ] denote extra information not in the text